# THE POLITICS OF THE PIAZZA

*For my students*

# The Politics of the Piazza

The History and Meaning of the Italian Square

Eamonn Canniffe

ASHGATE

Published by
Ashgate Publishing Limited
Gower House
Croft Road
Aldershot
Hampshire GU11 3HR
England

Ashgate Publishing Company
Suite 420
101 Cherry Street
Burlington, VT 05401-4405
USA

Ashgate website: http://www.ashgate.com

**British Library Cataloguing in Publication Data**
Canniffe, Eamonn
    The politics of the piazza : the history and meaning of the
    Italian square. - (Design and the built environment series)
    1. Plazas - Italy - History 2. Architecture and state -
    Italy - History
    I. Title
    725.9'0945

**Library of Congress Cataloging-in-Publication Data**
Canniffe, Eamonn.
    The politics of the piazza : the history and meaning of the Italian square / by
Eamonn Canniffe.
        p. cm. -- (Design and the built environment)
    Includes bibliographical references and index.
    ISBN 978-0-7546-4716-4
    1. Plazas--Italy--History. 2. Architecture and state--Italy--History. I. Title.

    NA9070.C36 2008
    711'.550945--dc22

                                                                2007041397

ISBN 978 0 7546 4716 4

**Mixed Sources**
Product group from well-managed
forests and other controlled sources
www.fsc.org Cert no. SA-COC-1565
© 1996 Forest Stewardship Council
FSC

Printed and bound in Great Britain by
MPG Books Ltd, Bodmin, Cornwall.

# Contents

# List of figures

## 7   Baroque: Scale, form and meaning

## 8   Neo-Classicism: Style and political ideology

All drawings and photographs by Eamonn Canniffe.

# Foreword

This book brings together many influences, haphazard circumstance and educational experiences which have joined to form my interest in the piazza. Having been born in a square (albeit a version of a green space far removed from the Italian examples I continue to study) I was aware from an early age of the sense of security and community, and the hierarchy of public and private, inherent in the form. Tantalizing television images of baroque ceremonial from Piazza San Pietro in Rome created a strong aesthetic impression of the theatricality of public space. These influences predated my discovery of architectural history in a library designated as part of a 'forum' (and situated in a space with the improbable name of Leningrad Square). During my university education I was privileged to attend lectures on Italian subjects (gardens, architecture and painting) from Peter Carl, James Ackerman and Sydney Freedberg which formalized my native instincts, while design projects for Sabbioneta (under Peter Eisenman) and Urbino (under Colin St. John Wilson) gave me the opportunity to explore the urban morphology of the Italian cultural context in a creative though distanced way.

When embarking on research on the subject of the piazza funds were provided by the University of Manchester for two study trips to Italy in 1993 and 1995. A Rome Scholarship in the Fine Arts at the British School at Rome in 1996 afforded a more sustained opportunity to examine the material *in situ*, and in particular to introduce some knowledge of archaeological remnants. Early encouragement for publishing parts of the present work came from my colleague Frank Salmon, and from Mehrdad Shokoohy through the pages of *Urban Design Studies*. My initial interest in the formal qualities of the piazza developed as I became aware of the political contexts in which the various principal examples were created. A period of study leave in 2006 from the University of Sheffield School of Architecture furnished time for the preparation of the manuscript of this book. Throughout this long period of evolution the preparation of lecture material and the teaching of studio design projects has afforded the opportunity to explore the form, meaning and potential of Italian urban space with many colleagues and students. Because, although this book is a history of its subject, its longer term intention has always been to provide a context for the understanding of urban form which is cognisant of the successful examples of the past, a continuity which any designs for future urban space would be foolish to ignore. In a situation where urban spaces are often banal and discouraging of any engagement how could I forget that first experience of the Piazza del Campo in Siena in 1979? Although the *palio* had finished, the crowds had dispersed and you could only faintly hear distant celebrations, the great brick bowl of space virtually pulsed with the life of the city.

Eamonn Canniffe
2008

# Introduction

By their very nature urban projects are engaging examples of direct political influence on building. The size of such an enterprise and the need for considerable coordination requires the sort of collective effort that only a political process can provide. This book explores the history of Italian urban space through the relationship between political systems and their methods of representation in architecture. Its broad historical scope, from antiquity to the present-day, will feature a series of examples where shifts between autocratic and democratic forms of government employ subtly nuanced spatial and iconographic languages to form the self-image of the *polis* and project an ideology onto a wider world. Within this context the piazza is a feature of the European urban inheritance which holds a place of affection in both the professional and the popular imagination. As a term it has been adopted in other contexts to denote some form of public open space, and even the use of the word has been regarded as enough to indicate the type of public life lived outdoors which is admired in the civic realm of southern Europe. It is the thesis of this book that the Italian examples of the genre present not only a consistent history of the morphological development of urbanism but also portray the story of change and continuity in the political situation of Italy. In addition the forms of different piazze, while establishing a continuous and self-referential tradition of public space, also act as a means through which the prevailing ideological system represents itself. The sequence of this book will therefore follow chronological order beginning with the Romans, and relate significant examples of Italian urban space to the political developments of a particular historical period in each chapter. Although towards the end of that story incomplete or unbuilt projects will appear, this is largely a history devoted to spaces which have survived through long periods of use, the robustness of the forms adapting to changes in political and social circumstance. These facts alone should be sufficient to indicate that there is no one-to-one correspondence between a space and the political system of the period in which it evolved. There are, of course, examples of direct political propaganda in the extremely expensive form of public open space throughout the book, but it should be remembered that, in a largely benign climate, public open spaces are a feature of Italian cities which are always valued, and has continued to be of benefit to the cities in which they survive long after the demise of their political creators.

If one accepts the connection between art and politics, however, the mechanism by which an image can be expanded into a space should also be considered. Iconography, as two and three dimensional visual images, as text and most importantly as commonly understood narrative ideas, might easily be exposed in a public space, and thereby find an audience for its specific messages. The forming of that public space is itself a product of an ideological process, most overt in spaces created by authoritarian regimes although that method is seldom a linear one. We seem intermittently aware of the layering of history which the city represents, with its manifestation of political conflict and change. But if, as described by M. Christine Boyer, *The City of Collective Memory* embodies the ambition for an authentic and resonant public realm and its simultaneous erasure, how might we define those urban spaces where history has been manipulated for political ends, based on narratives which are highly selective if not fictional (Boyer 1994)? It is necessary to explore how cultural and typological memories are exploited, and the study of Italian architecture and urbanism provides a fertile territory for exploration because of its direct exploitation of historical memory to support the political claim to power, and also the spread of those forms of expression to other cultures. It is also possible to question if, at a time when traditional methods of civic design have been largely eschewed in the aftermath of the apparent failure of post-modernism, it is a sign of political ambivalence or of maturity that examples of urbanism which operated successfully over a period of longer than two millennia should be deemed irrelevant for contemporary urban situations? In the historic situation the public nature of urban projects meant that the state and (in the specific cultural conditions of Italy also the significant political entity of the church) sought to produce architectural embodiments of the prevailing ideology through an often explicit iconographic programme. The pressures to manifest aspects of progress and renewal, while simultaneously relying on recognizable precedents culled from historical forms, produced curious hybrids. These divergent elements are often barely resolved but create the picturesque and disparate forms characteristic of Italian urban space, an aesthetic which has been widely admired since connoisseurship developed during the renaissance. In this regard periodization always presents a problem to an architectural historian, since the ties which bind an artefact to its era of production are not necessarily the only strong ones. In any creative discipline the aesthetic choice is seldom uninfluenced by contingent matters and the same is certainly true of urban spaces. The broadly held idea of historical progress being linked to the passage of time results in works which do not easily fit in the generally approved pattern, and perhaps being regarded as backward looking or provincial. Such assumptions need always be treated with a large degree of scepticism.

But firstly, to help define this situation in its context, the question should be answered as to what is meant by the city, the city materialized in its physically visible structures or the city as institution and political construct, the city of houses and monuments or the city of citizens? By concentrating on the piazza as a specific type of urban space these two aspects of the city, the architectural and the social, can be seen together in context, although the narrow focus on enclosed public space will here stand for the broader complexities of urban life. The practical qualities of the piazza, a central feature of any urban theory, have long been subject to intellectual interpretation and they can be grasped under three categories which establish principles, interpret space as part of a broader physical framework and attempt to accommodate it to the demands of modern society. In addition to these three groups ancient sources, renaissance thinkers and modern critics are responsible for providing the theoretical lens through which the tangible spaces might be understood. This duality, between the practical and the theoretical, will be further explained by introducing the four sections in which this book is presented, following a chronological sequence. The subsequent chapters will consider the development of Italian urban form, categorized by art historical and political periods. These fourteen chapters are grouped in sections dealing in turn with (i) traditions and

0.1   Campo San Giacomo dall'Orio, Venice. A typical Venetian space formed around the apsidal forms of the church.

0.2 Piazza Vecchia, Bergamo. A medieval communal palace with a ground floor communicating with the adjacent public spaces.

origins, (ii) renaissance and baroque developments, (iii) the nineteenth and early twentieth centuries and (iv) the post 1945 period.

In Part I, the representational quality of the public space of the ancient city initiates the dialogue between physical and architectural form and the political idea it embodies. Greek and Etruscan urban design influences will provide a starting point to consider the traces of ancient cultures which survive in Italy, most especially the fundamental legacy of the Romans. However, the distinction between theory and practice will be introduced through the comparison of the typology of the Roman forum (as transmitted by Vitruvius and visible in examples such as the Fora of Pompeii and Brescia) and the evolving form of the Forum Romanum, the central space of the Roman world. In this most complex and significant example, the transformation of the governing system from republican oligarchy to imperial cult is reflected in the increasing uniformity of architectural expression. Although the examples to be discussed will begin with the Roman forum, the pragmatic nature of Roman urban space had developed in an intellectual milieu which was indebted to Greek thought. The project of Vitruvius (dependent as the Roman author was on earlier texts which have not survived) represents a manual for imperial urban expansion, as the dedication of his work to Augustus indicated, and the fora of new colonial foundations would be the location of the imperial family cult. The continuity between the daily activity of the market and the political, military and religious life of the city will be considered through the forms which become the paradigm for subsequent urban spaces in the western tradition. However, the social instability brought about by the collapse of the Roman empire coincided with the establishment of Christianity as the official religion. Politically this period saw the withering of imperial authority and the rise of the church as a temporal power, expressed in the urban role of the bishop and the civic presence of his cathedral and fortified palace. In Chapter 2 urban form will be characterized by the transformation of Roman building types such as the basilica into their Christian counterparts which come to dominate the image of the city. With Augustine of Hippo, the splendour and squalor, idealization and pronounced inequality of the late Roman city became an experience against which the newly theorized celestial city of God could be compared, providing an intellectual framework that pervaded the creation of urban spaces, typically in relation to Christian churches for the next millennium. At Torcello in the Venetian lagoon, the ensemble of church, campanile, baptistery and martyrium forms a fragmentary image of the new settlements established as refuges from barbarian invasion. Conversely at Brescia, the periphery of the city developed as a Christian precinct which evolved into the central space of the medieval city. As stability returned the medieval Italian city-state represented its political autonomy in the forms of its public buildings and spaces. Although often built on earlier foundations, the radical form of these spaces responded to the political tension between civic and religious powers. This situation created a new urban identity in the form of civic palaces which dominated newly defined public spaces. In examples such as fourteenth century Florence, Siena and Perugia, the secular structure of the *comune* had control over the integration of religious elements into the civil order of the city, establishing the primacy of civic authority through architectural and urban form, and defining the typology of the Italian piazza.

The revival of ancient sources which took place during the renaissance did so by reaching back beyond the scholastic tradition which had developed out of Augustine's work to examine texts from the classical past, but also to diversify the fields of inquiry. Alberti's architectural theory was only one area of his research, but it was the work which was to have the greatest impact on how the renaissance court represented itself in built form. The political basis of such courts found a practical theory, albeit of a negative type in the work of Machiavelli, while the idealistic tendency was a product of the broad diversity of intellectual life in pre-reformation Europe. Part II commences in the fifteenth century with the tensions between feudalism and mercantilism which had characterized the middle ages being resolved in the political map of Italy into a series of dynastic states variously allied to papal or imperial authority. These small territories, often with fluid borders and shifting alliances, were the setting within which the ruling and highly cultured elite sought to express their own political systems and aspirations, the creation and redefinition of urban situations being only the most durable and largest scale example of this type of politically representative public work. In Chapter 4 the revival of classical culture fostered by the dynastic courts of central Italy signalled a shift in political systems towards the forming of autocracies. In urban form this process found expression in the creation of spaces which embodied the ideology of the ideal city, partially realized at Pienza, Urbino, Mantua and Ferrara. Characterized by perspectival construction, symmetry of form and the imitation of ancient precedents new value was placed on the clarity of urban structure as a representation of the hierarchy of renaissance society. As this culture proceeded, however, the turn of the fifteenth and sixteenth centuries saw the consolidation of revived Roman imagery (both republican and imperial) in the design of public spaces. The change in the outlook of European states between the collapse of the eastern empire, the discovery of the new world and the protestant reformation witnessed the development of urban models which reasserted confidence and continuity. Examples from this period include the establishment of a 'forum' at Vigevano, the redefinition of Piazza San Marco in Venice and the creation of the complex of public space and civic palaces on the Capitoline hill in Rome. The cultural value of antiquity was used as a specific form of political rhetoric to speak to the present, and the conscious use of perspective construction was an important representational tool. Later sixteenth century Italian states began to establish elaborate forms of civic ritual to validate political structures. In urban design this was manifested in the increased use of permanent scenography to define new and existing spaces, often supporting the social fabric of states by housing combinations of bureaucratic, commercial and charitable functions. Spaces in Florence, Bologna, Arezzo and Sabbioneta will be considered in Chapter 6. Repetitive linear structures characterize the first three examples and are used to create new urban spaces, define vistas and reinforce the existing civic realm. At Sabbioneta an entirely new complex of buildings and spaces furnish a setting for the self-image of a minor ruler. During the seventeenth century the political system of absolutism expressed itself in urbanism through the creation of spaces which sought to represent cosmic order within the constrained and irregular pattern of the city. The baroque period is often associated with the creation of new urban and architectural sequences on a grand scale, as at Piazza San Pietro in Rome, and regal centres such as Turin and Venaria Reale, indicative of the political ambitions of the House of Savoy. However, work at a minor scale, such as Piazza Santa Maria della Pace and Piazza Sant'Ignazio in Rome also exhibited the ingenuity with which designers attempted to make a form of continuity between everyday experience and the ideal, manifested in full-bodied urban theatricality.

Part III covers the modern period from the mid-eighteenth to mid-twentieth centuries, during which the Italian nation state was born. The dichotomy also became clear between the allure of contemporary techniques and the appeal to more ancient precedent which was the standard representational method for the

legitimation of a current power structure. With the shift from renaissance and baroque inventive reinterpretation of forms to the enlightenment cultivation of archaeology, the accuracy and authenticity of antique construction became of primordial interest at exactly the point, with industrialization, that traditional forms of city and society were about to undergo their most severe test. The nostalgia of ruins, despite its quality of *memento mori*, inculcated an appreciation of a well organized and ordered society the greatest artifacts of which were its public structures. However, from a distance of nearly two millennia how could the interpretation of such a history be accurate, since political expediency was likely to play a considerable part in the new interpretation? A past which was unquestionable and marvellous provided the strongest form of validation for the activities of the present. The archaeological interests of the later eighteenth century were to lead to a search for correct architectural forms which were recognized as having originary significance. Although architectural theorists of the period would eschew direct connections to the political turmoil which distinguished the revolutionary era, expressions of ancient grandeur reasserted the value of an heroic past. While Piranesi's decorative screen walls at Piazza dei Cavalieri di Malta in Rome presented a degree of ambiguity to the evocation of the past as ruin, examples such as the completion of Piazza del Popolo in Rome and the Piazza del Plebiscito in Naples evoked the modernity of the rapidly

0.3 Piazza della Signoria, Vicenza. Palladio's overcladding of the communal palace in a Renaissance interpretation of an ancient Roman *basilica*.

0.4    Piazza del Popolo, Rome. Valadier's treatment of the slope of the Pincian hill as a series of terraces in neo-classical garb above the Fountain of Mars.

changing nineteenth century city in simple antique dress. The eventual achievement of national unity under the House of Savoy saw Italian cities adopt new urban spaces which presented a confident image of modernity to nineteenth century Europe. The vistas of tight traditional urban spaces, photographed for the connoisseur and analysed for the professional by Camillo Sitte, could be contrasted with the regularity and expansiveness of new spaces carved out of existing fabric or planned in new districts. In this chapter examples include the enlargement of the marketplace in Florence (now Piazza della Repubblica), and Piazza Venezia and Piazza dell'Esedra in Rome, all monumental in scale and flamboyantly historicist in architectural dress. Within a few decades the urban situation in Italy in the first half of the twentieth century was dominated by the public works produced under fascism. Their monumental language came increasingly to depend upon the conceptual suppression of the time elapsed between the end of the Roman empire and the advent of fascism. Examples include Piazza della Vittoria in Brescia, which recapitulated the form of the city's ancient Roman forum, and the Piazzale del Impero in Rome which embodied urban space in the image of Mussolini. These spaces for mass gatherings were intended to promote conformity, places where individuals were moulded into an instrument of political will.

In the post 1945 period critical positions on the products of progressive idealism began to emerge. In the Italian context, the foremost route would be that outlined by Bruno Zevi, promoting an alternative type of architecture and urbanism indebted to the organicism of Frank Lloyd Wright. In Part IV the defeat of fascism and the arrival of the fluid political system of coalition government was marked by a chastened expression, loosely defined as neo-realism. The emphasis on social housing, the interest in vernacular architecture and the perceived political neutrality of technology combined to exclude an emphasis on the rhetorical expression of the public realm. However, this withdrawal, and the necessities of post-war reconstruction was to lead to a renewed emphasis on the careful reevaluation of historic public spaces, and the significance of urban morphology. The European tradition was reasserted for a new generation as political co-operation emerged from conflict, but it would perhaps be Manfredo Tafuri who defined the critical significance of contemporary developments against the profoundly researched historical context. The disavowal of modernist urban principles which took place in the 1960s was centred around Aldo Rossi's *The Architecture of the City,* where the contemporary debate over the neglected public realm came to the fore (Rossi 1982). His written work was indebted to the study of architectural typology, but placed emphasis on the formal coherence of the type irrespective of changes in function over time, and which was initially more influential than the images of his design projects which sought to retrieve meaning for architectural form which modernism had replaced by a utilitarian transparency of plan and structure. For Rossi memory, personal and collective, was the definitive analogy in which architecture and urbanism should be grounded. In Chapter 12 a distinction will be drawn between his theoretical and drawn work and projects which reached construction such as that at Fontivegge in Perugia from the mid-1980s. Here Rossi employed his familiar repertoire of forms in a space the political context of which was simultaneously bureaucratic inertia and Italy's identification as a global centre of design culture. But political turmoil continued as those born following the war and reaching majority in the late sixties were to encounter a changed political scene. The disputes of fascists and partisans from an earlier era resurfaced in the extreme actions of groups, neo-fascists and revolutionary marxists, whom the postwar consensus had failed to appease. In 1974 an explosion in Piazza della Loggia in Brescia killed eight people participating in a trade union protest, with many more wounded. A confusing pattern of responsibilities and intentions, as well as the ambiguous direction of the state during continued material prosperity provided the context for an act of urban remembrance from a famously reserved architect. In the final chapter the political expression of the public realm in the present time is one where the attachment to substance has been replaced by image. In this situation the diverse forms which this phenomenon takes will be shown to be united by the increased commercial presence in traditional spaces. One example is the use of spaces such as Piazza Navona and Piazza di Spagna in Rome as the setting for television spectaculars, sharing in an ambiguous

0.5   *Forza Italia* rally, Piazza del Plebiscito, Naples 12 July 2007.

way with the tradition of the ephemeral architecture of the festival. Another is the commercial exploitation of such sites of revered heritage as advertising hoardings for the products of global consumer culture encoding the long history of the culture of the piazza with the latest language of urban sophistication. A particular manifestation is offered by the use of such spaces for televised political rallies reinforcing a vague sense of national identity and historical continuity. And lastly the threat posed by the adoption of the North American model of the business district will be seen as an example of contemporary developments which place no value on the changeful and well proportioned qualities of the Italian piazza.

The principal method of research employed to produce this book, and which I would claim to be vital for any architectural historian, is not documentary or archival or bibliographic. Instead it has to be the experience of the place itself, not simply in its accumulated detail but in the generality of its effect, since juxtapositions and discontinuities play an important role in the aesthetic composition of the piazza. The relaying of the historical sequence which the structure of the four sections contain, however, suggests a succession of events which erase previously dominant orders. The adoption of this idea would give a misleading account of the Italian piazza since many individual spaces, as direct experience of them illustrates, contain evidence

of the simultaneous presence of various historical epochs. Examples of such phenomena are numerous and will be referred to throughout the book, but one instance is worth discussing to emphasise the historical complexity of even the most seemingly banal urban space. Piazza Sidney Sonnino in the Trastevere quarter in central Rome is situated on a crossroads between the traditional and the modern city in a district which has witnessed much political intervention (Canniffe 2003; Canniffe 2006: 97–101). The piazza contains in its visible forms, and some less visible ones, the chronological span to which I shall refer throughout the book. Its present form is perhaps too open, lacking sufficient definition to be regarded as the classic urban room. Yet the intensity with which the different elements of its history are incorporated would appear to reinforce the sense of place if one peels back the historical layers. The most immediate and intrusively apparent feature is the presence of Viale di Trastevere with its heavy traffic, tram lines and platforms, part of the late nineteenth century improvements to the functioning of the new national capital. The width of the thoroughfare essentially dissipates the sense of enclosure which was being identified during the same period by Camillo Sitte as being a significant element in urban well being, as will be discussed in Chapter 9. The commercial developments from the 1930s on the eastern side of the boulevard are generic buildings of their period, set back slightly

0.6   Piazza Sidney Sonnino, Rome. The *Casa di Dante*, the heavily restored fifteenth century Palazzo Anguillara adjacent to the nineteenth century boulevard Viale di Trastevere.

0.7    VII Coorte dei Vigili, Rome. The courtyard of the ancient barracks, at present at a subterranean level adjacent to Viale di Trastevere.

to create a wide pavement in front of them with lines of plane trees breaking up the space. The insertion of the road, though, was required to acknowledge the presence of historical remains in the objectification of the *Casa di Dante* as a relic of the medieval city (Robbins 1994: 170). To the informed observer, this juxtaposition of new development, building conservation and modern traffic planning epitomises aspects of the modern city, but one should also be aware that this only represents the present stratum.

Slightly further from Viale di Trastevere, within the depth of the block, but on the southern end in a subterranean zone are a set of rooms, the remains of Roman civic infrastructure in the barracks of the VII cohort of 'vigili' or fire watchers discovered by accident in the mid-nineteenth century and important evidence of the daily life of lesser functionaries in the ancient city. Presently roofed by a concrete slab, it is difficult to discern the historic situation, except to realise how the process of urban sedimentation has raised the street level of the ancient Via Aurelia several metres to the present Via Lungaretta, the medieval pilgrimage route to the Vatican.

On the other side of Viale di Trastevere and adjacent to that road is the church of San Crisogono, the oldest site of public Christian worship in the city, which dates from the fourth century and will be discussed further in Chapter 2. The present facade records the seventeenth century restoration of the church

under the patronage of the papal nephew Cardinal Scipione Borghese, but the columns, both on the porch and in the interior, are themselves *spolia* from other earlier pagan buildings, the most precious being the two porphyry ones which frame the apse of the church. The *cosmati* floor, with disks of marble sourced from the columns of earlier buildings, is another more complex example of spoliation, but this is only the present upper level. Again a subterranean zone on a slightly different alignment embodies the earliest historical layer of the basilica, while the campanile, the central vertical point of the entire space dates from the medieval rebuilding of the basilica. Such juxtapositions of historical layers as this single rather casual and down-at-heel piazza contains reinforce the political significance of an urban space, as a record of urban history, its survivals and its losses.

A contrast exists, however, to the use of urban space as a territory which was owned by the citizens or the *comune* that represented their interests and therefore served local needs, and examples where the piazza was presented as a rhetorical device that limited freedom for the population, but enhanced the control of the ruler, being subservient to his gaze or dependent on his presence, and examples of both types will occur throughout the following chapters. The immediate and apparent difference between the two types is expressed through the tendency of the latter type to adopt symmetrical

0.8  Piazza Sidney Sonnino, Rome. The early Christian basilica of San Crisogono with the inscription on its portico recording a baroque restoration.

0.9    Piazza Sidney Sonnino, Rome. An ordinary urban space adjacent to the basilica, and with a view towards the local church of Sant'Agata.

compositional forms which have their root in the principles of human vision. We should be wary of placing such expressions of social control firmly at the door of visual and compositional technique. As Robin Evans has warned, a causal relationship can be implied if never proved. Alberti confirmed this subjective impression when he compared the city layouts appropriate for a republic and a tyranny, as will be discussed in Part II. Evans commented that the two kinds of government require different terrains, and the differences reside in the way surveyability and accessibility are centralized and unified in the one, or multiplied and mutually linked in the other. 'When any vista cuts through the lives of others it is a political instrument of a certain complexion. And when architecture petrifies its passage and forces movement and vision into the same privileged paths, even more so is architecture politicized' (Evans 1995: 141). The politicization, or rather the reading with hindsight of deliberate political intent in various constructions, would be of dubious origin if it were not for the evidence from Alberti of architectural forms being so closely allied to social control, an idea more usually associated with post-Enlightenment thought.

It will be clear from the foregoing that the issue of urban space is not simply a matter of the absence of building, of space left over at the margins of construction. Such spaces are as unloved and as uncared for in Italy as in any contemporary urban culture. The piazza is almost exclusively a phenomenon of space defined by buildings, enclosed by their walls as if an external room, an enclosure and definition which brings with it a strong sense of identity and *genius loci*. In contemporary architectural practice the dependence on the object building is often tellingly revealed by the inability of new public spaces to achieve their designers' intentions because the relationship with the buildings to which they are adjacent is so poor, perhaps separated by traffic, or littered with attention seeking motifs, street furniture, signage, changes of surface materials. Despite the claims of their designers, nothing could be further from the tradition of the continuity of building and space, the sobriety of paving material and relative absence of furniture, and the focus on one or two elements of major significance and quality of execution which characterise the majority of examples discussed in this book.

It should be evident therefore that my purpose is twofold, both to account for the history of the development of this genre of urban space as a phenomenon dependent on the times in which they developed, and also to create a platform from which to critique the present ethos of public open space, assailed as it is by the demands of traffic, by increasing commercialization of space, and lack of appreciation as a phenomenon which is held in common and therefore requires some degree of decorum from buildings and people. Although, as will be discussed in the last section, the tradition of the piazza might be faltering under severe pressure of urban change, I do not believe it is in a terminal condition. The urban experiment of post-Second World War Europe remains fresh in the collective memory and the alienating consequences of the abandonment of conventional methods of the organization of civic life still painful enough to ensure that the value of a pragmatic use of urban space continues to be appreciated. However, that consideration remains for the end of the book, and will occur after the repeated appearance of a concept of space originating in the political structure of one city. Throughout the following chapters the idea of Rome as the urban exemplar and source of archetypes will occur with great frequency. In the spatial and typological transformations of a single rectangular form, the *forum*, with its local origin in the irregular Roman space, the persistence of the political image of urban space as a continuing tradition will be apparent. The longevity of that image, largely a memory rather than a direct experience, should serve to reinforce the value of adherence to an urban tradition which has survived successive political transformations and is therefore likely to continue to inspire.

# PART I

# THE ROOTS OF ITALIAN URBAN FORM

# 1

# Rome: The centre of the city as *axis mundi*

The history of Italian architecture and urbanism is haunted by the image of Rome and the traces of its rule. That presence is felt in different ways, either as the morphological origin of the contemporary urban pattern, as the source of a general attitude towards civic values often expressed through the imitation of its forms and iconography, or as a mythical ideal of urban order. These different legacies of the ancient culture to the cities which followed them, both within Italy and elsewhere within the scope of Rome's empire, are intricate and often hard to unravel, extending from archaeological evidence to fanciful speculation. However, the type of distinction between scientific research and retrospective imagination which we are able to make today is not necessarily useful to the meaning of the historical phenomenon, despite its relevance for the understanding of the contemporary urban situation. The decline of the interpretation of the natural and urban environment as a phenomenon charged with spiritual significance is intimately connected to the separation of the functional aspects of the city from the expression of any transcendent ethos. Historically the religious reading of the natural and physical world which underlay the construction of ancient urban situations predisposed the citizens to an appropriation of the city as a revealed truth (Fustel de Coulange [1880] 1955; Rykwert 1976). In that context the mythic interpretation of cities might be considered to have primacy over the broad facts of its form. To the ancient minds which created urban spaces there was a correlation, which would normally require expert interpretation, between their immediate physical situation and the observable phenomena of the wider world around them. Settlements were viewed as manifesting the direct intervention of the divine in the mundane, and therefore the spiritual function of cities – their role as theatre of the civic cult – has to be appreciated by the contemporary mind if one is to understand the range of their psychological as well as physical effects. This poetic life of the city has effectively been superseded by a combination of utilitarian and formal methods which have no anchor in any cultural tradition.

In the modern territory of Italy the traces of Greek, Etruscan and most especially Roman settlements represent a diverse range of spatial types which

1.1    Forum Romanum, Rome. A view from the floor of the forum towards the Capitoline hill, with the arches of the *tabularium* beneath the Palazzo del Senatorio, and the Arch of Septimius Severus to the right.

require brief consideration as the precursors of the type of Italian piazza we are familiar with today. Although Roman thought and practice was closest chronologically and physically to Italian forms of urban space, the influence of these earlier civilizations as interpreted through the Roman experience was also significant. Greek cities have been the subject of diverse interpretations, yet the fundamental influence of Greek urban culture underpins subsequent Western society, and in particular rooted itself in the Italian consciousness, so that the echoes of independence and democracy were to re-emerge, after the destruction of Greek settlements or their appropriation by Roman conquest and subsequent decay, in the rhetoric of the medieval city state. While Greek political ideas had a difficult relationship with the increasingly centralized forms of Roman government, they provided the language by which later cities could express their systems of authority and representation. This was manifested in the abstract quality of the spatial continuum which related the cities to the features of their vivid and specific landscapes, Greek urban space being characterized as generously dynamic, this dominant mode for the public areas and temple precincts contrasting with the rational grid method attributed to Hippodamus of Miletus (Martienssen 1956; Scully 1969). Although Hippodamian influence has been observed in later Etruscan settlements, their principal cities were designed to be both rational and in accord with a religious interpretation of the cosmos (Scullard 1967; Haynes

1.2 Forum Romanum, Rome. A view from the *tabularium*, with the columns of the Temple of Vespasian in the foreground and the portico of the Temple of Saturn to the right.

2000; Torelli 2000). Roman colonial settlements have clear geometrical relationships inherited from Etruscan layouts which were the product of divinatory practices that embodied their belief in human dependence on the otherworldly. The rituals which the Etruscans pursued in the process of city founding were maintained by the Romans in the forms of an augury reflecting the celestial order on the terrestrial plane to determine a favourable site, the tracing of the principal streets (*cardo* and *decumanus*) and in the ploughing of a ritual furrow to establish the divinely protected boundary (Rykwert 1976: 65–68). Etruscan planning practices, both religious and rational, were adopted by

Rome partly as a means of defining a distinct Italian character to their cities. Unlike the abstracted void-like quality of Greek space, the Etruscans placed great emphasis on surfaces, in particular surfaces which could be entered. In urban situations this reverence for the threshold conferred positive value on the exterior space adjacent to the elaborated entrance plane or portico. This close connection between building and immediate urban setting is a characteristic of Italian urban space which can be seen as an inheritance from Etruscan practice. Drawing on both Greek and Etruscan cultures, the Romans combined them to produce a distinct form of urban environment which prized the civic and military significance of the sacred public space.

From these necessarily brief assertions it should be appreciated that there is an ambiguity about the purpose and methods of spatial composition in these cultures. Furthermore the typology of Roman urban space had two distinct forms which it is necessary to define. The first strand is related to the *genius loci* of Rome and the topography of the Forum Romanum itself, where the circumstances which produced the central political space of the entire empire presented itself as an ideal for emulation. The Forum Romanum, although developed as an accretion of disconnected structures, achieved an integration of those individual monuments into a unified though never fixed urban space. The second form is the result of the use of a generic model for city planning which related all colonial outposts to each other and by implication to the centre, the mother city. In some examples, though, the density of layering of distinct urban cultures is compactly expressed, as at Pompeii, where the Roman city concealed earlier Greek and Samnite settlements (Richardson 1988). Emerging from a lengthy process of archaeological excavation, the clear figure of the Forum of Pompeii represents a type of public space which is recognizable in numerous examples from later centuries as the Italian piazza, which merge generic and specific forms.

Favro (1996: 4–11) has discussed the perceptual reading of the urban environment by the Roman population, largely illiterate but nuanced in their understanding of the form of the city and the iconography of its meanings. Although we live in a visually saturated society, it is a literate one which expects communication through the written word, and occasionally has difficulty with the comprehension of the codes of symbolic imagery, beyond their immediate aesthetic appeal. We can only assume that the sturdiness of tufa or brick construction, the precision of travertine and the refinement of marble all communicated distinctions of prestige to the buildings and spaces which they were combined to create. Despite its cultural importance though, (the historical state of the centre of the Roman world in the era of its greatest activity during republican and imperial eras having long vanished), the Forum Romanum is difficult for us to fully appreciate since its present state is a figment of the early twentieth century imagination, and is fundamentally different from the situations which preceded it during the medieval, renaissance and baroque periods. As an urban experience it is a site which offers little explanation, confident of its own significance. And that

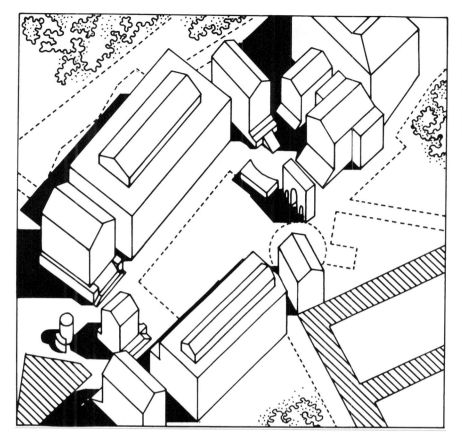

1.3 Diagram of the Forum Romanum with the Capitoline hill to the upper right. The new alignment of the later imperial fora is indicated at the bottom right.

confidence has been repaid by subsequent reinterpretations of the site itself and elsewhere as later public spaces sought to emulate the original model. The heterogeneous forms of the buildings which surrounded the Forum are its abiding legacy. The predominance of individual civic, religious or military structures and the proliferation of different expressions defining a precinct are the effects which have survived and continue to dominate, and which could also be seen as epitomising the Italian piazze which followed.

The foundation legends of Rome played their part in the location of the Forum. The story of the birth of the semi-divine twins Romulus and Remus, and the former's foundation of Rome in 753 B.C. was thoroughly documented by Roman authors. It combined Trojan origins, through the descent of the twins from Aeneas, and was therefore explicitly opposed through myth to Greek culture, but also featured Etruscan practice which made claim to native Italian origin. The inauguration of the city involved Romulus and Remus making rival augures from the Aventine hill. Their observation of the flight of birds resulted in the settlement of the Palatine hill and its enclosure by a ritually defined wall. This legend found a comfortable fit with the context of the historic city itself, and there was therefore a mutual validation which took place between myth and actuality (Carandidni and Cappelli 2000). The settlement of the Palatine hill was safe from periodic inundation by the Tiber which formed a natural defensive barrier, but land on three sides of the hill (roughly on the north western, south western, and south eastern sides) was marshy and particularly prone to flooding. The north eastern side, however, was less vulnerable and bordered the area of rival settlements of the Sabines on the Quirinal and Esquiline hills, and was overlooked to the north by the double hill of the Capitol and the Arx. Thus, after its use as a burial ground by the neighbouring tribes and in fulfillment of the narrative provided by legend, topographic convenience was to lead to the development of this valley as the Forum Romanum, the accretion of monuments eventually obscuring its natural state (Grant 1970).

Returning to the tension between the generic and the specific, the Forum Romanum, as the centre of the ancient city, represented both a physical model for rivalry in other colonial cities and a conceptual model to which other fora in those subject cities referred by analogy (Vitruvius 1999: 64). The conceptual framework of the Roman city, the structure of *cardo* and *decumanus* crossing at the forum familiar from these colonial cities was however hard to discern in the physical and social centre of the Roman world. Attempts have been made to interpret the surviving topography of the city in the geometry of the ideal conceptualization but with little success, and despite the efforts of skilled interpreters of classical archaeology, most especially in the nineteenth century (Grimal [1954] 1983): 29; Salmon 2000: 98–106). The physical form of the forum was much more clearly influenced by the geometry produced by attention to the topographic features of the landscape. The difficulty of describing a simple geometric figure, reducing it to a single strong idea would not to the modern sensibility be considered a fault and yet one has only to consider the long history of the design of precisely symmetrical spaces to be aware that the pervasive association of ideal geometric space with political power was overturned in this particularly potent place and concept.

The actual space had a threefold purpose whose overlapping characteristics were at the root of its complexity. Firstly it was a religious place, the home of the city's most sacred objects guarded by the Vestals. Secondly it was a political space, site of the meetings of the assembly in the Comitium, a vaguely circular open space overlooked by the Rostra adjacent to the Senate House. Beneath the Comitium, the so-called *lapis niger* was discovered, a Greek black marble pavement covering an earlier shrine the position of which emphasises the connections between the religious and political spheres. And lastly these roles were supported by the site's military function, as the scene for the commemoration of victory through the erection of monuments, the celebration of triumphs and the holding of gladiatorial games on the pavement of the Forum. This tripartite function of worship, debate and expression of power was to survive into later Italian examples. In addition commercial life was also accommodated in the shops which lined the space and were later enclosed within the basilicas.

The pragmatic draining of the land for the Forum around 600 B.C., with the construction of the *cloaca maxima* (the great drain) and the paving of the ground surface, should not obscure the spiritual significance of its elements surrounding the most sacred site of the city. The Forum, arranged along the path of the *via sacra*, spanned between the two most important temples in Rome, that of Jupiter Optimus Maximus on the Capitoline hill (consecrated in 509 B.C. at the start of the republic), and that of Vesta on the valley floor itself (the present remains of which date from approximately 200 A.D.). Between these two poles, representing at one end an Etruscan legacy (with the celebrated pedimented temple, its gilded roof and sculptures), and at the other end the civic cult of Rome (in the eternal flame of Vesta, the hearth of the city in its circular temple the form of which recalled its original pastoral construction of willow and thatch), this urban space was loaded with political significance which established Rome's right to pre-eminence. This meaning was reinforced by further limits to the space of the Forum which were established by two further temples, those of Saturn and Castor. Built at the foot of the Capitoline hill, and facing across the Forum to the Comitium the columns of the Temple of Saturn (rebuilt from 43 B.C.) survive to testify to its importance as both the state treasury and the site where laws were displayed. Adjacent to the complex of the Vestals, the Temple of Castor and Pollux was built on the site where the heavenly twins were believed to have appeared to water their horses at the pond of the *lacus jaturnae*, following the battle of Lacus Regillus in 499 B.C. The high podium of the Temple of Castor was used for balloting of the citizenry, and its three standing columns provide one of the great picturesque elements of the present-day archaeological site.

In the complex transition from republican to imperial systems of government the aesthetic contrast between these distinct elements was reduced by the creation of a series of three civic structures the consistent and repetitive treatment of which did much to unify the space. Straddling the saddle of the hill between the Capitol and the Arx, the Tabularium was an arcaded structure built from 78 B.C. to house the city records. The lower areas of this building survive as the foundation for Michelangelo's Palazzo del Senatorio, the seat of contemporary Roman civic government which faces on to the Piazza del Campidoglio. The engaged columns and arcades of the Tabularium were complemented by the similar elevations of two buildings now vanished and the impact of which is harder to imagine, the Basilicas Aemilia and Julia, which functioned respectively as business and legal centres. The Basilica Aemilia was earlier in date, (179 B.C.) and it was this structure which was complemented across the Forum by Julius Caesar's Basilica, completed under Augustus (54–46 B.C.). The remaining open side of the Forum was enclosed by the construction, also by Augustus, of the Temple of the Deified Julius (dedicated in 29 B.C.) adjacent to the Regia, his former residence as *pontifex maximus* (high priest) and the site of cremation of the assassinated dictator, with its own Rostrum facing the repositioned rostrum adjacent to the Comitium. The solar positioning of this new temple, and its alignment on a line between sunrise on the winter solstice and sunset on the summer solstice extended out to impose a new meaning on the circumstantially developed forum, but would perhaps remain obscure to other than the most informed citizen (McEwen 2003: 175–8). As the temple was so aligned that the sun entered the *cella* at sunset on the summer solstice, the centre of the Roman world was overlaid with a cosmological significance which associated the space with both Augustus's adoptive father, Julius Caesar, and his reputed father, the sun god Apollo. The development of the Forum under Augustus, its gradual enclosure and visual homogenization brought about a reinterpretation of the space, so that in diametric opposition to its original orientation towards the Capitoline complex, new emphasis was placed on the other direction towards the Temple of the Deified Julius.

As the imperial system was consolidated the flight of significant daily activity to the new fora initiated under Caesar, Augustus, Vespasian, Nerva and Trajan emphasized the sacred aspects of the original Forum Romanum. New temples were dedicated to the deified members of imperial dynasties, and arches recorded their military triumphs. The Temple of Vespasian and Titus was constructed perpendicular to the Temple of Saturn and next to the Temple of Concord so that it faced along the Forum to the Temple of the Deified Julius and the Arch of Augustus at the other end. Three of its columns survive, but there are more complete remains in the elevated portico of the Temple of Antoninus and Faustina (built from 141 A.D.) facing across the Forum overlooking the Regia and the Temple of Vesta. Its subsequent life as the church of San Lorenzo in Miranda ensured the preservation of many of its elements. The Arch of Augustus (29 B.C.) which spanned between the Temples of Castor and the Deified Julius, which enclosed the southern corner of the Forum Romanum and acted as a screen to the Temple of Vesta, has not survived. More substantial is the Arch of Titus (81 A.D.) restored in the modern era and standing outside the Forum proper, positioned on the *via sacra* in relation to the House of the Vestals. However, within the Forum, between the Rostra and the Comitium, the African emperor Septimius Severus confirmed his ascendancy with the erection of a magnificent three bayed arch with engaged columns in 203 A.D. The subsequent half-burial of his arch during the centuries of the city's decline was a considerable help in its survival.

The periodic maintenance and rebuilding of the structures of the Roman Forum became an accepted method by which different republican officials, dictators and eventually imperial dynasts sought to exert political power. This would take two forms, a direct one and an implied one. In the first instance rededication and amplification by a ruler to project his own claims to power as exemplified by the planned construction of the Tabularium by Sulla, the restoration of the Temple of Jupiter Optimus Maximus claimed by Julius Caesar, the initiation of the latter's own forum and the building of that of Augustus represented the most apparent form. More subtly the second form served to emphasise the dynastic ambitions of various rulers, for example Augustus's completion of Julius Caesar's projects and the dedication of a temple to him, and the completion by Hadrian of the projects of his

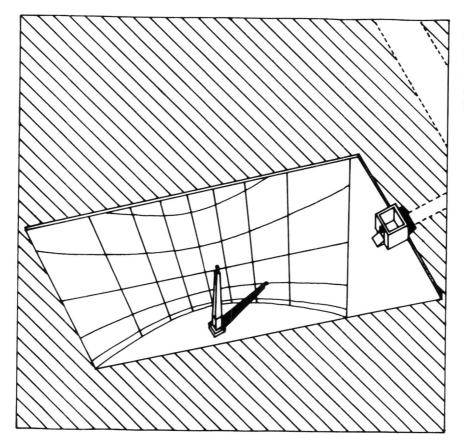

1.4 Diagram of the Horologium Augusti, Rome. The Ara Pacis Augustae stands at the edge of the paved precinct.

predecessor Trajan associated specific families of rulers with the city's destiny (Zanker 1988; Boatwright 1987). An unintended product of the thwarting of these ambitions, the significance of the Forum Romanum as an antecedent for Italian public space is in its ambiguity of functions and their coexistence. Change was a constant as structures were embellished, either in pious restoration or significant enlargement and through the introduction of new monuments. The general direction was towards a continuity of enclosure but the individual rivalries ensured a variety of expression. Inevitably the space was overawed by the major manifestations of political patronage, but extended periods of social instability had created discontinuity in the urban fabric, a discontinuity which provided aesthetic relief and variety in the urban scene which would remain a positive feature of subsequent piazze.

While Roman pragmatism found uses for the magnificent monumental areas constructed by numerous emperors, there was also the use of unadorned space itself as a display of power, no more amply expressed than in the complex of the Horologium Augusti, or Augustan sundial erected in the area of the Campus Martius to the north of the city, and built in relation to the mausoleum of Augustus and his altar, the Ara Pacis Augustae inaugurated in 9 B.C. The marble panels on the exterior of the altar enclosure instructed the Roman citizens in the benefits of Augustan rule and the imperial destiny of his heirs, making claims to dynastic political supremacy as being divinely sanctioned through its reference to Aeneas. The altar stood at the edge of a marble pavement measuring 160 by 75 metres with bronze inlaid lines mapping the hours of the day and months of the year, times indicated by the shadow of a massive 30 metre high red granite obelisk transported here to symbolise Augustus's conquest of Egypt. On his birthday, 23 September, the shadow of the sundial's gnomon was cast across the entrance to the enclosure of the Ara Pacis, linking the space of the city with the life of the emperor in a dramatic display of apparently cosmic power. Here was a further instance of the personal mythology of Augustus as offspring of Apollo being expressed in physical terms through the solar animation of an urban monument.

As the imperial system of government was secured the pattern was established of the imperial fora extending out to the north of the Forum Romanum, the link being the Forum of Julius Caesar (dedicated 46 B.C.) constructed for the transaction of business as a symmetrical frame to the temple of Venus Genetrix. The regular rectangular plan form derived from Hellenistic precedents but had already been adapted for use in colonial cities. The dedication of the temple to Venus, from whom the Caesars claimed descent, suggested an exclusive experience of control without the competitive display of rival monuments so characteristic of the original Forum. With their different expressions and contrasting irregularity and regularity between these two spaces the basic typological division of the subsequent Italian piazza between 'organic' and 'inorganic' forms could be discerned adjacent to each other. But while the Forum Romanum would remain a foundational idea for the conceptualization of future piazze, the idealizing uniformity of the Forum Julium would inspire numerous often incomplete imitations in subsequent centuries. The completion of the projects of Julius Caesar by his heir and eventual successor Augustus would provide the source of his own project of the Forum Augustum where the precinct was provided for the temple of Mars Ultor (42–2 B.C.), and the rectangular precedent was supplemented by apsidal transepts dedicated to the civic ancestor-founders Aeneas and Romulus. Constructed perpendicular to the Forum Julium, the Forum Augustum presented through its iconography a more explicit programme of justification for the divine status of the *princeps* (Favro 1996: 95–98). However the relationship to the existing city was somewhat problematical, their internalized nature and protection by great walls (such as the surviving fire wall of Augustus's Forum) suggested an exclusive image of citizenship. The pragmatic reasons for such separation between city and public space, between the brick, timber and stucco urban fabric and the glistening marble forum, reinforced the political status of the ruler, described on his monument as *pater patriae*, father of his country. This complex in turn would lead to the layout over a century later of the Forum of Trajan, on an axis perpendicular to that of

Augustus (Packer 1997; Wightman 1997). The substantial survival of parts of this complex, the markets of Trajan, give the modern day visitor some idea of the extent and qualities of these imperial constructions in contrast to the less easily legible remains of the Forum Romanum.

1.5   Forum of Trajan, Rome. The largest of the imperial fora, this view shows the hemicycle of Trajan's Markets built against the Quirinal hill.

The Forum of Trajan's scale was complemented by the complex sequence of spaces arranged along and across its axes. The earlier fora of Julius and Augustus were essentially unitary spaces with columned temple porticoes dominating rectangular spaces but the Forum of Trajan (constructed 107–13 A.D.) only commenced with a rectangular forum surrounded by colonnades. An equestrian statue of the emperor was positioned in the centre and the cross axis was extended beyond the rectangular enclosure by apsidal spaces similar in size to those employed by the Forum Augustum. That on the north east of the Forum of Trajan was itself surrounded by the elevated exedra of the markets which form a boundary with the Quirinal hill. In place of the usual terminating temple, though, was a public hall, a basilica that served as a library, the Basilica Ulpia which was itself terminated at its short ends by two more apsidal spaces. Beyond and towering over the library was Trajan's column, the commissioned account of his Dacian campaign in the form of the spiral narrative wrapped around the shaft. Trajan's statue on its summit was visible from the *fornix*, or gate, of the forum, and therefore it acted as a focus for the visitor's journey through the complex (Davies 2000: 127–35; Wilson Jones 2000: 161–74). Beyond the column and completing the axial sequence was the customary temple to the deified emperor conjectured to sit within a columned apse. The extent of this

1.6    Forum of Pompeii. A colonnade lining the forum, which is oriented towards Vesuvius in the distance.

sequence with contrasting scales of spaces which vary between the extensive and constricted, the directional and the cross axial, combines the unitary typology of the early imperial fora and the variety of form typical of the Forum Romanum itself. The culmination of the sequence though was not the view of the cult image within the cella of the temple, but the view from beneath his image at the top of the column (see Figure 9.6). Of course, this view would have been subject to restricted access but would have provided a spectacular view of the city under the patronage of Trajan and has been thought to have helped determine further imperial monuments in the city under his successor Hadrian (Davies 2000: 158–71). The entire complex of the Forum and the markets of Trajan presents the most splendid example of a planned forum in the capital of an empire at its apogee. During the later empire the ancient irregular space of the Forum Romanum was neighboured by the ordered magnificence of the imperial fora, the orientalizing luxury of their scale, symmetry, and regularity in sharp contrast to native Roman austerity and the haphazard growth of the central urban space of a world empire. The influence of the newer complexes on later generations was largely literary as their topographical position buried them under subsequent medieval accretions or their form disintegrated as, for example, their great series of identical columns became the building components of early Christian basilicas, as will be discussed in the next chapter.

As the remains of the Forum Romanum and the imperial fora were uncovered systematically by architects and archaeologists from the eighteenth century onwards the scale of the urban enterprise and the political will of the ancient city became evident to newer industrializing societies. Outside the city of Rome, in other colonial foundations in Italy and beyond more modest examples provided further demonstrations of the typology of urban space, and presented more typical examples of the Roman urban experience. Also uncovered during the archaeological campaigns of the enlightenment, the Forum of Pompeii presented one version of this type of prosperous colonial city, frozen on the day of its destruction by the eruption of Vesuvius in 79 A.D. The best surviving example of a Roman public space, both in terms of its overall typicality and the atypicality of its individual elements, Pompeii is less difficult to read than the excavated remains of the Forum Romanum, or the examples which survive embedded within cities with continuous histories of inhabitation. At Pompeii not only did the volcano preserve a substantial example of Roman public space but also the process by which the forum was being renewed and enhanced following its earlier destruction caused by the earthquake of 62 A.D. Although there were earlier settlements on the site, it developed as a significant urban development from the second century B.C., and witnessed an acceleration of the urbanization process with the establishment of a colony of army veterans in 80 B.C. The forum is untypically exaggerated in form, its length being more than four times the width, proportions which would not have met with the approval of the contemporary authority Vitruvius (1999: 64, 239). The northern end of the forum is dominated by the footprint of a temple of Jupiter, positioned to relate to the silhouette of Vesuvius beyond it. Other temples and public structures lined the forum with the basilica placed at the lower end, but with an unusual asymmetrical arrangement. Unity for the diverse structures forming the space was provided on the eastern side by a series of similar porticoes. On the western side a continuous portico was under construction when the volcano struck (Richardson 1988: 88–99, 191–210, 261–76).

A more generic example is provided by the remains of the forum of Brixia, located in the historic core of the Lombard city of Brescia, (which in this book will provide examples of piazze from different historical periods up until the twentieth century). Set within a gridded *castrum* plan, the axial arrangement of the forum of Brixia, disposed between capitol and basilica at the crossing of *cardo* and *decumanus* ensured its survival as a public space within the town after the fall of the Roman empire although, as in Verona, medieval building was to shrink the dimensions of the open area to a form of wide street of irregular limits, the present day Piazza del Foro. Our knowledge of the Roman remains comes from the first serious excavations in the 1820s, when the region was under Austrian control. As illustrations from the period show, a fair degree of licence was used to produce a sufficiently impressive silhouette to the *capitolium* so that it could inspire an appropriate awe and melancholy, in accordance with romantic aspirations which would turn

1.7   Forum of Brixia (Piazza del Foro, Brescia). A view northwards to the reconstructed portico of the capitolium.

eventually to thoughts of national unification (Springer 1987). This nostalgia reached its propagandistic apogee in the 1930s with the reconstruction of a fragment of the portico of the *capitolium*, and the present Piazza del Foro therefore has an explicit political meaning in the use of an urban memory which was intended to reinforce ideas of continuity, at precisely the same time as a Fascist urban centre was being created at Piazza della Vittoria in a more modern quarter of the city (Canniffe 1997). The actual state of the ruins of the *capitolium* was integrated into a fictional ruin the appearance of which was intended to support the contemporary political order of Fascism as well as display evidence of past glory. Within this complex layering of references, the original representation of its excavated state owes much to the tradition of the romantic views of ruins which conditioned the popular image of Rome at that time. This publication during a period of Austrian rule, presented a pacific and elegiac aspect to these discoveries (Saleri 1838). The bronze statue of Victory, the most significant find, presented a magnanimous face, but a hundred years later it was the martial aspects of Roman civilization which were seen to be of most importance. The reconstruction of the portico in the 1930s and the creation of the archaeological zone produced dead public space, where significance as a museum exhibit took precedence over its life as part of the city. This situation, where the new/old portico is itself recovered from the existing urban context of Brescia, is extreme but it took place at a time when archaeological remains in Rome were themselves being freed from

1.8    Piazza del Foro, Brescia. Diagram of the disposition of the *capitolium* and the basilica, with the profile of the bronze figure of Victory excavated there.

their 'decadent' accretions to serve as contemporary propaganda, as will be discussed in a later chapter.

Always suitable for exploitation for political purposes, the nature of Roman public space would gradually be eroded and transformed during the long decline of the empire, but its forms would persist, and not only the forms of public open space. The reuse of substantial structures through dismemberment and reassemblage will be discussed in the next chapter. New forms of occupation, with abandoned structures being used for a number of different

1.9   Piazza Navona, Rome. The modern day piazza, built on the footprint of the Stadium of Domitian, is dominated by the church of Sant'Agnese in Agone and centred on the obelisk which surmounts Bernini's Four Rivers fountain.

functions would leave their mark in subsequent cities. The persistence of these forms would be described by Aldo Rossi in his 'theory of permanences' (Rossi 1982: 57–61). Famous examples of this process which exerted an influence on urban form include the reuse of amphitheatres in Florence and Lucca, the former densely built over and recognizable by the curving street pattern produced by the memory of its presence, close to the present day Piazza Santa Croce. In the example in Lucca the original impact of the elliptical amphitheatre survives as the Piazza Anfiteatro at the centre of a circuit of housing built over the substructure of the raked seating (see Figure 2.1). However, the most dramatic example of this phenomenon of public space growing organically from previous monumental buildings is Piazza Navona in Rome, the central public space of the modern city which occupies the footprint of the Stadium of Domitian (c. 92–96 A.D.). Its position in the Campus Martius, the area of the ancient city reserved for large sporting and leisure facilities meant that the ruins of the stadium remained in the sparsely occupied post-imperial city largely unused for the best part of a thousand years until the fifteenth century (Krautheimer 1980: 243). Its presence today, as an enclosed but expansive public space, owes much to the elaboration of its constituent buildings which did not appear until the seventeenth century. This period saw the construction of the huge domed church (1652–72) dedicated to the Roman martyr Agnes, reputed to have been put to death in the stadium. Sant'Agnese in Agone adjoins the Palazzo Pamphilj (1646–49), and the square is given focus by Bernini's Four Rivers fountain (1647–51) the obelisk of which simulates the sort of monument which would have ornamented the *spina* of the ancient race track. During the Mussolinian period the resonant utilitarian underpinnings of this exuberant baroque space were exposed at its northern end by the opening up of the half-submerged archaeological remains. But this dry exercise in imperial history could not dispel the popular use of Piazza Navona which had seen it host numerous festivals including deliberate flooding. Its present use as one of the foremost tourist sites of the city, with photo opportunities, market stalls, amateur artists and portraitists, buskers, living statues and the occasional television spectacular keep the tradition of the ancient forum alive in the modern city. However distant from each other in time, those two phenomena are connected by a process of political and social transformation which begins with a fundamental change of values at the centre of the Roman empire, signalled by the rise of a new religion. But beyond that immediate change the republican and imperial iconography of Rome was to find itself reinterpreted by later cities as *the* means by which to express independence, dominion and power.

# 2

# Christianity: The development of new urban forms

The fracturing of political stability which occurred in parallel with the collapse of the western Roman empire provided the Italian city with a new phase of development which laid the foundations for the urban culture which we still recognise as specific to the country. There were particular circumstances which produced this situation. The patronage of the hitherto persecuted cult of Christianity by the young emperor Constantine was the major change. This followed his victory at the Milvian Bridge on the outskirts of Rome in the year which became designated as 312 A.D. when the Christian calendar was introduced. The previous focus on a single emperor had already been dispensed with through the introduction of the tetrarchy by Diocletian in 293, with pairs of co-emperors ruling western and eastern empires. Constantine's strategic decisions would have consequences beyond Rome itself, especially with his refoundation of Byzantium as a new imperial capital, Constantinople, in 324. The power vacuum created by the eastward shift in the centre of gravity of the Roman empire left Italy increasingly vulnerable to barbarian attack, a situation exacerbated for Rome itself by the adoption of Ravenna on the Adriatic coast as effective capital of the western empire during the fifth century. When subsequent barbarian invasions undermined the authority of imperial control, especially after the sack of Rome in 410, the only efficient jurisdiction which survived to fulfil the roles of civil administration was the relatively newly established episcopate which had been mapped on to the Roman bureaucratic system. The unified network of previous Roman colonial settlements instead gave way to a transformed scene. Cities returned to a more independent status than had been the case during the empire. Within cities, old centres and structures were abandoned in favour of new centres. And the status of the city as a refuge within a hostile landscape became reinforced as control of the surrounding territories fluctuated or fell under the domination of hostile powers. The apparent fulfilment of apocalyptic prophecies in the political and social turmoil of the period would only have served to reinforce the role of the church as the protector of cities, and the city as a reflection of divine order. From this era of conflict produced by internal and external threats which tested the survival of urban civilization, and through a prolonged process of development lasting the best part of a millennium, emerged the confident arena of the public realm as the clearly defined urban space with its towers, portals and arcades; the piazza.

Throughout these dramatic changes the physical significance of Rome was drained of energy, yet the political idea of the city would be maintained under a very different guise. The city's relationship to its origins was the first concept to be transformed. If the city represented a significant component of imperial administration and identity, and even its form was a type comprehensible across the empire, the institutionalization of Christianity had the effect of rupturing this universality. Centres of pagan worship, the very focus of Roman cities, were now subject to disuse or even destruction in favour of the construction of new meeting places often located in the marginal sites of previous religious persecution. Replaced by Constantinople as the new centre of the empire, the paradigm which provided the model for emulation was no longer Rome but Jerusalem, the urban epitome of the Judaeo-Christian tradition which was itself a metaphor for Paradise.

This reflects the difference in meaning between the two Latin terms for city, *civitas* and *urbs* where the former indicates the sense of civic values and the latter refers to the physical entity and the former the political identity. In an era which saw public aspiration focus on the afterlife, under the influence of Christian eschatology, the split between the two terms, representing the actual and the intangible was the subject of interpretation by the most perceptive observers even as this division became apparent. Following the sack in 410, Augustine of Hippo produced a theological justification for this division in *On the City of God against the Pagans*, provocatively questioning the claims to divine origin of Rome itself, and the cities which claimed her inheritance.

And yet who ever believed in the divinity of Romulus except Rome, and that when Rome was small and at the beginning of her history? Thereafter it was inevitable that posterity should preserve the tradition handed down from earlier times, and the community, as we say, drank in this superstition with its mother's milk. Then the city grew in power and attained a great empire; and from this height of power she diffused, from that higher level, as it were, this belief among the other nations, whom she dominated. Those nations professed this belief, without indeed believing it, to avoid giving offence to the city to whom they were enslaved, in the matter of that city's founder. They would have given offence by differing from Rome about the title of Romulus; for Rome's belief in his divinity did not spring from a love of error but from an error of love. In contrast, although Christ is the founder of the eternal Heavenly City, that City's belief in Christ as God does not arise from her foundation by him; the truth is that her foundation arises from her belief in Christ as God. Rome worshipped her founder as a god after she had been built and dedicated. Rome believed Romulus to be a god because she loved him; the Heavenly City loved Christ because she believed him to be God. Thus Rome had already an object of her love, which she could readily turn from a loved object into a final good, falsely believed in; correspondingly, our City had ready an object of her belief, so that she might not rashly love a false good but with true faith might set her affection on the true good. (Augustine 1972: 1030)

This passage neatly qualifies the divine sanction of Roman urbanity by replacing the role of founder of the heavenly city with that of its destiny in the form of union with Christ. Augustine's text was written after disaster had struck Rome, but Constantine's policy in the previous century had been to renovate the fabric of the city through the construction of new Christian structures, notwithstanding the conservative opposition of an initially lukewarm civic bureaucracy (Krautheimer 1980: 3–58). The topography of Christian Rome was to be created from two sources, from above and below in the social hierarchy, using imperial family properties (as at the Lateran basilica, founded in 312) and the existing sites of the veneration of Christian martyrs (as at the basilica constructed between 317–332 at the Vatican cemetery where the apostle Peter was believed to be buried). Removed from the historic centre of the city in the still largely pagan Forum Romanum, the new publicly visible structures, symbols of the political ascendancy of the new religion, redefined the city from their peripheral locations. In a possible echo of the traditional forms of *cardo* and *decumanus*, the axis between the Lateran and the Vatican, and that between the later churches of Santa Maria Maggiore (circa 420) and San Paolo (384) formed a cross centred on the Colosseum, now held sacred as a notorious site of persecution and martyrdom (Guidoni 1990: 3–36). The change of interpretation of such a symbol from a device of pagan divination to that of Christian sanctification indicates the whole process by which the new holy city was created out of the carcass of ancient urban practices.

The typological variety of the urban complexes of this period, of course, disrupt the common notion of the Dark Ages, achieved as they were in a period of less than obvious technological and infrastructural sophistication. Although to later eyes they were not in the van of architectural innovation the substantial structures of this period would continue to provide the core of later medieval and renaissance cities (Elsner 1998). The new typologies, most notably the longitudinal Christian basilica and the polygonal baptistery or martyrium were transformations of antique types but were quite radical in these mutations. As cult buildings they broke from the pagan past by encouraging collective worship within the body of the building, through the complex metaphor of the church as the body of Christ. In accordance with numerous late antique examples, decorative expression was concentrated on the interior, with mosaic, fresco and the use of coloured marble, while exteriors continued to be austere. While this distinction supported the designation of the church interior as sacred, the threshold between the public space and the interior would become a significant zone of articulation.

The specificity of these new types of Christian urban form grew with the development of ritual practice during these centuries. The social situation which saw mass public conversion required urban spaces rather than the essentially domestic spaces of an era of persecution. For example the need for an entire urban population to be with their bishop for the major Christian feast of Easter meant that public space had to be employed, if only as overspill for occasions such as this when the church building had reached its capacity. In the process of conversion the distinction between full participation and the preparatory status of the catechumen required a spatial division which manifested itself in the development of the baptistery as a distinct building form. Typically independent of the body of the church proper, their characteristically massive polygonal structures transformed the typology of the circular halls of late imperial palaces, such as that of Diocletian at Split. However, the specific archetype, where function and form (in this case in a columned octagonal hall) would appear to be the Lateran baptistery initiated by Constantine himself adjacent to the new basilica on his family property the latter described as 'an audience hall of Christ the King' (Krautheimer 1980: 22).

While imperial patronage provided the means for new building, previous religious architecture could not provide the model, and the characteristic form of the basilica therefore was adopted from civic structures, but also from a reinterpretation of public space which was to have an enduring influence. The basilica of San Crisogono, referred to in the introduction, is amongst the earliest known public site of Christian worship in Rome and the assumed appearance of this early church established a pattern which would become embedded in subsequent church building practice (see Figure 0.8). In the relatively free urban pattern of Trastevere, the first church took the form of a large rectangular hall, borrowed from the secular building forms of the period, with a pitched roof and arched openings on its eastern side (before the normative west to east pattern was established) leading ultimately to the longitudinal axiality of Christian churches. On either side the long outer walls were protected by long porticoes of piers and lean-to roofs. Openings in these walls communicated between the church proper and these protected exterior spaces, and it has been assumed that they indicate the social division among the Christian community between the baptized and the catechumens who were allowed to listen to the reading of the scriptures but could not participate in the eucharist (Krautheimer 1971: 5–6). Through the development of spaces such as these porticoes, the church complexes began to exert an urban presence which would form significant spaces as the new religion rose in its social and political status, with boundaries between clergy, congregation, and those in the process of conversion resulting in ambiguous and hierarchical architectural forms.

The transformation of the pagan urban world into the rather less politically ordered Christian world had consequences for every form of social expression not the least the city. The civic cults associated with paganism had placed emphasis on the combined power of origins and centre as a reflection of celestial order. The form of the city was a sign of paganism and the new religion therefore could not be indifferent to urban form, whatever the expectation of imminent salvation. The rise of Christianity was dependent on two elements, however, a popular and personal faith which had adherents at all levels of society, and an imperial champion in Constantine who could use the power at his disposal to promote its cause. The combination of the two elements would mean that urban form could be transformed from above and below, by imperial fiat and popular action to overturn the pagan city. If the civic temple in the typical forum had a reduced status, that could be contrasted with the enhanced role of sites of Christian worship, particularly those of martyrdom and burial. Their geographical location, often on the periphery implied the changing of a centripetal model to a centrifugal one, as Elsner remarks

Establishing a new sacred topography around the outside of the city involved a radical redefinition of the ritual patterns of urban life. Instead of the sacred focus being concentrated in the centre (as had been the case in pagan Rome), it would forever be directed to the city's periphery. In due course, the forum – the very heart of ancient Rome – would become little more than an easy quarry for reusable stone. Exactly the same transformation took place in Milan, where apart from the cathedral in the city centre, the major churches and their relics surrounded the city's outer walls. (Elsner 1998: 141)

In northern Italy the city of Milan had risen in status as an imperial residence during the rule of Maximian Hercules, who had served as Diocletian's co-emperor between 293 and 305. Its strategic position for routes across the empire helped it maintain its pre-eminence as a western capital throughout the fourth century leaving significant early Christian remains buried within the fabric of the modern industrial city. Most prominent amongst them is the basilica of San Lorenzo, to the south west of the centre. The basilica, unlike the rectangular hall from which the term derives, is a complex of polygonal structures gathered around a central domed space is a product of the period when the city was dominated by the personality of Ambrose, bishop of Milan between 374 and 397. His involvement in the theological disputes of the period, and in the struggles regarding the relationship of the emperor and the church would dominate different aspects of urban life, but would have an enduring impact through the establishment of significant churches, such as that in which his body lies, Sant'Ambrogio, and San Lorenzo Maggiore. The precise origins of the latter church, either as a product of Ambrose's party, or of the pro-imperial group to which he was opposed remains difficult to determine. Krautheimer has speculated that it was the latter, with the subsiduary chapel of San Aquilino planned as an imperial mausoleum (Krautheimer 1983: 69–92). Whatever the precise truth, the complex of adjacent churches, chapels and towers, with no significant religious relics, was approached via a great atrium with a portico of fluted corinthian columns which survive adjacent to the present-day tram lines. The presence of an arch in the centre of an otherwise trabeated colonnade has been considered a sign of its imperial origins, and the magnificent scale and geometrical complexity of what was built continued the design strategies of late imperial residences, but here devoted to the more popular and public use of the new religion.

Whereas the type of the Roman forum had been characterized by the rectangular arrangement before a pedimented temple front, the civic structure of the basilica and the ranges of colonnades which adjoined them, the piazza which came to supersede it had a distinctly different family of elements. The Christian basilica's ornamented facade, with its adoption of the language of

2.1   San Lorenzo
Maggiore,
Milan. A view
through the
surviving
colonnade
towards the
octagonal
basilica.

military triumph to the representation of the gates of the heavenly Jerusalem
was now the dominating element, its typical orientation being at the east of the
new urban space (Smith 1978: 79–96). This arrangement was reiterated in the
interior, with parallel rows of columns forming a public space, a nave, before
a triumphal arch framing the altar in its apse, the chancel. The materials for
these buildings, both structure and decoration, were provided by the *spolia* of
pagan structures, particularly marble columns and panels. The longitudinal
axis connecting the public space to the altar was then marked by a series of
elements which indicated the enhanced status of each zone. Pairs of columns,

2.2 Sant' Ambrogio, Milan. A view from the atrium towards the basilica and the campanile.

typically objects of spoil, would flank the door and in more complex and later manifestations would be mounted on the backs of recumbent lions to support projecting portals marking the boundary between sacred and profane space. Strategies for this type of demarcation would often be replicated internally to signify the separation between laity and clergy, exploiting the iconography of the triumphal arch to signify Christ's victory over death. Decorated tympana, or panels of mosaic would show the enthroned Christ while the surface of the facade would be pierced by major windows, often becoming circular in form in later examples, and articulated by tiers of arcading. The facade was often an independent entity conceptually attached as much to the body of the piazza as it was physically attached to the volume of the nave, collapsing the iconographic programme of the interior onto the exterior surface. A further zone of distinction might be provided by an atrium around a fountain or well head as survives at the basilica of Sant'Ambrogio in Milan. Such enclosed public spaces became elided with different social functions, in one direction, that of enclosure and tranquility, becoming the source of the cloister once the monastic system was established, and in the other, as a place of gathering prior to religious activity becoming another precursor of the medieval piazza.

In addition to the baptistery and the basilica, clerical accommodation, either as a canonry or bishop's palace would often accompany these sacred structures, and later perhaps would be supplemented by a centre of civic government (Miller 2000). Lastly rising over all and providing a vertical accent to the ensemble would be a campanile, housing the bells that summoned the faithful to prayer and providing a lookout for signs of political trouble. Far less formally coherent than the types of urban space which had preceded it, the explicit connection between function and form, the typological family of urban elements would mean that each city would assume a more distinct identity, rather than being reflections of the identity of the mother city, Rome. The space between such structures, largely religious in character if not actually sacred buildings, then became the focus of processions and festivals both penitential and celebratory which marked the liturgical year. In a culture where literacy was very restricted, the representation of the mysteries of Christianity in the spaces of the city would be a major means by which the secular world was connected to the sacred, and the heavenly Jerusalem manifested in the everyday urban environment. The civic nature of such urban places was reinforced by the encouragement of specifically local cults, where the presence of the relics of a saint provided some guarantee of divine protection. This might take the form of an internationally significant saint, such as the evangelist Mark, his body stolen by the Venetians from Alexandria in 828, or that of St. Nicholas similarly taken from Myra in Asia Minor and presented to the southern Italian city of Bari in 1087, partly to thwart a rival plan by the Genoese. More typically the relics were those of a local early Christian saint, perhaps a martyr, but often an early bishop such as San Ercolano in Perugia and San Geminiano in Modena whose veneration signified a desire for urban continuity with the historical past.

Whatever the spiritual benefits of such devotions, there was an undoubted commercial motive to town and clergy through the institutionalization of pilgrimage. In the great centres this activity would be truly international in character, but would have a regional impact for local centres, reinforcing the link between city and territory and extending the influence of and

identification with the patronal saint. This phenomenon in turn might be a source of competition in regions with several urban centres, leading to a form of cultural rivalry expressed in a higher tower, a broader nave or a grander fountain. In such situations civil and religious authorities made common cause, but the city benefited generally from the increase in prestige. Of course, the construction of the civic and religious complexes were not short term affairs. Progress on a single project was subject to delay by economic, social or political difficulties, while the changing occupancy of an episcopal see, and sometimes extended periods of vacancy, could mean the abandonment of the more ambitious projects. Changes of political allegiance might lead to a renewal of interest as the benefits of adherence to either the papal or imperial cause was announced in architectural and urban form. However, the extended period of political and religious change after the end of the western empire was characterized by two types of urban settlement. Firstly in many instances there was the continuation of existing settlements but often with different configurations, and secondly in more extreme cases the abandonment of cities vulnerable to barbarian attack and the establishment of new towns of a completely Christian identity. While the former type would exploit the regular structure of Roman cities, as occurred in the example of Brescia, the

2.3   San Marco, Venice. The burial of St. Mark depicted in the original mosaic decoration of the basilica, the domed and columned form of which is represented in great detail.

2.4   Piazza del Duomo, Brescia. Diagram of the *broletto* and the summer and winter cathedrals, with the original footprints of the religious structures, including the baptistery which stood on the opposite side of the piazza.

foundation of a new town such as Torcello could be seen to indicate the future form of urban space.

In Brescia, Piazza del Duomo epitomises the transition from late antiquity to the medieval world and grew up towards the western edge of the Roman town, the forum still being used as a market (Canniffe 1997). It started as a religious precinct that assumed a civic character as well, in common with urban spaces in other cities in Lombardy such as Como. To contemporary eyes it presents an apparently casual arrangement of space running north to south before a series of highly individual monuments. From the south there is the round nave of the *duomo vecchio*, then the baroque mass of the *duomo nuovo*, itself on the site of a previous Romanesque basilica, and the medieval *broletto* or town hall, with its crenellated tower. The two cathedrals conform to the type of the double cathedral, and while now largely constituting later rebuilding, they are known from excavations to have been built on a pair of earlier structures which can be dated to the fifth or sixth centuries. Their designation from at least 838 as winter and summer cathedrals, and dedication to the Virgin and St. Peter conforms to the pattern of other double cathedrals both within Lombardy, in Milan and Pavia, and further afield (Krautheimer 1971: 161–180). The present situation is perhaps the result of the extension

2.5   Piazza del
Duomo, Brescia,
showing the
tower of the
*broletto*, the facade
and dome of
the cathedral
and the sunken
rotunda of the
*duomo vecchio*.

of a cleared space between the cathedrals and the baptistery whose remains survive under the western side of the square. A Christian precinct of the first millennium, because of its appropriation as public space grew to include a communal function in the second millennium, and like other communal palaces of its time and date, the *broletto* was a product of a particular medieval interpretation of *civitas*, examples of which will be discussed in the next chapter. Although the forms of the present cathedrals are very different from their original incarnations, their distinct characters preserve the individual identity of each building, roughly a basilican type and a martyrium. Some physical indication of the historical transformation of this complex is provided by the dramatic change of level between the piazza and the nave of the *duomo vecchio*, a good storey height, which embodies the passage of time over more than a millennium. As an urban space, though, Piazza del Duomo (officially renamed Piazza Paolo VI after the locally born pope) follows the pattern established by the earlier Roman forum in the town in its general orientation, combined with the Christian topography of a space opened to the west of the new buildings oriented perpendicular to the axis of the space.

Brescia was a typical city of the mainland of Italy, which could be compared with many other examples, such as Verona, Parma or Florence, which grew on Roman foundations. Torcello in contrast was founded as a refuge from barbarian incursions on an island off the coast in what would be subsequently identified as the Venetian lagoon. Its isolated location ensured physical protection, and lack of previous substantial structures allowed the city to be developed in an ideal manner, bearing in mind the difficulties of construction. Because of attack, the bishopric of Altino on the mainland was transferred here and the settlement established. In political and ecclesiastical terms Torcello was under the authority of Constantinople, and in ecclesiastical matters the city of Venice which succeeded it was to remain proudly independent of control from Rome. As Ruskin noted in *The Stones of Venice*

...in the minds of all early Christians the church itself was most frequently symbolized under the image of a ship, of which the bishop was the pilot. Consider the force which this symbol would assume in the imaginations of men to whom the spiritual Church had become an ark of refuge in the midst of a destruction...a destruction in which the wrath of man had become as broad as the earth and as merciless as the sea, and who saw the actual and literal edifice of the Church raised up, itself like an ark in the midst of the waters. (Ruskin [1853] 1981: 65–66)

Still a dramatic presence in the lagoon, the island of Torcello presents to the contemporary visitor the surviving fragments of a once significant centre. Depopulation has left three major monuments, a cathedral, a church and a campanile, and a cluster of lesser structures which highlight the values of a civilization which saw itself as vulnerable to barbarian attack. The cathedral of Santa Maria Assunta takes a basilican form compatible with its foundation date of 639 and its reconstruction in 1008. Adjacent to its simple linear form the complex centralized church of Santa Fosca is connected by a continuous arcade dated to the twelfth century, the appearance of which has suggested the intention to evoke similarities to sites in the Holy Land. Overlooking this pair of structures, the campanile served the additional purposes of lighthouse and refuge. In a characteristic Byzantine manner, the undecorated exterior surfaces contrast with the rich mosaic images of the interiors, especially the great image of Mary, Mother of God in the cathedral apse, and the Last Judgement opposite it on the entrance wall which backed on to the now ruined baptistery. This arrangement emphasises in architectural and decorative form

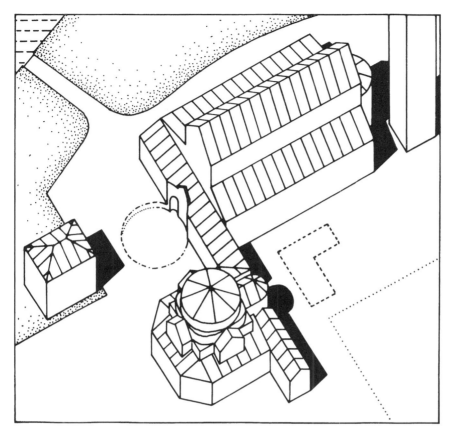

2.6 Diagram of principal structures of Torcello. The circular ruins of the baptistery, the basilical form of Santa Maria Assunta (with its campanile), and the polygonal form of Santa Fosca, connected by a portico.

the separate status of the unbaptised prior to entry into the church both as a community and as an urban monument. So the baptistery represents Christian rebirth, followed by passage through the wall with the Last Judgement, and its vivid portrayal of the testing of the faithful, through to consummation at the high altar beneath the image of Virgin and Child in the golden field of heaven. As a collection of architectural types, (basilica, martyrium, campanile, baptistery) this piazza foreshadows the elements of more populous cities which developed on the Italian mainland into the medieval period.

Although the present basilica is a later rebuilding, the difference between Christian worship and the pagan ceremonies which preceded them are apparent. As has been previously discussed, the basilica had developed out of Roman civil structures for trade and the dispensation of justice but the Christian basilica internalized the language of Roman public space with the perimeter colonnades and triumphal arch. In some instances the columns would themselves have previously lined fora and other public spaces so we can assume that early Christians would have been aware of the connection, and the isolation of Torcello underlines the importance of this difficult appropriation of urban material to make a Christian city. Similarly the form of

2.7   Santa Fosca, Torcello, with the basilica and campanile in the distance.

the apse, particularly with its image of Christ or the Virgin would have taken on the inheritance of triumphal imagery with traditional figures of victory replaced at Torcello by images of the Annunciation. Such use of physical and conceptual *spolia* represented the triumph of Christianity over the pagan past, and in the Venetian context specifically her succession to the Byzantine and Roman empires. This tradition of cultural appropriation is also evident in Santa Fosca, a later addition to the complex, in the form of a martyrium, or centralized church based on Byzantine precedents. Its separation would allow for the creation and display of processions. Deborah Howard has suggested that its form, especially with its encircling porch is intended to evoke structures in Jerusalem such as the Dome of the Rock, or the church of the Holy Sepulchre. This is the period of the Crusades in which the Venetians were heavily involved, especially the Fourth Crusade in 1204 when Constantinople was sacked and much ancient material transported to the newly emergent city as symbols of her claim to *imperium* (Howard 2000: 213–15).

In this shifting political scene, the church had the enduring jurisdiction and was the predominant heir of expressions of temporal power. The imperial office had been revived in the west for Charlemagne in 800, but now without the same political coherence and under the express sanction of the church. Civil command ceased to have an iconography which was not interpreted through Christian appropriation of earlier forms. This scenario would eventually lead to political and religious conflict over the appointment of bishops epitomized by the excommunication of the Holy Roman Emperor Henry IV by Pope Gregory VII in 1076 and periodically thereafter. To the modern mind the causes of and effects of the investiture crisis, the struggle between papal and imperial authorities over episcopal appointments, might seem arcane, not the least with regard to their impact on urban form. But the bishops were typically the most powerful civic authorities and therefore control over them was an important means of co-opting urban centres into a feudal system largely dependent on the ownership of land. The cities, as the centrepieces of the different feudal territories therefore had significant symbolic importance and the occupant of the see a major role in the supervision of civil society. Positioned equidistant between the papal centre in Rome and the imperial territories in Germany, northern and central Italy were the regions most affected by the conflict and it is no coincidence that this distinctly political dispute should have a later consequence in the creation of strong city states in the same territories (Spike 2004: 220–224).

One of the implicit aspects of the investiture crisis was the revelation that secular power was dependent on religious power, and had little identity other than a military one. The political expression of civil authority had lost its independence and would have to be reinvented through appropriations of images and spatial forms to create a new language of civic statehood. Augustine's vision of an eschatological urbanism as described in *City of God* had failed to materialise, its perfectibility compromised by the political vicissitudes of the first Christian millennium. The end of time, and the return of Christ was not yet at hand. In the readjusted expectations of the twelfth and thirteenth centuries a means of living in this world had to be found, which would see a transfer of political power from bishops to civic officials, and which would have its physical expression in the development of new urban spaces and new civic palaces. Maureen Miller in her study of the development of bishops' palaces has made the following observation.

The most significant factor influencing the siting of communal palaces is the power of the bishop within the city in the precommunal era and his relations with the commune as it emerged. In cities where bishops really exercised comital authority within the walls – as in Brescia, Bergamo, Cremona, Modena, and Reggio – the period of power sharing and cooperation between bishop and commune was long, and one ecclesiastical and one civil centre developed. In cities where the bishop's authority was limited, particularly by the presence of strong counts – as in Verona, Bologna, Mantua, Florence, and Treviso – the commune's ascendancy was established early, and an independent civic center emerged. (Miller 2000: 120)

Whatever the nuances between different cities, the dominance of church structures in the public spaces of early medieval Italian cities is indicative of the strongly political role ecclesiastical authorities played. The creation of a specific topography of urban form can be distinguished, albeit one where, distinct from his cathedral church, the major secular structure might be the bishop's palace. The public space between them, flowing both into the great sanctified space of the cathedral and the courtyard of the palace, served to emphasize the all pervasive nature of the authority exercised by the bishop in both the spiritual and temporal

2.8  Pisa. The ensemble of Campo Santo, baptistery, cathedral and campanile (the leaning tower) is emblematic of a medieval religious precinct.

spheres. The continuity of this experience, where the sacred and the secular were often difficult to distinguish, indeed did not require distinction, developed in a situation which was far from benign. Cities lived in fear of destruction by seemingly friendly powers as well as sworn enemies. Social norms did nothing to prevent violence occurring even on holy ground. Buildings, even churches, continued to have a defensive architectural character even well within city walls. The closed and compartmentalized nature of such urban forms separated and accommodated different functions but did so within the same types of massive structure. Although the political situation would remain dangerous the new confidence of secular urban authorities which would develop in the thirteenth century would see the growth of distinct building types and iconography which spoke of the city's place in the world. However, the communal palace would be a later development, an addition to the family of urban elements, the basilica, the baptistery, the campanile, the combined presence of which would come to define both the generic image of Italian urbanity and the identity of individual cities. While the cities would host different factions of papal and imperial partisans, respectively the guelph and ghibelline parties that formed in the wake of the investiture crisis, the overriding idea under which governing coalitions would be forged would be that of civic independence. After centuries of urban decline, and from the chaotic situation of conflict between the different temporal and spiritual powers, the cities themselves would emerge as independent powers, embodied by the formal definition of their central spaces.

# 3

# The Middle Ages: From the city of God to the city of man

The thirteenth and fourteenth centuries would see the formation of a distinct pattern of civic government in Italy, and also the creation of a series of spaces which would subsequently be identified as the definitive image of political urbanity. Yet, as has been referred to in the last chapter, this aesthetic unity emerged from centuries when the diplomatic tensions in Europe were played out on the Italian peninsula in the disputes between the guelph and ghibelline parties which with the personal ambitions of papal and imperial figures continued to form a backdrop to issues of territorial control. In many respects the two parties did not represent great ideological divides, as had at least been the official pretext for the investiture crisis. Instead they often represented local factional disputes which became embroiled in the larger political shifts of allegiance and control, a reflection of the instability of each grouping. Although Rome under the authority of the popes in theory represented a point of fixity, the brevity of successive papacies and the election of rival anti-popes removed any certainty from one side of the dispute. On the other side the occupation of the imperial title by northern Europeans meant that their infrequent presence south of the Alps could also be a source of periodic destabilization (Waley 1988).

Since the south of the peninsula was under the quite distinct monarchical system of the kings of Naples and Sicily, the cities of northern and central Italy were therefore able to occupy the political void with a series of city states, nominally under imperial suzerainty, the interests of which could be served by validation of their own identity and independence. Of course this process was only gradual, subject to changes of political control and occasionally to sack by enemy forces, but generally working towards amplification of urban facilities and monuments, and a consequent enhancement in status. One positive outcome of the competition between cities would be the erection of new communal palaces complete with towers (to rival the dominance of the cathedral campanile) and elaborately ornamented public *logge* and fountains, the appreciation of such urban elements requiring ample cleared space (Cunningham 1995). Each city produced its own unique architectural solution to express its own system of government. Assemblies of citizens

3.1 Palazzo
della Ragione,
Padua. The
arcaded
communal palace
is adjacent to the
market square
Piazza delle Erbe.

were complemented by appointed non-native officials such as the *podesta*
and the *capitano del popolo* in whom were invested civil and military
authority. Depending on the balance of power between local oligarchs and an
independent magistracy, the political complex could take the form of separate
buildings, or a single structure accommodating different functions, the latter
solution having the advantage of creating a more unified image of government
for the edification of the citizenry. In either case though, the relationship to
public space was a necessary component which could be cemented by the
provision of intermediary spaces in the form of arcades or dramatic flights

of steps. The examples of buildings and spaces which will be discussed, from Padua, Perugia, Florence and Siena present the civic values of this period individually and collectively, through distinct but related architectural and urban expression.

While each of these cities had specific systems of government and would have specific destinies they conform to a pattern which placed civic authority in a pre-eminent position in the perceived world (whatever the pious expectations of the next). The republican image of government, although essentially oligarchic in nature, represented a form of communal stability which was clearly different to the centralized and monarchical south, the impotent or exiled papacy, and the tyrannies ruled by various warlords. The architectural form of the civic palace developed from the great halls of military commanders and adapted crenelation as a decorative motif to imply political power. But instead of a defensive plinth to protect the hall at the upper level, there were often open arcades and vaults, or commercial premises, which communicated directly with the urban space around it. In many examples the decoration of the great hall underscored the political message of this spatial and conceptual openness by situating the city in its cosmological and historical frame and transferring these images of harmony onto the plane of the everyday, advising the governed and the governing about their good behaviour not solely for the delayed benefit of eternal salvation but for the immediate benefits of social harmony, what we now call civil society. The rule of law was identified with urban well-being rather than an abstract entity separated from lived reality. Although personal piety was highly prized, through the example of contemporary and local saints such as Francis of Assisi, Anthony of Padua and Catherine and Bernardino of Siena, the institution of the church was not as well regarded, leaving the vacuum into which these new symbolizations of temporal power could flood.

In the first example, from the northern Italian city of Padua, the complex of the Palazzo della Ragione, standing between the Piazza delle Erbe and the Piazza della Frutta, presents an early example of the genre of the communal palace in a process of transformation towards a recognizable type. Morphologically it has an unusual trapezoidal form straddling across a roughly rectangular space which it divides into the two tapering piazze. The pragmatic nature of this form is entirely appropriate since the structure originated in the booths of the markets which still operate on the site. Constructed as a series of stone cells, they formed the base of a great hall, *il Salone*, where justice was dispensed. The multi-level arcaded nature of the hall, facing on its two long sides towards the market squares was surmounted by a great barrel vaulted roof which defines the uninterrupted central space, behind the layers of arcades and market stalls. There is therefore an incremental intensification of the functional relationship from the space of the market to the space of the hall, and a direct continuity between the daily life of the city, the higher functions of civil society and the sense of the city's own history through the reuse of earlier structures. The *Salone* was begun in 1218–19 which places it in the very early phase of this process of urban self-representation, when other communes were building less substantial civic palaces. The Paduans grounded the extent of their ambition by tying the new structure to the mundane world of the market. However, by the time the great hall was cleared of internal divisions and the roof raised in 1306–09 there could be no concealing the status the civic authorities sought for themselves, despite the additional layers of arcades added in 1318 over the external staircases. Any visitor would be impressed by the programme of internal fresco decoration which completed this phase of civic beautification from 1370–80, although by that date the communal government had effectively been superseded by rule by the Carrara dynasty. As both a commercial and a civic building, the cohabitation of different functions in a single structure is a phenomenon which has only been reidentified as of positive benefit in urban design relatively recently. Foremost among its advocates was Aldo Rossi who identified the Palazzo della Ragione (in addition to the Roman remnants referred to in Chapter 1) as an example in support of his 'theory of permanences', in its survival and transformation over time (Rossi 1982: 29–32). But as an image of civic authority the political message emitted during the period under consideration was one of transparent government, close to the daily concerns of the population and presiding over them in a sheltering way. As other examples of the communal palace developed, a more robust defensible model would evolve which reflected the *realpolitik* of the conflicts which affected the peninsula.

A second example of the municipal buildings and spaces which developed in response to such struggles, particularly between church and civic authorities is the ensemble of the present day Piazza IV Novembre in Perugia. Unlike the low lying topography of Padua, Perugia's dramatic position on its hill, commanding the Umbrian territory around it, is the testimony of its strategic importance from Etruscan times. Its epicentre, however, is not a position from which the surrounding landscape was visible, but rather a set of enclosed spaces, the public interiors of civic and religious centres, and the urban room of the piazza. Far from representing isolation from the topographical context, this separation serves to distil the essential elements of the civic structure, at the centre of the urban labyrinth. Piazza IV Novembre (previously Piazza San Lorenzo and Piazza del Municipio) forms the terminus of the city's main thoroughfare, Corso Vannucci. The space is composed by the conjunction of the Duomo and the Palazzo dei Priori, the principal religious and civic edifices, and the organic shape of the piazza is virtually emblematic of the relationship between the different components of medieval urban life. Yet this irregular arrangement rests on a planned framework from the Etruscan period whose lines can still be traced (Scullard 1967: 159–165). In accordance with the celestial pattern which governed Etruscan planning a *cardo* ran north–south (along the line of Corso Vannucci), while it was crossed by a *decumanus* (along the routes of the present Via dei Priori and Via Fani). This cruciform framework was connected to the system of gates which encircled the settlement on its summit and themselves remained in use following the Roman period. The persistence

of this urban pattern provided the underpinning on which the two principal medieval buildings of the piazza are placed.

The paired structures are positioned somewhat apart, so that each maintains its independence, but are moulded into a single urban space by the continuity of the surrounding buildings. The space of the piazza is roughly triangular, the wall of the cathedral forming the shortest side, while the palazzo is placed perpendicular to it. The third side then gradually deflects so that it runs past the facade of the Duomo, unusually in this instance positioned on its eastern end. The surface of the space rises gently as it opens, climaxing in the flank wall of the Duomo with its grandstand of steps. The perpendicular disposition of the Duomo and the Palazzo dei Priori contrasts with the irregular urban wall which encloses them, but the space is focused around the Fontana Maggiore with its allegorical representations of the zodiac, the liberal arts and the saints (White 1970). The fountain and the steps to both monumental buildings heighten the nature of the bowl of this space, yet the size and prominence of the fountain does much to organise the relationship between the two major elements. Its position allows it to be visible roughly on the axis of Corso Vannucci, but its size allows it to easily dominate the space volumetrically, unlike the other incidental statuary and sculptural decoration visually or physically attached to the cathedral. This ensemble of elements is essentially a product of the *trecento* although the campaign of urban development extended from the commencement of the paving of the piazza in 1253 through to the effective

3.2   Palazzo dei Priori, Perugia, dominates one side of Piazza IV Novembre.

3.3   Piazza IV Novembre, Perugia. The flank of the *duomo* of San Lorenzo and the Fontana Maggiore.

completion of the cathedral in 1487. The complex and distinct histories of the fountain, palazzo and duomo require individual consideration to help expose the processes of the self-representation of Perugian society during the period of the city's greatest political power.

The history of the formation of the present space commences with the principal focus and chronologically earliest element of the piazza, the Fontana Maggiore (1278). With its broad circuit of steps and two levels of basins it has been encircled by railings from 1301 to protect a commodity that was essential to life but had only been brought to this elevated point in the town by means of aqueducts constructed at considerable cost to the municipality. Engineered by Fra Bevignate, the beauty of the ornamentation which adorns the fountain, the work of Nicola and Giovanni Pisano, attests to the significance with which this important amenity was regarded by the populace. The political tensions between religious and civil powers could be subsumed by the overriding need to sustain life in the centre of the city, these waters being forbidden for animal and laundry use. The structure of the fountain forming a pyramidal whole, the lower basin, some 10 metres in diameter has twenty-five sides, each divided into two panels making a total of fifty low relief depictions of the months, myths, biblical scenes and intellectual pursuits. Above this, and at two thirds its diameter is an upper basin which is twelve sided, including

3.4  The Fontana Maggiore, Perugia.

allegorical representations, biblical figures, saints and contemporary figures such as Matteo da Correggio and Ermanno da Sassoferrato, respectively the *podesta* and the *capitano del popolo* for the year 1278. A bronze dish provides the topmost element, with intertwined figures of three water carriers standing above it. These were originally surmounted by four beasts, two griffins and

3.5 *Duomo*
facade, Perugia,
with Palazzo
dei Priori in
the distance.

two lions, respectively the Perugian and guelph symbols which emphasized
the city's political allegiance (Neri 1988).

South of the fountain the Palazzo dei Priori places its bulging flank to the
Corso, and turns its entrance to the space between it and the cathedral. Its
fabric is constructed with some refinement and its sheer walls betray the
defensive nature of its origins. The ground floor to the Corso contained the

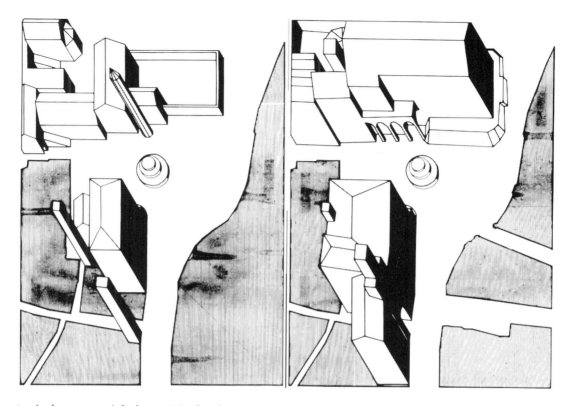

typical commercial element its lowly position required, with two generous bands of fenestration punctuating the crenellated wall above, this redundant feature of defensive architecture being adopted as a reference to the political authority represented by the great halls of the nobility. Despite the regular and complete nature of the facades, the organic development of the palazzo between the thirteenth and fifteenth centuries is evidenced by the irregular profile, the addition of extra bays to the original facade, and the inclusion of the earlier defensive tower which marks the opening out of the Corso into the piazza. On the northern elevation the entrance to the Sala dei Notari, the principal meeting hall at first floor level, is approached by the generous flight of steps which complement those on the cathedral. The doorway is flanked by two projecting sculptures in bronze, a griffin and a lion reinforcing the support of the civic authorities for the papal cause.

The site for this new type of structure, flanking the ancient Etruscan *cardo*, was at the centre of the civic, religious and mercantile complex, although the existing offices of the commune were distributed in various palazzi in the vicinity. The development of a central administrative building on the *isola della piazza* followed the construction of the fountain, and was established next to the Romanesque church of San Severo di Piazza, the site of the church being included eventually within the curtilege of the new palazzo in 1319 (Gurrieri 1985: 10–11). The fire of 1329 which destroyed the existing municipal

3.6   Diagram of the development of Piazza IV Novembre, showing the growth of the civic and religious structures from earlier collections of smaller buildings.

Palazzo dei Consoli, consolidated the significance of the new structure which was only occupied by the Priors in 1353, with a further extension to the south constructed between 1429 and 1443 (Martini 1970).

To the north of the palazzo the flank of the cathedral effectively closes the progress of Corso Vannucci, but the rising ground plane allows the interior of the church to be entered more easily on the perpendicular facade. Its bulk and dramatically unfinished appearance throws into sharper relief the few sculptural elements which decorate it, such as the red and white marble diapered surface which acts as a backdrop to S. Bernardino's pulpit, from where the Sienese saint sought to revive the faith of the citizens when he preached in 1425. Tradition records that the early cathedral was built on the site of a temple of Vulcan (Lunghi 1994: 14). By the period in which the piazza began to take its definitive form, the area occupied by the present cathedral consisted of a series of individual structures. The church of Ss. Lorenzo ed Ercolano oriented north–south was adjoined by the chapel of S. Ercolano where the civic patron's relics were venerated. Accompanying this group was an octagonal campanile, removed in 1375 and the *canonica*, the residence of the cathedral clergy. Following an initial project by Fra Bevignate from 1300, the present cathedral developed as a fifteenth century *hallenkirche*, its new orientation east to west (the reverse to the typical arrangement) determining the occupation of the footprint of the previous church as the new transept. The political turmoil of the period resulted in a lengthy period of construction before the reinstallation of San Ercolano's relics in 1487. To the left of the southern entrance, and on the axis of the Corso Vannucci, sits the enthroned bronze figure of the Pope Julius III (by Leone Leoni), the sculpture's benediction greeting the opening of street into square. The statue was erected in 1555 by a populace grateful to him for the restoration of privileges removed by his predecessor, the Farnese pope Paul III, when he crushed the Perugian rebellion over the salt tax.

The boundaries between these buildings and the piazza are blurred by intermediate zones, elements such as the steps and the loggias attached to both buildings. These elements of use unite buildings and piazza, and accentuate the subtle modulation of the space. The concave loggia attached to Palazzo dei Priori (proposed by Gurrieri as a remnant of San Severo) balances the convexity of the flight of steps reconstructed in 1902. Facing it across the square, however, the Loggia di Braccio attached to the cathedral appears as a clumsy *quattrocento* attempt to mediate the scale of the duomo with that of the *canonica*. The self-confidence with which the two principal structures confront each other in the piazza represents the antagonistic medieval history of the rival civic and religious powers, a story eloquently told by the defensive nature of the Palazzo dei Priori and the denuded state of the *duomo*. The mundane urban fabric which provides the backdrop to the major monuments performs its subservient role without rhetoric, its only overtly rhetorical elements being the treatment of the corners of the existing buildings as a triumphal entrance where a wider street, Via Calderini, was cut through to connect the political arena to the former market place at a lower level in the town in 1591.

However as an embodiment of the relations within medieval society, what fundamentally distinguishes this urban ensemble from those which preceded and succeeded it is the dynamism of the overall arrangement and its elements. At its centre point, the growth from three-sided to 12 sided to 25 sided in the descending levels of the Fontana Maggiore creates an invitation to circular movement around the focus of the piazza. The central level of guardian figures, in John White's proposed reconstruction, creates a plan relationship with Eulixstes (the city's mythical Trojan founder) on the north and the city's personification as *Augusta Perusia* on the south, crossed by that between St. John the Baptist on the east and the personification of Rome on the west. This geometrical configuration, echoing that of the *cardo* and *decumanus* as a centring device or *axis mundi* can be extended to include the correspondences between the eight other major figures, who stand above bestial faced waterspouts. Civic values are represented on the north by the trio of Eulixstes between Matteo da Correggio and Ermanno da Sassoferrato. Correspondingly on the south the city is personified between her two patrons San Ercolano and San Lorenzo. Revealed religion is represented by the Baptist, a pivotal figure between old and new testaments, placed between David and St. Benedict, while organized religion under the papacy is represented by Rome between Saints Peter and Paul, this group greeting many visitors when they entered the city from the Porta Conca. Here on the western side this level of divinatory geometry is keyed into the more contingent sequence of panels at the lower level despite their misalignment. The enthroned figure of Rome presides above Romulus and Remus, the legendary founders of the urban paradigm.

Other than this instance, correspondences are more difficult to discern between the level of intercessionary figures and that largely composed of representations of physical and mental disciplines. However, below the metaphysical imagery of the water carriers at the summit, the allegorical plan relationships of the upper basin connected to the cardinal points has its physical counterpart in the sectional configuration of the fountain. The topography of the piazza is such that the sequence of the twelve months corresponds visually to the elevation of the fountain on a plinth that negotiates the fall between the fountain steps and the piazza. From this aspect the figure of San Ercolano presides as central intercessor on the upper basin, thus establishing the relationship between terrestrial and celestial realms, time and eternity. The geometrical knot which such a reading of the fountain's narrative provides can be interpreted as a balancing of civic and religious values. As a mnemonic and divinatory device whose influence extends beyond the physical confines of the fountain, the line connecting the figures of San Lorenzo and Matteo da Correggio can be extended towards the doors of the later Palazzo dei Priori and the Duomo respectively, as if exchanging these figures as ambassadors to the opposing power.

3.7    Detail of the Fontana Maggiore, Perugia. In this image the city's patron San Ercolano is shown presiding over scenes representing the activities of the summer months.

The visual appropriation of urban space which these arrangements facilitated underpinned the political identities with which medieval society represented itself. It was such a society in Perugia which was capable of conscious self-examination, individually and collectively. During a period of regional religious fervour the city had been the location of one extraordinary instance of collective piety which affected its daily life. The interests of rival parties and classes were put aside in the great flagellant movement of 1260, which saw the suspension of all daily activity for 15 days (Becker 1981: 163). Scourging encouraged the citizens to publicly identify themselves with the suffering Christ, as a means of repenting the sins which urban life encouraged. Despite the upheavals of the subsequent decades, this act would have remained in the collective memory of the population during the creation of the Fontana Maggiore and the transformed urban realm which grew around it. The self-reflective but momentary gesture of mass flagellation was succeeded by the more permanent ensemble through which the citizens could read the relationships between the civic and religious powers.

Urban design and political structures express their intentions through narrative, and the Fontana Maggiore has a complex iconography which makes a dynamic unity out of disparate social elements. Such allegories are a common feature of figurative sculpture, yet it is a more dispersed and sometimes incidental element in urban ensembles. With this qualification, however, it can be seen that the complexity which the fountain embodies between the civic and religious spheres, the celestial and terrestrial and the daily and the metaphysical, have their echoes in the broader urban space projecting from it. If such a symbolic construction is to succeed as urbanism, it needs to undergo a process of transformation from object to space. Far from utilitarian structures which were the result only of technological innovation, the Palazzo dei Priori and the *Duomo* consciously manifested these social structures. They were rooted in an ancient physical context which itself was deemed to have had a divinatory origin, the principal spaces being mythically situated and their surfaces adorned with symbolic elements such as lions and griffins as if they were the political decoration of an urban room. A citizen could therefore actively inhabit a symbolically vivid space, in a fuller manner than he or she could appropriate the Fontana Maggiore which ultimately remains an avoidable object of contemplation.

If this Perugian example represents the rivalry between church and civic powers in very direct terms the form of Piazza del Campo in Siena presents a situation where secular authority was without challenge. In the form of the Duomo, the church had a distinct and not inconsiderable presence in another part of the city, and therefore the Campo, and the Palazzo Pubblico which dominates it had a pre-eminent role as the focus of political life. The ensemble, which in any thorough assessment would also have to include the programme of didactic fresco decoration on the interior, embodies a consistent attempt on the part of civic authorities to project both an image of the urban ideal, and to go as far as possible to create it in reality (Bowsky 1981).

Piazza del Campo is essentially another vessel of space with the slightly concave facade of the Palazzo Pubblico forming most of its eastern edge. Its topographic situation as land falls away to the surrounding countryside means that the seat of civic government acts as a point of mediation between the city and its territory, a position reinforced internally by the subject matter of Ambrogio Lorenzetti's frescoes which divide themselves between images of good and bad government in both town and country (Feldges-Henning 1977). This place of surveillance in both directions is complemented by the descending entries of streets which issue into the Campo and reinforce the theatrical qualities of the *cavea*. Treated as an unadorned brick surface the pavement dishes down to a central drain over a subterranean cistern. That drain, in the form of a shell, sits in front of the facade of the Palazzo Pubblico begun in 1297 and largely completed in 1310, a brick mass rising above a stone base crenelated and with a raised central section, the *torrione*. The division of the facade into three elements expressed the tripartite nature of the functions accommodated. On the left was the residence of the *podesta*, in the centre (separated by a narrow lane dropping nine metres down to the Piazza del Mercato) the Sala del Consiglio for the city council, and lastly the wing for the apartments of the Nine, the ruling group of citizens. The side wings had an extra storey added in the sixteenth century although the architectural language of two centuries earlier was maintained. In 1325 the Torre del Mangia was commenced to the left of the tripartite facade and was completed in 1344. This period of self-confident development was brought to a temporary halt by the effects of the Black Death, an event commemorated by the construction from 1352–76 of the open chapel at the base of the tower.

The Campo had been paved in nine sections in 1333–34 to signify the ruling Nine, and its fan like form focused attention on to the Palazzo Pubblico, the last monumental element being the creation of a fountain eventually taking the form of Jacopo della Quercia's Fonte Gaia (1409–19) with its elaborate sculptural programme. The form of the Campo's other buildings were governed by the decisions taken regarding the Palazzo Pubblico's appearance, with the characteristic use of the *trifore* windows. But although these devices regarding architectural consistency were overlaid on a space which had been defined organically before the construction of the present arrangement, there are some dimensional relationships which suggest the attempt to apply an optical ordering system in the design (Cunningham 1995: 41). These perceived relationships between plan and elevation in Siena supplement the possibility that the geometrical layout of Piazza IV Novembre is implicit in consciously expressing the ordering of its elements, but it is in Florence, the fourth example in this chapter, that the controlled arrangement of space becomes apparent through measure.

There, Piazza della Signoria and the Palazzo Vecchio within it, have been discovered to have a geometrical relationship which predates by a century the quantifiable composition of space associated with the demonstration of the laws of perspective by Brunelleschi in the 1420s. The piazza is dominated by the Palazzo Vecchio, a massive fourteenth century block surmounted by a tower whose slender form rivals Giotto's campanile on the city's skyline. The relative blankness of the sheer walls of of the palazzo underscore its ambiguous formal nature in relation to the piazza. Although physically it

3.8  Piazza del Campo, Siena. The Palazzo Pubblico with the Torre del Mangia and the open chapel at its base.

creates an edge to the clear space of the square that has developed around it, the geometrical solidity of the palazzo suggest that it is in the process of occupying the square. Conversely the L shape of the piazza implies a virtual rectangle of clear space out of which one corner has been subtracted by the looming presence of the palazzo. Although this interpretation is a misreading

3.9  Piazza del Campo and the Fonte Gaia viewed from the Palazzo Pubblico.

of the actual process of development, it accounts for the curious ambiguity of the form of the piazza, where a geometric understanding of the spatial relationships are inverted by perceived reality. The geometry of the piazza has two distinct grids to accommodate. Within the urban network it resolves the conflict in alignment between the orientation of the Roman *castrum* on the cardinal points, and that of the *centauratio* surrounding it defined by the ancient field patterns aligned to the course of the Arno, although the internal geometry of the square is simpler.

Marvin Trachtenberg (1997) in his work on the Florentine *trecento* piazza has asserted that the geometrical structure conforms to three urbanistic principles. In accordance with his first principle, space is deemed to expand from the monument. Secondly, the regulation of the space is geometrical. And lastly the relationship of this space and its monuments to the major streets from which it is entered conforms to a third principle of a 'street-connected' ideal viewpoint. In the case of Piazza della Signoria, though, what that view consisted of was the massive defensive bulk of a civic palace which of all the examples discussed in this chapter appears the most prepared for urban conflict. It had been planned in 1285, but construction did not begin until 1299 and the structure was complete in 1318. Its site was at the southern edge of the tight pattern of the ancient *castrum*, and had been expropriated by the city government from a condemned family. A small piazza existed to the north of the present palazzo but another was cleared as part of the

3.10   Piazza dell Signoria, Florence, dominated by the Palazzo Vecchio.

initial building campaign between 1299 and 1306, the final form of the space being achieved between 1343–56. The clearing of this massive space showed considerable political will, but also demonstrated the aesthetic concerns of the city government to provide a clear view of the huge tower that reared up from the massive facade of their palazzo, rivalling that of Siena. The view of it from the north-east corner of the piazza where Via Calzaioli enters the square creates a 45 degree angle to the top of the tower, just one of the relationships which suggests that the proportioning of buildings and spaces was consciously planned. This harmonization of solid and void reflected the

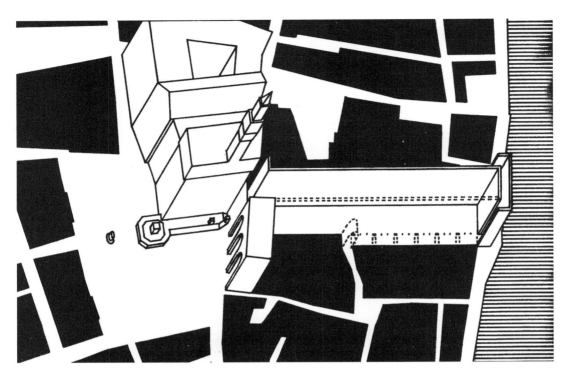

3.11   Diagram of Piazza della Signoria, Florence, with the Palazzo Vecchio, the Loggia dei Lanzi and the later intervention of the Uffizi.

aspiration to balance the different factions within the city for the benefit of a greater whole.

As Derek Heater suggests in his discussion of citizenship (1990), the positive aspects of community which relate to shared values and beliefs have their counterpart in the separation of one group from another, just as the civic and religious institutions in Piazza IV Novembre can be clearly distinguished. For every citizen who recognises the symbols that constitute the code to his or her civic identity, the interpretation and understanding of those same symbols by an outsider will serve only to confirm their exclusion, or at least their inability to participate in a system which invited an unusually high degree of involvement. Citizenship in late medieval Italy would have a visual and spatial identity, characterized at a more local, parish level as *campanilismo*, association with and pride in one's immediate community visible to outsiders through the prominence of the church tower or the towers of rival civic palaces. At an urban level the silhouette of the city, often represented as nestling in the arm of a local patron like their saintly attribute, or within the sheltering cloak of the Virgin, was supported by a rich iconographic language which defined such identities. Although these identities survive in some cities along with the rivalry between their different quarters, as in Siena with the annual reenactment of the horse race the *palio* around the Campo, the intensity of such a relationship between neighbours is hard to appreciate from an era of global expectations. In a medieval city the whole of life's experience and the hope for the next world could be inscribed within one set of walls or even a few streets. The visual field within which a typical citizen lived his or her life was essentially their whole world, leading to an intense familiarity with the city which would have no difficulty in considering the urban environment as a unified entity. The continuity with which this world was expressed architecturally placed the citizen in a situation as clearly identifiable as that of the figures in a Giotto fresco. The environment could be represented in geometrical form, its crystalline nature speaking of an ordered world. However, in the subtle forms of the "City of Good Government", Ambrogio Lorenzetti depicts the space of the city of Siena extending from the foreground piazza into distant parts of the town, a regular rhythm of towers and cornices composing the recession into an organized whole. The visual order of a centralized composition, an ideal city is shown under construction by builders visible on the rooftops.

The correspondence between methods of architectural design and those of pictorial representation comes into focus at this point in urban history because of the growth of a systematic depiction of space especially evidenced in the great fresco cycles. The lives of Christ and the saints were depicted in ordered narratives against backdrops of urban scenes and interiors which were themselves highly composed, with the consistent application of techniques of spatial recession and illumination creating a unified entity from often quite disparate material. This same tendency to unify separate elements can be perceived in the desire to create urban complexes of palaces, *logge* and piazze, although evidence of their origin in a single conceptual method is scant. What was certainly apparent was the significance of geometry as both a practical method by which large building projects such as the civic palaces could be disciplined, and at a conceptual level as the ordering system by which knowledge was organized. There was, therefore, a structural link between physical, perceivable reality and an otherwise hidden order which could be used to define urban space. The role of vision as the mechanism by which such an order might be revealed would come to dominate the design of the city in the following few centuries, the urban consequences of which will be discussed in the next section.

# PART II

# THE EARLY MODERN CITY

# 4

# Early Renaissance: Perspective, representation and the ideal

The cultural legacy of fifteenth century Italy and its 'rebirth' of classical themes is a phenomenon which continues to exert a huge attraction, as witnessed by the ever expanding tourist industries which draw crowds to the main centres of Florence, Venice and Rome. The cities create an illusion of cultural production as being universally valued in sophisticated urban societies, yet this impression is to ignore the political tensions of the time. The strains between feudalism and mercantile democracy which had characterized the medieval period gradually resolved large sections of the political map of the peninsula into a series of states, variously dynastic or republican, allied to the rural papal or imperial powers. These small territories, often with shifting boundaries and alliances were the arenas within which autocrats sought to express their own political systems and aspirations, the creation and redefinition of urban space being only the most extensive example of this type of representative public work. (Martines 1980)

The most politically stable of these centres, the Republic of Venice, would face a readjustment of its role in the eastern Mediterranean following the fall of Constantinople in 1453 and the emergence of Ottoman power. At the same time this maritime power was extending her power on the Italian mainland through expansion of its borders at the expense of the Duchy of Milan. Contemporaneously the city of Florence was falling under the influence of one dynasty, the Medici, who would come to be most strongly identified with her rise in political importance. And Rome, following the election as pope of Martin V and his return to the city in 1420, would see its role as home of the unrivalled papal court renewed after schism and the Avignon exile. Although only a sad echo of her ancient state, the presence of the court, especially under builder popes such as Nicholas V (1447–55) would foster direct knowledge of ancient architecture which has had an abiding influence on our surviving image of the *quattrocento* city (Westfall 1974). The political rivalries which underscored this period of great change would appear not to have impeded the development of coherent Renaissance aesthetic values. But the urban ideal which cities were designed to reflect had also shifted from the contested space of the medieval city, with its rival spiritual and secular models, to one which sought affirmation in the emulation of the ancient city, as described in surviving histories and narratives and imaginable from the newly valued fragmentary remains. Here essentially was a world of ideas in which new city spaces could be projected through the language of the past into the present.

Renaissance urbanism, as will be explored in this and the next two chapters, was the product of the overlaying of many influences of which we can readily identify three significant strands: the development of linear perspective, the desire to describe the 'ideal', and the interpretation of antiquity. The matrix of perspective construction and perception found embodiment in the harmonious proportions and rhythms of the design of space in depth. With perspective it became possible to prescribe the urban drama in measurable space, and by manipulation of the conventions of perspective construction to subtly heighten the effects of that space (Damisch 1994). Urban composition extended to include not only the delineation of the piazza in plan, but also through perspective the control of visual, spatial and hence social relationships. Platonic geometric forms could be used to express the ideal, where the purity of the form could be understood as a manifestation of a cosmic harmony. And lastly, through the study and application of the orders, the revival of classical forms facilitated the creation of fora whose regularity and control were the result of classical precedent, filtered through perspective vision, and striving for the ideal.

Brunelleschi's demonstrations of his discoveries in theoretical and physical constructions in perspective were to lead to doctrines that would be knowingly manipulated by later generations of artists. The fact that the descriptions of experiments with which Brunelleschi proved his codification of the laws of perspective in the 1420s should be concerned with the two most important piazze in Florence is, in this regard, of immense importance. His artificial construction of convincing pictorial representations of the Baptistery and the Palazzo della Signoria and the spaces in which they stand, confirms the relationship which during the Renaissance was understood to exist between space as an abstract and quantifiable entity and the actual fabric of cities. By means of reflections, peepholes and silhouettes Brunelleschi replicated perceived reality, although these were only the methods of the fairground trickster masking the mathematical basis of his visual alchemy. The framework by which these illusions were achieved was abstract but not uniform. As Panofsky observed:

homogenous space is never given space, but space produced by construction; and indeed the geometrical concept of homogeneity can be expressed by the postulate that from every point in space it must be possible to draw similar figures in all directions and magnitudes. Nowhere in the space of immediate perception can this postulate be fulfilled. (Panofsky [1924–5] 1991: 30)

While post-Cartesian thought has seen Brunelleschi's work, founded on the evenly marked pavement, as prefiguring the postulation of space extending homogeneously to infinity, the sites of his experiments as given spaces

4.1   Piazza
Santissima
Annunziata,
Florence, viewed
from the loggia
of Brunelleschi's
Foundling
Hospital.

would suggest otherwise. They are spaces chosen because of their specific
characteristics of familiarity and recognisability, and which his audience
knew intimately. Their replication must have been all the more startling, and
the consideration of them as abstract realms all the more unlikely. However,
it is the existence of the intellectual apparatus of perspective which makes

4.2   Campo
Santi Giovanni
e Paolo, Venice.
The ornate facade
of the Scuola
Grande di San
Marco features
a series of low
relief perspective
panels.

these different readings possible. Perception in perspective consists of two elements which alternate as the prime focus of the construction. Inevitably, measured extension in depth, because it mimics visual perception, is the first phenomenon which should be considered. But it has to be realized that the ground for the construction of the illusion is the plane from which it is projected. This duality of depth and surface is not a pair of conflicting oppositions but rather a symbiotic relationship which conditions the creation and appropriation of the new spaces which followed. The development during the sixteenth century of Piazza Santissima Annunziata in Florence from the model provided by Brunelleschi's loggia of the Foundling Hospital (1419–26) is indicative of the interpretations possible through perspective construction.

An unusual example from Venice might serve to express how the new methods of depicting and conceiving of urban space began to appear in cities, where the aesthetic problem of the perspectival articulation of an urban wall received a singular treatment at Campo Santi Giovanni e Paolo. Here, adjacent to this important civic basilica a facade was created for the Scuola Grande di San Marco (1489–94) where through the iconographic programme of a series of sculpted marble low relief panels, a virtual extension to the actual space was created which mediated between the life of the city and that of its patron saint. It is all the more extraordinary because of the sober but essentially unadorned facade of the adjacent gothic basilica. The scuola's position as one of the great confraternities of the city meant the ostentatious display of wealth was seen within a specific social context of charitable provision. At ground level, pairings of scenes in barrel vaulted and flat ceilinged spaces by Pietro and Tullio Lombardo are carved from the wall plane in controlled perspectives which resonate with the antique language of the equestrian monument to Bartolomeo Colleoni. The sculpture of the *condottiere* commissioned from Andrea Verrocchio in the 1480s had been intended to stand in Piazza San Marco but the republic demurred from bestowing this honour on someone who was not even a Venetian. The length of the facade with its six bays was such that the perspective illusion takes place around two centres and with two different horizon lines (McAndrew 1980: 358–63). The circumstantial alliance of these two different elements within the same space, and in the presence of the richly iconographic Santi Giovanni e Paolo, was to reinforce a connection between the saintly acts of the Evangelist and the military power of Venice, explicitly conjoined in the second most important space of the city in a way that was less possible in the more venerable Piazza San Marco (which will be discussed in more detail in the next chapter).

While the ordering of painted space is the aesthetic practice most immediately associated with fifteenth century Italy, the conceptualization of the urban context in which perspective depiction operated was arguably to have as much significance, as visual coherence became associated with political representation. As a new intellectual ideology, humanism would come increasingly to depend on the institution of the dynastic court to develop advances in urbanism rather than the free republics of earlier centuries. Humanism's devotion to the recovery of ancient knowledge would find its architectural expression in the revival of classical forms in the appropriate use of the orders as described by Vitruvius and visible in the numerous structures remaining from the Roman past (Wittkower [1949] 1971). The very survival of such remains endowed them with an aura of almost divine approval which went beyond their pragmatic issue of strength of construction. Their proportions and details were held to indicate a divine agency, but as Lauro Martines has observed their use had a more immediate social purpose.

In effect, the rediscovery of Vitruvius was grounded in quattrocento experience: in upper-class demand, in the building craze, the ideology of magnificence, and the rising awareness that elites could reapportion or remake the urban space if they so willed. So was born the Renaissance interest in 'the ideal city'. Here power and imagination united and the ensuing vision of space was domineering, moved by a faith in men's ability to control the spatial continuum. (Martines 1980: 380–81)

The revival of interest in the pagan world as a prefiguration of Christianity would lead to the combination of the two systems of thought in quite an ambivalent way which would in turn produce periodic religious reactions against humanistic influence. In addition the identification of renaissance rulers through claimed descent from, or emulation of, ancient heroes suggested both the scale of operation and the classical dress in which new urban commissions were imagined. This practice was facilitated by the dependency of both perspective construction and proportional replication of classical orders on the use of modular dispositions of building elements and the intervals between them (Wittkower 1953). This underlying discipline would lead to the extension of the co-ordinated rhythms not only within a building's parts in plan and sectional modules but also between different buildings, creating co-ordinated urban ensembles, or at least projects for them. As discussed in the last chapter, the designed relationship between *trecento* buildings and spaces remains obscure. But in the spaces of the fifteenth century, painted, projected or built, the creation of a harmonic whole is apparent, even when only completed in a fragmented manner. Given the greater degree of political control required for the implementation of consistent urban projects, the qualities of space in both building and urban elements are treated as equivalents, expressions of the same harmonic order. The culture of the renaissance court presents an acceleration of tendencies which had been apparent in previous centuries, but which became centred on a series of dynasties which moved in a few generations from merchants and mercenaries to hereditary rulers. The transformation of urban space therefore played the role of reinforcing the claims to power of specific rulers in which the motif was the memory of Rome, or rather the reappropriation of Roman dress for contemporary purposes.

The opportunity to present different aspects of society – ruler, church, bureaucracy, people, commercial interests – in a single space and in a co-ordinated fashion suggested that there was an underlying order in which the ruler was the key responsible element, the figure on which the rest of the political edifice depended (Machiavelli [1531–32] 2004). While this would have negative political consequences for Italy, as the rival European states sought continued control or influence over the various states in the peninsula, the sophistication of the Italian courts' patronage would be exported to other cities which also wanted to reclaim the mantle of Roman *imperium*. The revival of antiquity would become a pervasive cultural theme in Europe for the next five centuries but in Italy itself the scale of its urban manifestation would take the form of spaces which remain potent expressions of political intent. The spaces which will be explored in this chapter, in Brescia, Pienza, Ferrara and Urbino present a range of different political situations from a city subject to new rulers, a city created as a personal project to beautify a papal birthplace, to two examples of dynastic urban design, but all represent the new concepts of the explicitly ordered renaissance city.

A further example from the compendium of historical urban types which Brescia contains, Piazza della Loggia is the quarter which contains the city's principal renaissance monuments and is representative of the mercantile culture of the Venetian Republic which conquered Brescia in 1428 (Canniffe

4.3   Piazza della Loggia with the Palazzo della Loggia, Brescia.

1997). The space is oriented east–west and is positioned in the westwards expansion from the Roman core of the city which took place during the middle ages. Running north to south an arcaded mercantile loggia bounds the eastern side of the square, and is ornamented by a clock tower, the *orologio*, crowned by figures of Moors striking a bell which echoes the similar arrangement in Piazza San Marco in Venice (see Figure 13.1). The western side of the square is occupied by the Palazzo della Loggia, the centre of civic administration. Three arches, the fruit of Filippo de' Grassi's initial project of 1492, front the elevation to the square and support the major internal space on the *piano nobile* beneath the reconstructed lead vault. This structure bears a strong similarity to the basilica in Vicenza, and indeed Palladio was consulted with regard to the completion of the upper storey in 1550 (Puppi 1975: 286), although the building was completed by Lodovico Beretta. The square also hosted, as was common in the outposts of the Venetian *terra firma* and overseas territories, a column with the Lion of St. Mark on the northern side of the square. Forming the southern edge, the new financial institution of the Monte di Pieta asserted its claims to antiquity by the inclusion in its walls of a fragment of an ancient Roman inscription (C. IULIUS CAESAR PONTIF) placed there in 1480, and intended no doubt to invoke the ancient precedent of Brescia's Roman forum for this project of contemporary urban regeneration. The arrangement of the ensemble exemplifies the prevailing attitudes of the period and the fundamental impact perspective had in the envisioning of the space in both pictorial and architectural forms. The classical articulation of the buildings

4.4   The mercantile *logge*, Piazza della Loggia, Brescia. To the right is the tower of the *broletto* in the adjacent Piazza del Duomo.

having a specifically local resonance, the axial arrangement of the two principal elements, the Palazzo della Loggia and the *orologio*, ties the piazza into broader urban developments most especially the significance of the depiction and control of urban space in the development of methods of linear perspective in the first quarter of the 15th century. In Piazza della Loggia the authenticity of the urban experience is heightened by the replication of arched forms across the square, providing in real space that index of distance through repetition which pictorial composition employed to create the illusion of depth.

It is also significant that the conscious manipulation of perspective should be the medium through which these compromises between the antique, the pragmatic and civic beautification could be achieved. The order and control in the division of space which perspective construction implies has the effect of solidifying the geometric divisions into physical structure, limiting architectural language to that pure volumetric form most suited to representation within its rules. Panofsky argued that

whether one reproaches perspective for evaporating "true being" into a mere manifestation of seen things, or rather for anchoring the free and as it were, spiritual idea of form to a manifestation of mere seen things, is in the end little more than a question of emphasis. (Panofsky [1924–5] 1991: 71)

In an example such as that in Brescia, freed from the constraints which marked the great centres, the framing of civic elements in a reciprocal relationship in

4.5   Piazza della Loggia, Brescia. Diagram showing the perspectival relationship between the mercantile *logge* and the Palazzo della Loggia.

quite a pure and direct way demonstrated the pervasiveness of the search for the ideal. That quest required a considerable degree of control, which had already been demonstrated in the mid-fifteenth century in an exquisite example which had the totalizing focus of a personal project.

The creation of a new centre for the papal court in Tuscany under Pius II (1458–64) produced one of the most remarkable examples of urban composition, the town square (now named after the pope) of the freshly renamed Pienza, bringing a sense of civic grandeur to a hitherto unremarkable medieval hilltop settlement of Corsignano. The square, with its cathedral, palaces and town hall framing its sides marked an entirely fresh type of

4.6   Piazza Pio II, Pienza. The cathedral viewed from the loggia of the communal palace.

space, the unity of which (not the least because of its largely classicizing architectural language) suggested the recovery of ancient values. This reading was by no means inappropriate since the patron of the project to aggrandise his birthplace, Aeneas Silvius Piccolomini, was a foremost humanist prior to his election as pope (Mack 1987). The ideological composition of the new city is easily legible from the disposition of its elements. The cathedral occupies the central position, its three bayed facade marking the principal axis. To the right of this view a grand civic palace was created for the papal family by Bernardo Rossellino, while to the left, less architecturally fashionable, was the palace of Cardinal Rodrigo Borgia, the future Pope Alexander VI. Behind the viewer, and removed from an axial relationship to the cathedral was the communal palace marked by a loggia and a crenelated tower which identified it as a seat of civic authority, albeit here in a subservient role. This arrangement underscores the primacy of view marked out by the emphatically gridded pavement. Yet the space itself is not square or even rectangular in plan but a very marked trapezium with the cathedral occupying the larger of the two parallel sides. This device is a conjunction of the topographic condition of the existing town, structured along a gently meandering route along a hilltop ridge, and the optical principles of perspective defined by Brunelleschi a few decades earlier. This marriage of circumstance and conceptual definition meant that the impact of the space was all the greater, the subtle distortion of the perspective box making the cathedral appear bigger, and giving the right hand flanking palace a greater length on which to display authority on its elevation as it leads toward the magnificent view of the landscape. (As will be discussed in subsequent chapters, this distortion of spatial expectation through the use of a trapezoidal plan would be replicated down the centuries. Within Rome there are examples at the Campidoglio, at Piazza San Pietro, Piazza del Popolo and eventually Piacentini's Piazza Pio XII at the mouth of Via della Conciliazione completed in 1950, although all these successors inflate the intimate scale of the original demonstration at Pienza).

The geometrical underpinning which is exposed to the viewer, an entirely appropriate term for such a scenic conception, is the relationship of the gridded pavement to the facades, particularly those of the Palazzo Piccolomini and the cathedral (Furnari 1995: 130–33). Divided into nine rectangular units, three across and three deep, the different dimensions accord with the bay structure of both the cathedral and the rhythm of the three right hand bays of the Palazzo Piccolomini. Proportionally the entire cathedral facade sits within a square, and if folded down into the piazza the summit of the pediment would land in the middle of the street, at a point from which an ideal view is possible, if one were to follow Trachtenberg's method of one to one spatial relationships in plan and section outlined in the previous chapter. The Palazzo Piccolomini's proportions are rather more complex the palace being a rectangle of seven by eight bays, its height effectively matching that of the summit of the cathedral. The principal entrance facade is oriented to the street rather than the piazza, with the partially obscured eight bay facade to the piazza having two minor entrance bays placed between three sets of paired bays. However, the entrance on the left is merely a facade treatment which masks an awkward internal division. Only visible at the periphery of the ideal view, the maintenance of such an artifice underscores the scenographic intention of the design. This

4.7   Piazza Pio II, Pienza. The cathedral, with the fountain.

observation is not merely to attempt to downplay the architecture as a form of permanent stage set since, as will be discussed in subsequent chapters, theatrical attitudes were a significant component of renaissance urbanism. Pienza's individual buildings are quite distinct, their architectural languages consciously different from one another, and in the case of the cathedral different between the facade and the body of the church (the latter following

4.8   Piazza Pio II, Pienza. Palazzo Piccolomini.

the pattern of the *hallenkirchen* Pius II had seen in Northern Europe during his travels as a papal legate). However, the common architectural language between the facades of the cathedral and Palazzo Piccolomini, a normative classicism, indicates the tendencies which would prevail in subsequent urban projects. Around the rectangular stabilizing element of the gridded pavement the principal street, the cathedral steps and the two subsidiary tapering zones

4.9    Piazza Ariostea, Ferrara. The central space of the extension to the city planned under Ercole d'Este.

connect the vertical and horizontal surfaces, the zone on the right occupied by a well head. This small element within the space is positioned so as to connect views along the street, and out towards the landscape, emphasizing the continuity of this idealized space with the other elements of the physical environment. With Pius's death, though, the papacy's interests deserted this small city, leaving it to an isolation which has helped preserve it as a built example of *quattrocento* concepts.

The intimacy of scale of Piazza Pio II is in extreme contrast to an urban product such as Piazza Ariostea in Ferrara, just one example of how the ambitions of the Este family were marked out in their dynastic aggrandisement, strategic alliances with other major courts and conspicuous display of largesse. Martines describes one such example of charitable activity from Duke Ercole I

Once a year he went around Ferrara with cap in hand, humble airs, and a crowd of courtiers, begging food at the doors of citizens. Whatever he gathered – pies, capons, gamebirds, and cheeses by the hundreds – was given over to feed the city's poor. The exercise made a candid use of power, but it was interestingly combined with a self-image turned upside down, as in the pairing of prince and dwarf. The prince put on mock airs and became a beggar. Power became theater and ritual. But all the provisions collected by the begging Ercole went to prop up his magnanimity: a weak if sincere gesture that could not make up for the oppressive fiscal machine, as Ercole (d.1505), in the course of his reign, stepped up his political ambitions and splashed his resources around on grand building schemes. (Martines 1980: 321–2)

One such building scheme was the desire on the duke's part to expand a property such as the city of Ferrara itself through the extension undertaken in the 1490s, and centred around the ample new piazza. The court architect Biagio Rossetti created a generous environment for courtly life, with plots for the palaces of courtiers unencumbered by existing buildings. The gridded nature of such a town extension, rationally planned, however, also meant that the new piazza was vast, suitable for chivalric displays in the joust but essentially suburban in the context of a small city (Rowe and Satkowski 2002: 271). Its effect is therefore somewhat dispersed, and the concentrated effects of urban space in support of dynastic ambitions find their finest example not in low lying Ferrara but in an isolated location on a hilltop in Marche.

Urbino's fame as a renaissance court can partly be accounted for by the record of courtly values there left by Baldassare Castiglione in *The Courtier* provides a memoir of the rule of Federico da Montefeltro, Duke of Urbino (Castiglione [1528] 1967). Secure in his military prowess, the duke created a court the painting and architecture of which occupied the minds and hands of some of the most significant artists of the age. The piazza before the ducal palace serves as part of a sequence of increasingly confined spaces which encapsulate the status of personal power. Communicating with the magnificent loggia overlooking the landscape, the duke's *studiolo*, famous for its *trompe l'oeil* intarsia panels is only the most intimate and intense of these spaces. In between there is the *cortile*, a demonstration of harmonic perfection in a space which provided the heart of court life. The creation of a piazza, flanked on one side by the cathedral, and on two by the folded wall plane of the palace facade provides the most public element. These three spaces graded in their rights of access to the duke might be seen to accord with the three distinctions of person that Federico insisted was maintained at his court through forms of address (Martines 1980: 325).

Although the cathedral is a later structure (rebuilt by Giuseppe Valadier in the 1780s following an earthquake), the walls of the palace provide a severe public front which articulates the dignity with which court life represented itself, the ground floor expressed as a stone surface above which sit classically detailed window frames. The defensive character of the building is supplemented by a long stone bench at its base providing a waiting space for the duke's clients. Above all the piazza epitomises how the cultured renaissance ruler was to be presented to his people, in control of the city state through the authority of his image or name (inscribed above the openings) and represented by his architectural works. The piazza was only the outer surface of densely packed strata of ritual and elaboration around the person of the prince, but where he and those he favoured had maximum exposure, and therefore the greatest audience to impress.

In the development of the intellectual framework which produced these spaces, two distinct sources can be discerned. Political treatises such as that by Machiavelli, which dealt with the good governance of the state provided a rationale for the political structures, while ancient and contemporary architectural treatises offered direct examples for emulation in new urban developments. Leon Battista Alberti spanned both these disciplines. *De re aedificatoria*, his most celebrated and influential book, was only one of the texts on social matters that he produced. Although, as Mark Jarzombek has noted, it is difficult to find exact concordance between his written and built architectural works, let alone between his architectural and political texts, Alberti was characteristically forthright about his views on the architectural expression of political systems:

> For each building and even the city itself should differ when under the rule of those called tyrants, as opposed to others who take up their command and care for it like a magisterial office conferred on them by their fellows. For the city of a king it is sufficient defense to be capable of holding off an enemy attack. But for a tyrant, his own people may be just as hostile as outsiders, and he must therefore fortify his city against foreigner and fellow citizen alike, and the layout of the fortifications must allow him to receive outside reinforcements, even some of his own men against their fellow citizens. (Alberti 1988: 5,1,117)

Without expressing a preference for either system, Alberti makes typological distinctions that ally urban form and political realities. To a twenty-first century audience such moral ambivalence might seem reprehensible, if disarmingly frank, but it confirms that the perceived link between political and architectural forms, a source of much debate in the last century, was a part of the modern political ideas surfacing in the renaissance. The passage reflects aspects of Alberti's own career, whether with the papal court, those of Ferrara, Mantua or Urbino, or especially that of his patron Sigismondo Malatesta, the tyrant of Rimini. Jarzombek raised the issue of the ostensible conflict between the idealism of Alberti's instructions on best practice, and the reality of tyranny, questioning: '...would that not offer an opportunity to make manifest the dialectic between the humanist program and the frenzied world' (Jarzombek 1989: 172).

We should be wary, though, of assuming that the architects who produced buildings and spaces for these various states were consciously exploiting the paradox which underlay the production of ideal urban environments, and the far from benign regimes which provided sources of patronage. The hierarchical view of society, reinforced by the teaching and structure of the church, remained largely unquestioned, and creative artists were regarded as little more than jobbing craftsmen who, whatever their intellectual abilities, were expected to produce work that flattered or reinforced the authority of their clients. If, as Alberti asserted, architecture should merely reflect the political reality, then it becomes evident that authority will be directly expressed in major constructions such as those discussed. The need for external defence was a commonplace in renaissance urban theory and practice, but the desirability of such direct internal security would find few echoes in contemporary utopian descriptions. From a pragmatic viewpoint, however, autocratic regimes have always tended to provide willing architects with a broader scale of project than the more democratic and incremental alternatives. Architects and their patrons therefore had a mutual interest in

4.10  Piazza Duca Federico, Urbino, showing the corner of the Ducal Palace.

the projection of large scale developments, enhancing the status of both while the needs of those expected to inhabit such new urban spaces would be only a secondary consideration.

Alberti's writings, as a prime example of the fusion of architectural and broader intellectual thought, were a source much consulted by succeeding generations. In the princely courts of Italy, persons whose knowledge could be exploited for an overlapping series of academic, artistic and social purposes provided a number of services. Tutorships to the younger members of the court accounted only for the most mundane tasks, in contrast to the provision of intellectual justifications for military, diplomatic and dynastic manoeuvres, and the ideological framework for the temporary and permanent works which celebrated those events. In parallel to artists and architects, the task of these intellectuals was to provide support for authority, and not to question the validity of political decisions. Festival constructions, and edifices commemorating alliances and victories could be formed and decorated to convey the most precise and topical messages, but a broader social situation could be defined by the ruler for the ruled by means of public works which, typically in renaissance and baroque times, imitated Roman scale and style in such a way that the imperial pretensions of the particular dynasty were explicitly communicated. Antiquity was seen as providing the model both for architectural languages and the successful society.

A direct connection could be made through geometry. The pyramidal structure of a courtly society, with a broad base but one pinnacle is only the most banal of analogies. This structure was replicated in other states, as well as being echoed in the perceived structure of the known world. It was therefore only a short intellectual step for emphasis to be placed on the importance of geometrical coherence in the success of civic functions, and the relationship between clarity of urban form and social structure. The reflection and replication of a cosmic order in the human sphere was a fundamental tenet of the theological vision of society, but in the renaissance the role of geometry is enhanced with the definition of the visual pyramid and the dissemination of perspective methods. A tool which could remake the image of the world, as well as change the way it was perceived, presented a political weapon to those who exercised power (Evans 1995: 141).

The court philosopher held the role of interpreter of phenomena in support of the regime. The fiction under which this operated was a self-reflexive one. The order of the world as derived from ancient sources was mirrored in the hierarchical order of society, of which the order of the court was itself a microcosm, while these social structures were themselves projected in the physical constructions which the regime promoted. This tendency towards 'ideal' structures in society found its clearest tool in this use of geometry, which was simultaneously transformed into an instrument of aesthetic rigour, constructional coherence and social control. The revelation and creation of structures which reflected a divine order required a geometrical definitionpossessing both clarity and meaning so that functionality could be assured without the loss of opportunity to reinforce the political *status quo*. Perspective construction, in which perceptual simulation combined with geometrical abstraction, was, to the early modern mind, the manifestation of the hidden order of the world and the artist's and architect's point of entry into that order.

Beyond the picture plane, the urban scene could be surveyed in two species. While the quantities of space, in distance and dimension could be measured, so could the qualities of the citizen be assayed by the prince. Perspective provided proof of the geometrical order of the world, while the clarity of the spaces projected, despite the complexities of historical reference and iconographical meaning, afforded evidence of the privileged viewer's control. The piazze discussed reveal the projection of sophisticated urban strategies as part of a political campaign of absolutism, the subsequent demise of which does little to diminish their spatial impact. In all these cities the urban culture of adornment had a political purpose which went hand in hand with the aesthetic refinements. While antiquity was to continue to be the principal model, the intention was to equal if not surpass it. Nostalgia played little part in a culture where despite the threat to Christendom from the Ottoman Turks, horizons were expanding in the culture, science and knowledge of the world.

# 5

# High Renaissance: The modern city *all'antica*

The growing sophistication of the culture of the Renaissance court had encouraged the development of the language of public space in a more obviously systematic form than its medieval predecessors. However, it would be the major Italian states, such as Milan, Venice and the Papacy, which would articulate the architectural spirit of the period in an urban form which adopted the scale of antique precedents. The principal characteristic of the spaces they created would be the dominant presence of the architectural figure in the form of the classical column or pilaster, constructed on the basis of ancient usage. The consistent, inventive and symmetrical use of the orders was intended to evoke the Roman world by direct reference or to create an allusive reinvention of their vanished meanings. While the use of superimposed orders, as at the Palazzo Piccolomini in Pienza could be derived from Alberti's theoretical reconstruction of ancient practice, the development of the giant order was a new interpretation of classical precedent which in turn would be identified subsequently as pointing the way to later architecture and urbanism. The inflation of the size of architectural elements also had urban consequences, in the extension of distance across which urban scenographic effects were to be noticed (Burroughs 2002: 176–93).

The idealization of these architectural figures with the creation of symmetrically defined spaces owes much to the classicizing tendencies of renaissance art and particularly the concentrated attention to the body which characterized the work of the major creative figures of the period. With no clearly defined system of professional boundaries, patrons were often happy to employ as urban architects men whose skills had previously been demonstrated in painting, in sculpture and in scenography. The central gaze, as required by perspective construction, and the creation of axially arranged complexes to accommodate it would become one of the defining effects of the architecture of the period. It represented a strongly marked discipline through which the configuration of the body was mapped onto the city in two forms, an explicit method and an implicit one. In the first the comparative display of figurative sculpture and architectural members has the effect of creating hierarchies of modeling and volume which animate surfaces. In the latter the metaphorical connection was expressed through the arrangement of buildings paired along a spine in the form of a route or space and terminated by a single structure serving the role of a head. Although the corporeal basis of such arrangements would not necessarily be directly expressed, the frequency with which it would occur during the period suggests that such ideas were common in the practice of urban composition, spread by the newly available architectural treatise (Adams and Nussdorfer 1994; Rowe and Satkowski 2002).

The ideology of the state, and the practical measures through which it was expressed in the form of urban beautification, depended on the frequent reinforcement of the personification of the state, as a mythical abstraction or in the person of the ruler, as discussed in the previous chapter. The growth of bureaucratic institutions in the consolidation of state structures required accommodation, but also demanded representation. The language of the classical past, especially when juxtaposed with the medieval context, provided an ambivalent form of validation, the regular, symmetrical architecture rising pristine and new amongst an irregular context and, especially in Rome itself, emphasising continuity with ruined antiquity. The articulation of this modern architecture, based only on the scantest archaeological research and the aesthetic speculation of theorists was a mixture out of which innovative forms could grow, with the prevailing conditions encouraging a liberal exploitation and combination of trabeated or arcuated forms, the repetition and variation of rhythms, the articulation of corners as massed and overlaid columns and pilasters and the introduction of series of sculptures adorning the cornice line. The superabundance of these motifs, with interrupted cornices and subtle accents of centrality provided a connection between body and city through the articulation of scale.

Although the concept of artistic development is often described through the distorting mirror of a prevailing ideology, the use of defining moments or personalities to focus discussion is inevitable if the material from a long historical period is to be assessed in a manageable fashion. Erwin Panofsky held that when work on certain artistic problems appears unlikely to bear fruit there is often a recoil or reversal of direction, accompanied by a return to apparently more "primitive" modes of representation (Panofsky [1924] 1991: 47). This assertion of a recoil mechanism by which such development is effected had its origin in his attempt to account for the philosophical origins and cultural ramifications of the application of a codified perspective to artistic production in the *quattrocento*. In addition, as Wolfgang Lotz has observed, this artistic use in architectural production would be replaced by a reliance on orthographic projections in the period of the high renaissance (Lotz 1977a). Using these arguments, we may suggest that the development of urban spaces as representations of the body related to these apparently primitivising tendencies, manifestations that also include antiquarian concerns, the reassessment of medieval types and the exploitation of the linear, planar and volumetric forms upon which perspective construction was founded. The three piazze considered in this chapter all feature assertive interventions into

5.1 Piazza Ducale, Vigevano. Diagram combining downward and upward looking views of the space.

the principal urban spaces of their respective cities, the violence they must have done to their contexts serving to reveal the nature of the political use of space. The scenographic intentions of these urban works, in Vigevano, in Venice and in Rome arose from the desire of the power elite to project an ideal which would have the traits of the antique and the self-consciously rational. In each case the scale of the work was substantial, an attempt to return to civic and administrative structures the dignity which Vitruvius described them as

5.2  Piazza Ducale, Vigevano. The arcade lining the piazza and the Torre di Bramante viewed through the street doorway of the baroque facade of the cathedral.

enjoying in ancient times. The abstract and geometrical language of perspective was therefore the perfect method by which an assumed past grandeur could be projected onto the present. But one should also be aware that the piazza was a medium through which authority was communicated directly to a population. In a passage from contemporary history which he refers to as a digression,

Machiavelli recounted the actions of Cesare Borgia in using the central urban space of Cesena for the unannounced but chilling display of the dismembered body of a discarded confederate (Machiavelli [1531–32] 2004: 30–31). Through such a blunt action the nature of tyrany could be unequivocally demonstrated in the piazza, and no more so than in the first example.

The town of Vigevano, situated south-west of Milan across the River Ticino, and is commanded by the fortress developed by successive Milanese rulers (Canniffe 1998). It was the birthplace in 1451 of Ludovico Maria Sforza, also known as *il Moro*, the Regent and Duke of Milan who developed the new piazza in a single campaign between 1492 and 1494. A centre of courtly patronage in the later decades of the fifteenth century, Milan had attracted the presence of figures such as Leonardo da Vinci and the mathematician Luca Pacioli, but it was through the work of the painter and architect Donato Bramante (144–1514) that the influence of antique precedents was brought to bear on the design of this 'forum' below the ducal fortress (Lotz 1977b). As it survives today, Piazza Ducale is very different from Bramante's original scheme, although it is still largely defined by the arcades he introduced. They form now a continuous range around north, west and south sides of the piazza, which measures roughly 50 by 130 metres, with the concave baroque facade of the *duomo* forming the fourth side. In their original condition, however, the arcades would have been broken in the south-western corner to provide an access ramp to the ducal *rocca*. As Bruschi states, Bramante seemed to take a consistent interest in the theme of defined and delimited space – cloister, courtyard, piazza – which he saw to be significant for the experience of towns as entities. His early experiences at Urbino would surely have helped form this idea. The art of architecture was no longer to be restricted to single buildings. As a part of the city the individual buildings gained in value, and the arrangement of spaces became full of implicit 'urban' allusions: 'a cloister or a courtyard was, ideally, a piazza, a "forum", of a city; and conversely, a piazza like the one at Vigevano was a courtyard, an open-air hall' (Bruschi 1977: 62). The use of arcades to define the edges of the square and house commercial life provided a dignified framework for civic life. A constant rhythm of columns and arches unifies the disparate functions, emphasises the value of the collective urban room over the rivalries of individual buildings, and borders the piazza with a covered external route akin to a cloister. The upper surfaces are decorated with painted antique architecture, including triumphal arches which indicate the connections to adjacent streets.

The current situation, however, should be balanced against Bramante's actual construction rather than the results of the amendments made in the 17th century. The Piazza Ducale as it stands bears some formal similarity to the Cortile del Belvedere in the Vatican, which Bramante commenced ten years later. Furthermore Tafuri has related both complexes to the ancient precedent of the palace-hippodrome complex (Tafuri [1992] 2006: 68, 95). However Bramante's original interventions did not present the same degree of comprehensive enclosure which we experience today. Instead the piazza was bounded by a more discontinuous set of arcades, with apparently clear breaks between them, while the existing church, on a different alignment from the new piazza, had a rather more detached relationship than the present *duomo*. The contained space of the piazza would therefore have been perceived less as a clean geometrical figure, than as a void between distinct though similar ranges of arcading. According to Bruschi, the layout of the piazza in Vigevano bears comparison with that described by Filarete in his *Treatise*, written in Milan between 1460–65:

– the piazza is in the middle of the city. ...its width is 150 braccia and its length 300; the latter runs from east to west, the former from south to north. ...At the eastern end I will build the cathedral, and the royal court at the western. ...In the northern part of the piazza I will make the merchant's piazza. ...On the southern side of the piazza I will make another piazza that will be a sort of market where edibles can be sold, ...and other things necessary to the life of man. ...At the head of this I will make the Palazzo del Capitano on the corner nearest the court, so that only the street separates them. (Filarete 1965: VI, 42v–43r)

Filarete's description of the proposed city of Sforzinda, dedicated to *il Moro's* father Francesco Sforza, comprises his narration of the details of the city's planning and constituent parts. The audience for this lengthy story is Filarete's interlocutor, a princely patron, and therefore Bramante's work, whether directly derived from Filarete or not, has at least an ironic echo of his desire to enhance his prince's reputation by the design of the new city as a demonstration of cultural patronage. Sforzinda remained unbuilt, but Vigevano reflects some of the ideas it embodied, although with a more sinister character since it had a real political context. As Lotz has shown, the relationship between piazza and fortress was a direct one, the feudal relationship between prince and people expressed itself in the visual control of the urban space maintained from the tower of the fortress. Furthermore, Lotz comments that, as a rule, the medieval municipal palaces in the free communes of the Po Valley stand either between two squares as in Padua and Vicenza, or they project on three sides into squares as in Piacenza, although their forms varied as a result of differences in political jurisdiction. He adds that nothing is known of the appearance and site of the medieval town hall of Vigevano, which was torn down to make room for the new piazza, but the fact that the community received the relatively large subsidy of 1,000 ducats from *il Moro* for the new building would indicate that the old one was sizeable. The new town hall is located at the centre of the long, north side of the square, with the municipal coat of arms on the facade distinguishing it from the adjacent buildings on either side. If it can be assumed that the destroyed building, like surviving examples of the type elsewhere, was partially or completely free-standing, thereby symbolising the independence of the commune, then the incorporation of the new Palazzo Comunale behind the continuous facade of the piazza had a specific, political significance; it bore witness to the end of communal independence (Lotz 1977b: 126).

Subsumed, therefore, within the range of building on the north side of the new square, the new Palazzo Comunale could be both reduced in visibility

5.3 Piazza Ducale, Vigevano. Detail of the arcade with the nineteenth century decoration.

towards the citizens, and be overseen from a distance by the fortress, with the clear space of the piazza between ducal and civic centres. The subsequent additions to the square, most notably the creation of the apsidal facade to the duomo, the removal of the ramp and the joining of the ranges of arcading, serve to reinforce the coherence of the civic space. These were the work in the 1680s of the bishop and amateur architect Juan Caramuel de Lobkowitz. The disjunction between the alignment of the duomo and that of the piazza, although contrary to the symmetry and balance of post-perspectival space provided the opportunity for a remarkable example of baroque ingenuity. The construction of a concave facade to the cathedral, allowed the piazza to be closed by a shallow *exedra*, a form echoed in the segmental pediment that terminates it. However, the central axis of the piazza does not meet the new facade on a magnificent central doorway as would have been expected. Instead it is marked by a central line of structure, a spine, which, within the cathedral, is continued by the left-hand nave arcade. The new facade thus has four bays, the outer two single-storey, but supporting volutes that frame the upper central storeys and pediment. Each of the doorways is given equal weight and treatment, and therefore leads into a different condition beyond the facade. From the left they frame, firstly Via Carlo Alberto which runs along the northern flank of the cathedral, secondly a doorway into the left-hand aisle (at the cusp of the facade curve and the orthogonal geometry of the cathedral), thirdly, via a small vestibule, the central axis of the nave, and finally a small external shrine created out of the space between facade and nave. The generous concavity of the facade is contrasted with the shallow relief of the paired pilasters, and the peristyle of eight free-standing columns which frame the doorways. The layering and plasticity of the duomo facade provides the terminus to the piazza's enclosing surface whose sheer plane has only illusionary articulation in the form of the vaguely *trompe l'oeil* murals.

Even without this baroque embellishment, considered as an example of political architecture the piazza bears comparison to Alberti's description of the differences between tyrannical and 'democratic' urban space referred to in the previous chapter.

> But this is how they differ: A royal palace should be sited in the city centre, should be of easy access, and should be gracefully decorated, elegant and refined, rather than a house. But that of a tyrant, being a fortress rather than a house, should be positioned where it is neither inside nor outside the city. Further, whereas a royal dwelling might be sited next to a showground, a temple, or the houses of noblemen, that of a tyrant should be set well back on all sides from any buildings. (Alberti 1988: 5,1, 121–22)

The *rocca* at Vigevano could not be mistaken for a mere house. Its elevated position and proximity to Piazza Ducale reinforces the political message of the sugjugation of communal liberties to despotic rule. The clearing of the space for the piazza might well be an attempt to meet Alberti's injunction that such a tyrant's dwelling be set well back. Such a clear range of fire from the castle at Vigevano did not, however, prevent *il Moro's* overthrow in 1499 during the French invasion which Machiavelli saw as the inevitable consequence of the political machinations of Pope Alexander VI as he attempted to create a dynastic state for his son Cesare Borgia (Machiavelli [1531–32] 2004: 26–35).

The 'ideal' geometrical condition of the piazza belies its historical context. In Vigevano the effect of the cumulative work of generations of architects is to mask the irregularities and inconsistencies of existing structures and relationships to produce a coherent urban space with the illusion of geometrical consistency. Although there is a clear distinction between the zone for occupation by the citizens and that for the tyrant, their relationship is one of convenient adjacency heightened by the possibilities of surveillance. The organic nature of their proximity is a condition which is only marginally effected by the geometrically controlled public space created by renaissance and later architects. At Vigevano the presence of the Duke as the protagonist is explicit in the visibility of the *Torre di Bramante*, (framed in a view through the baroque facade) and there is little ambiguity as to who is the actor and who is the spectator. The aesthetic power of the 'forum' begun by Bramante ensured its completion as an enclosed public space for gathering. The geometry and stability of this example, therefore, underscores the implications of the physical embodiment of the city for the society which it contains. At Vigevano, the 'completion' of Bramante's project by the creation of continuous facades and the consequent screening of the entering streets reinforces the defined nature of Piazza Ducale and indicates the direction of development in future examples which will feature in later chapters.

In the context of the French occupation of Milan, at just this point in the 1490s new elements would also begin to be introduced at Venice into Piazza San Marco, marking the commencement of a long campaign of urban renovation. As with Vigevano, the point of cultural reference was also Rome, although indirectly filtered through the culture of Byzantium. The role the city republic had in the Mediterranean as the major maritime power and eventually as the bulwark of Christendom against the Ottomans had only developed out of its earlier role as an increasingly ambitious trading partner of Constantinople. With that city's fall and the relative weakness of the papacy, Venice saw herself as assuming an imperial mantle as a new Rome. This would be manifested in the reconstruction of its major public space, the conjoined areas of the piazza and piazzetta, in an architectural language which spoke directly of those Roman aspirations (Howard 1975: 8–37). If the piazza, the great space focused on the shrine of St. Mark, had a function which replicated that of an ancient Roman forum (inspired by the longest surviving example of the genre still in use in Constantinople), the piazzetta's role as ceremonial entry point to the city would be enhanced during this period. The site developed its cultural significance as the location of Venetian government with the Doge's Palace positioned at the mouth of the Grand Canal, from which point a straight route across the city's islands could be traced to the Rialto, the centre of trade. Next to the Doge's Palace the basilica of San Marco had grown up not as the city's cathedral but as the private chapel of the Doge, where the body of the evangelist Mark (following its theft from Alexandria in the early ninth century) was housed in a cruciform church directly inspired by that of the Holy Apostles in Constantinople, its facade adorned with elaborate mosaics and the gilded horses plundered from Constantinople during the fourth crusade (see Figure 2.3). Opposite the junction between church and palace marked by the Porta

5.4   Piazza San Marco, Venice. Arcade of the Procuratie Vecchie with the base of the campanile in the distance.

della Carta (1440s) stood the immense bulk of the campanile, itself forming a hinge between piazza and piazzetta. At the opposite end of the piazza, and forming a terminus to the processional route was the church of San Geminiano. The distance of approximately 600 feet had been set in 1172 when Doge Sebastiano Ziani doubled the original size of the square by ordering the removal of the orignal church further way from the basilica to enhance its importance. Between them on the north stretched the regular rhythm of the Procuratie Vecchie, the headquarters of the shrine's numerous officials, while on the south side were a variety of structures including a pilgrimage hostel. The whole space was depicted in detail by Gentile Bellini in 1496 in the painting *Miracle of the Holy Cross in Piazza San Marco* originally commissioned for the confraternity of the Scuola Grande di San Giovanni Evangelista (and now housed in the Galleria dell'Accademia) (Fortini Brown 1988: 142–52). Despite the obvious propaganda value of such a work, depicting the splendour of the city and its governing elite, the political power represesented is deliberately undersold in contrast to the religious power. The ritual life of the city, as perceived in the renaissance has the function of expressing not merely the prevailing civic order, but by implication also the divine, and that identity could be celebrated both by temporary human action through processions or by permanent architectural and urban ensembles.

5.5 Procuratie Vecchie, Piazza San Marco, Venice.

Despite the evident scale and grandeur of this vision of their major public space at the close of the fifteenth century, successive Venetian administrations sought to enhance the physical majesty of the space beginning, as Bellini's great documentary record was completed, with the construction of the Clock Tower in the 1490s to designs attributed to Mauro Codussi (d. 1504). This structure, in the latest classical manner, made a terminus both for the view from the entry point to the city and was a triumphal ornament to the densely packed route through the city to the Rialto. The adjacent structure of the Procuratie Vecchie was rebuilt with an extra storey following a fire in 1512. The foreground of that increasingly idealized view into the city along the piazzetta was itself transformed with the construction of the library of St. Mark (1537 onwards), designed by Jacopo Sansovino on the west side of the piazzetta, a design based on the remains of the ancient theatre of Marcellus in Rome and forming an unequal pair with the Doge's Palace (Johnson 2000). The framing arcades and upper level galleries provided viewing spaces for civic rituals, from public executions between the paired honorific columns (also erected by Doge Ziani in the twelfth century), to ducal ceremonial, especially the processions which emerged from the Porta Della Carta and turned into the square in front of the new Loggetta at the base of the campanile. This triumphal adornment had been made possible by the significant decision by Sansovino to free the campanile of surrounding encumbrances and move the southern boundary of the Piazza back to create the Procuratie Nuove. The unresricted view towards

5.6   Piazzetta San Marco, Venice. A view towards the *bacino* of San Marco with Sansovino's library on the right.

the basilica was widened by the new structure which extended the regular rhythm as a more classically ordered pair to the Procuratie Vecchie. The work however did not commence until 1582, 12 years after Sansovino's death, the construction being commenced by Vincenzo Scamozzi and completed by Baldassare Longhena around 1640. Sansovino's new facade to San Geminiano (demolished with the construction of the Napoleonic palace between 1807–13) completed the renovation of the square in this period (Goy 1997: 130–43).

The theatrical aspect of political representation as exemplified by Piazza San Marco had its frequent expression in the most elaborate civic ritual, often expressed through the form of ephemeral architecture for festivals (Muir 1981). While the renovation of major civic spaces was often directly connected to such festivals, the influence of their combination of architecture and symbolic content had the effect of creating an architecture rich in expression where the surfaces which defined public space had begun to be treated explicitly as a form of urban signage. The increasing scale with which this was articulated would lead to the extension of the impact of such facades across urban distances, a technique of civic design demonstrated in Rome toward the end of the sixteenth century by Domenico Fontana's replanning of the city for Sixtus V as an aid to pilgrims. However, such an extensive and influential planning scheme with its exploitation of vistas, urban sculpture and architectural backdrop to a spiritual journey had its origins in a secular work in Rome from half a century earlier.

The project to remodel the Capitoline Hill in Rome originated under Pope Paul III and his diplomatic efforts to cement an alliance with the Holy Roman Emperor Charles V (Argan and Contardi 1993: 213–230, 252–263). Imperial forces had sacked Rome in 1527 and the city was still in the process of slow recovery from its devastation. The construction of the new basilica of St. Peter's was proceeding, albeit at an unhurried pace, but the pope required a setting of suitable civic grandeur for the entry in 1536 of the first emperor to visit his official capital since 1452. The centre of municipal government on the Campidoglio, overlooking the ruins of the Forum Romanum had the requisite resonance, although its actual state represented a far from dignified view. Two palaces formed an open space on the summit of the hill overshadowed by the huge medieval church of Sta. Maria in Aracoeli. The palaces, that of the Conservators (the councillors, dating from the fifteenth century) and that of the Senator (essentially the mayor, first recorded in use in 1151) were typical medieval communal palaces, although the latter was unusual in being built upon the remains of the ancient Tabularium which dominated the valley of the Forum referred to in Chapter 1 (see Figure 1.1). The palaces consisted externally of the usual elements of towers, *logge* and staircases, and the site was further ornamented by the display of ancient statuary, some the result of recent excavations and presented to visitors

5.7 Piazza del Campidoglio, Rome. The Palazzo del Senatorio, with the statue of Marcus Aurelius.

5.8   Piazza del Campidoglio, Rome. The new palace, built as a pair to the existing Palazzo dei Conservatori.

from the 1470s as relics of Rome's vanished pagan magnificence (Hart 2006: 61–63). These included several significant figure sculptures such as *Lo Spinario* (a small-scale bronze of a boy picking a thorn from his foot), marble statues of reclining river gods, a huge gilded bronze statue of Hercules, and fragments of colossal imperial statues in the form of two heads, one in bronze, one in marble thought to be of Constantine. These disparate elements were required to be integrated into any new project and its author therefore had to produce a work which had political significance, civic decorum and quasi-museum functions. The design which developed was initiated by Michelangelo but was not completed until long after his death in 1564, his posthumous reputation ensuring that the extensive subsequent work was a faithful reproduction of his recorded intentions.

The political dimension was served not only by the location of the work, but by its orientation, turning its back towards the Forum Romanum, because of the practical necessity of maintaining the Senator's palace, but also framing the new direction of view towards the modern Rome that was developing, with the massive structure of St. Peter's emerging on the horizon. This reorientation served to emphasise the city's dependency on papal power rather than its notional independence as represented by its ancient origins. The decision to relocate the ancient bronze equestrian statue of Marcus Aurelius from

the Lateran in 1538 also meant that the antiquarian character of the existing sculpture collection was to be superseded by an emblem of imperial power, foregrounding images of rulership over communal democracy.

The existing context, accessed by the dramatic staircase which leads up to the Aracoeli, has also been seen as representing a spiritual dimension to Michelangelo's work. The new route which was provided from street level to the newly defined piazza offered a gentler ascent than that directly to the church, suggesting the civic realm as a resting place on the path of salvation (Argan and Contardo 1993: 216). But whatever the authenticity of such a metaphor, the sculptural quality of Michelangelo's architecture suggests a corporeal reading of a space which, when considered in plan terms has a head, arms, chest and trunk like a vast recumbent figure, a personification of the city on an even bigger scale than that present on the site in the form of the fragments of ancient sculpture. We know from Michelangelo's drawings that the interchangeability of architectural and organic form was a recurring motif and therefore even in the constrained circumstances of an urban renovation one could read its architectural members as equivalent of limbs and organs (Hall 2006).

The compositional techniques by which the final ensemble was achieved included an implicit acceptance of the existing situation, especially the acute angle formed by the two palaces, as a key into the site's transformation. The creation of a new axial route perpendicular to the Senator's palace and stretching down to street level positioned both the site for the equestrian statue and the line of symmetry along which a new palace could be projected as a pair

5.9 Piazza del Campidoglio, Rome. The pavement of the piazza, shown following the removal of the statue of Marcus Aurelius for conservation.

5.10  Piazza del Campidoglio, Rome. Detail of the statuary at the Palazzo del Senatorio, showing its integration into the structure of the new staircases.

to the conservators' palace. Giant orders of pilasters are then used to lend a dignified and united scale to the facades, strongly marking the paired palaces with their ground floor colonnades and applied across the upper storeys and the prominent ends of the Senator's palace. The elliptical pavement swelling up within a slightly lowered central space then provided the footing for the equestrian statue, helped deceive the eye as to the non-rectangularity of the plan, and provides a symbolic language for Rome's claim to be the centre of the world (Ackerman 1961: 176–93).

The Campidoglio's impact, (which will be seen reflected in one example in the next chapter), springs from the completeness of the experience and the variety of its elements. A knowledge of the historical origins of the present situation is not necessary to recognise the skill with which the space is controlled. A place has been created which speaks of the exercise of power, however illusory that was in practice, the prospect from the piazza commanding the city to submit. This control is reinforced by the integration of the gestures and attitude of the sculptures selected for arrangement on the site. As the supreme sculptor of the period, (although one recognized as having a fluctuating record when required to produce more than one figure) the sculptor's skills were exploited only in the handling of the architectural detail, and the placing of work by other, anonymous, ancient hands. The plinth and pavement for the equestrian statue, the integration of the river gods against the staircases and the display of horse

5.11 Piazza del Campidoglio, Rome. The facsimile of the statue of Marcus Aurelius which occupies the centre of the space.

tamers and trophies against the open edge of the space all helped heighten the drama of the site. The approaching visitor passes through the figurative screen framed by the horse-tamers, under the blessing hand of Marcus Aurelius to reach the staircases behind the river gods. The totality of that experience, as a figure moves among other sculpted figures, is as fundamental a part of its urban design as the use of the giant order and the zodiacal pavement.

These three insertions into existing urban spaces, designed within a few decades of each other, share many characteristics. They represent the successful completion of urban spaces by the introduction of strong, radically contemporary structures based on ancient precedents into venerable environments. The arcades they all employ have three distinct sources, a vernacular practicability, a civic purpose, and a classical representational role. The medieval type of the arcaded urban building, with residential accommodation above workshops or other commercial spaces was a commonplace on the urban scene in Italy, its virtues of convenience for shelter and proximity between workplace and home attested to by its widespread application. There was, in addition, the tradition of the civic loggia, used for the dispensation of justice and the embodiment of the active roles of public authority. On to these roots was grafted the classicizing influence of theorists such as Alberti, with his description of the ideal, colonnaded urban space, derived directly from Vitruvius, and suggesting the elevation of convenience into the cladding of the dignified urban room.

The Greeks would make their fora square; they would surround them with a generous double portico, adorned with columns and stone beams; on the upper floor they built a gallery. Here in Italy our fora had a width two-thirds their length; and because they had long been the traditional sites for gladiatorial displays, the columns to their portico would be spaced farther apart...

Nowadays we prefer to make the area of the forum a double square; the portico and other surrounding buildings must have dimensions that relate strictly to those of the open space, so that it appears neither too extensive and the surrounding buildings too low, nor too confined if hemmed in by the buildings stacked up all round. The ideal roof height would be between one third and a minimum of two-sevenths the width of the forum. (Alberti 1988: 8,6, 25–26)

Alberti's proportional prescriptions could not be applied with any consistency in these existing urban contexts, but the examples discussed in this chapter display the transformation of the ground floor colonnade into a dignified device for the framing of a space. Transforming its medieval precedents and differentiating itself from the language of the urban palazzo facade which favoured the closing in of ground floors, the colonnades maintained the concept of the public realm into the language of space intended to evoke state power. While the monumentalization of this device will be discussed in the next chapter, it is worth emphasising that this dignifying of daily life took place initially in the context of the representation of power, shared through the reinvention of the 'forum'. One of the examples had no need to strain to emphasise its connection to the concept as it was positioned next to the original version of such a public space. At Vigevano and Venice, the longitudinal relationship between urban space and 'temple' was quite direct in its reference to Roman precedent. But at the Campidoglio civic authority enclosed the space but directed the view towards the new 'temple' of the apostle Peter across the city, signifying the scenographic direction in which the design of the piazza was developing as an element of a broader cityscape.

# 6

# Mannerism: The theatre of the city

The aftermath of the sack of Rome in 1527, the new cultural constraints of the counter-reformation, and the extension of artistic languages in the wake of Raphael and Michelangelo have been seen as representing a distinct tendency if not a definite style, Mannerism (Hauser 1965). In architecture and urban design, the evidence for the coherence and dominance of this style is sparse since (with the exception of the villa and the garden) the period was not particularly innovative in the development of spatial types. Radical changes to the urban environment which did occur relied for their effect on the theatrical devices of the growing art of scenography to which the development of perspective was closely allied. In a broader context Richard Sennett has argued that society's image of the city as a theatre of human action is one of the underpinnings of attitudes to the organization of traditional urban life (Sennett [1977] 1986: 35). If we delineate Sennett's three purposes of urban theatricality the connections between city and theatre which he asserts are reinforced. His description of 'illusion and delusion' has an immediate similarity to the development of linear perspective, in its knowing manipulation of vision as referred to in Chapter 4. The detachment of human nature and social artifice can be compared to the quest for, and belief in, the 'ideal' represented in the examples in Chapter 5. And finally, his assertion of the value of roles, that is the assumption of a received convention, has parallels with the adoption of classical antiquity as the datum against which contemporary phenomena were to be judged. The four spaces under discussion in this chapter are products of the middle to later years of the sixteenth century, three of them being the work of two of its most significant figures, Vignola and Vasari, and the last one being closely associated with its patron. All of them employ the linked phenomena of perspective and theatricality to control urban space. The insertion of a new structure, such as those which will be discussed in Florence, Bologna and Arezzo, changed the space to which it was added by its presence as a stabilizing and ordering backdrop to the urban scene, exploiting a reinterpretation of the loggia-type (Canniffe 1995). The form was associated with banking or money-lending institutions, with civic edifices for the dispensation of justice, as well as providing cover for traders and customers. However in a situation such as

6.1 Piazza della Signoria, Florence. The Palazzo Vecchio, the Uffizi and the Loggia dei Lanzi.

Sabbioneta, where the entire small city was designed with theatrical intent, the political nature of the spectacle was intended to be even more convincing (Canniffe 2001).

It would seem appropriate to commence in Florence, the city associated with the development of perspective, and return to the Piazza della Signoria, one of the locations of Brunelleschi's demonstrations, and the extension to the space produced by Giorgio Vasari (1511–74) in the form of the Uffizi (Satkowski 1990). Both the Piazza della Signoria and that of the Uffizi have an internal coherence which is independent of the connections made between the two spaces by vistas, volumetric oppositions and markers such as the numerous statues. If the basic form of the Piazza della Signoria is understood as a void rectangle from which one quarter is occupied by the mass of the Palazzo Vecchio, the renaissance developments gather around a line which bisects the square and, with a slight deflection, is roughly perpendicular to the course of the Arno (see Figures 3.10 and 3.11). This line is populated by the statues arranged along the front of the Palazzo which terminates in the equestrian monument to Cosimo I de Medici, referring to the precedent of the Marcus Aurelius statue in Rome. This arrangement results in a procession of figures which issues from the perspective space of the Uffizi.

6.2    The statuary of Piazza della Signoria, Florence framed against the Uffizi. The statues include Bandinelli's *Hercules* and the facsimile of Michelangelo's *David*.

The complex of the Uffizi was commissioned by Cosimo I to house the offices of the magistracy, and from this utilitarian function the court architect Vasari conjured an urban composition which produced city-wide resonances. Its extended form was cast like a projection of the tower of the Palazzo Vecchio from the southernmost corner of the Piazza towards the Arno. Despite the obviously public nature of its form as an attenuated nave inviting access from the citizenry, from the earliest times of its construction in the 1560s the Uffizi also had a darker political side. As Fricelli has observed, the wide street flanked by parallel palaces serves as a device to telescope the relationship

6.3   Piazza degli Uffizi, Florence. View along the Uffizi towards the Palazzo Vecchio in Piazza della Signoria.

between the hub of Cosimo's urban power in the Palazzo Vecchio, and his military might in the Forte di Belvedere on the Oltrarno, thereby standing as an expression of authority (Fricelli 1984: 61–63). Conversely, in 1565 Vasari was instructed to connect the Uffizi via an elevated and concealed passageway, the *corridoio*, to the Palazzo Pitti also on the other side of the river, a route which provided convenient private access for the ducal family and court between their principal residences, and a secret escape path should Medici rule be challenged.

The architectural language in which Vasari constructed the Uffizi and which does so much to contribute to its urban impact is derived from that developed by Michelangelo in the Laurentian Library forty years earlier. The three storeys of the elevation decrease in public emphasis as they ascend. The ground level public loggia follows ancient and medieval precedents, while the compressed mezzanine above houses windows which light its vault. The major offices are articulated by tall framed windows with alternating triangular and segmental pediments, while the upper storey, now glazed, was originally an open though private loggia at the level of the *corridoio*. This transmutation of the architectural expression in each bay contrasts with their serial repetition along the extended length of the elevations, virtually replicated on either side of the central street. As a terminus of the space, however, Vasari broke the rhythm in the screen across the Arno elevation. The sober trabeation of the lateral elevations meet in a triumphal arch which forms the bridge between the two wings and frames the view of the Belvedere across the river. This triumphal motif, at a reduced scale, also forms the theme of the *piano nobile*, with the addition of an extra arched bay at either side. The five bay sequence of alternately arched and trabeated elements is repeated and forms the pattern for the elevation of the Uffizi, where it protrudes into the quayside of the Arno with the generous saucer-domed river loggia, the view through which frames the Palazzo Vecchio.

The statuary of the square forms two distinct series. While the Loggia dei Lanzi houses statues as a collection in the form of a grand external museum, emphasizing their artistc value as opposed to their content, those which occupy the zone of the axis of the Uffizi have a more didactic role. From the Arno to the centre of the Piazza the sequence of figures represent a variety of political messages. Michelangelo's David, and also Donatello's Judith refer to the revived tradition of Florentine republicanism in the years around 1500 during the Medici exile. Bandinelli's Hercules and Cacus and Ammanati's Neptune Fountain, as the product of restored Medici patronage, have a subtler signifiicance. Hercules, as a mythical founder of Florence had a specific civic identity, although here he is portrayed in a scenario which celebrates the suppression of rebellious forces. This admonitory image is contrasted with the Neptune Fountain that forcefully displays Medici benevolence in the provision of a new water supply to the city. Finally, in the two statues of the patron by Giambologna, Cosimo I, in military guise presides twice over the scene. In the statue above the Uffizi triumphal arch where he assumes the garb and posture of Mars, he gazes towards the piazza, which he also dominates in Giambologna's equestrian monument, the revolutionary spirit of the earlier statuary being overclad with images that reinforce Medicean autocracy.

This urban renovation was roughly contemporaneous with another project implemented by a different political authority. As the principal space of the

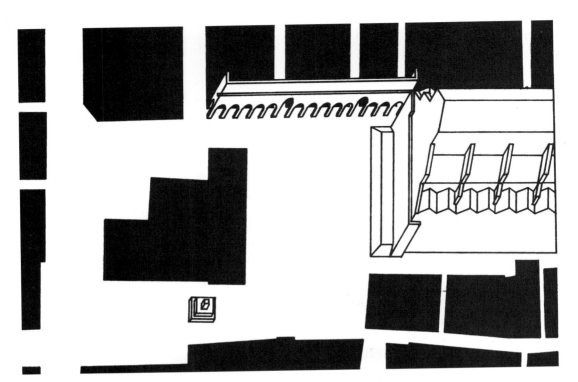

6.4   Diagram of Piazza Maggiore, Bologna showing the Neptune fountain, the Facciata dei Banchi, and the cathedral of San Petronio.

second city of the papal states, Piazza Maggiore in Bologna was the subject of the political expressions of various popes. It reached its approximate current state in the 1560s after a series of extensive urban renovations. These included the clearing of the area to the north of the piazza to produce Piazza Nettuno, with its elaborate new fountain, another work of Giambologna, and the refacing of the Portico dei Banchi by Jacopo Barozzi da Vignola (1507–73) which housed the moneylenders, on the eastern boundary of the square to create an enhanced urban edge to the city, opposite the centre of papal government in the Palazzo Comunale. These interventions complemented the major existing structures on the north and south of the square, respectively the Palazzo del Podesta and the Basilica of San Petronio. Adjacent to the latter and the Palazzo Comunale in the south-west corner is the much smaller Palazzo dei Notai.

Vignola's facade consists of fifteen bays of a monumental composite order, with an attic storey above. The continuity of the regular bay structure is interrupted in the sixth and twelfth bays by higher arched portals marking the issuing of existing streets, Via Pescherie Vecchie and Via Clavature, into the piazza, dividing the facade into a series of respectively five, five and three bays each. As has been observed by Richard Tuttle, Vignola's 'triumphal iconography' for the Facciata dei Banchi translated 'the temporary triumphal arches *all'antica* that were regularly erected in wood, canvas and stucco to honor visits by important state and church dignitaries' into 'a permanent piece of celebratory display'. 'Virtually all triumphal entries into

Bologna culminated in the Piazza Maggiore, where the most elaborate of such ephemeral decorations were deployed, many at the mouth of the Via Clavature' (Tuttle 1993: 83).

6.5   Piazza Maggiore, Bologna with the Facciata dei Banchi.

The Neptune Fountain is Giambologna's masterpiece as a monumental sculptural group, and its positioning keys it into the urban framework of arcades and piazze. It stands on the boundary between Piazza Maggiore and the clearing of Piazza Nettuno which it was created to ornament. The full width of its marble base occupies nearly a third of the neck of space between the two piazze, and is aligned on the arcade which runs behind the Palazzo del Podesta and continues the line of Via degli Orefici. Despite the asymmetry of the relationships between the elements that bound the piazza, a series of correspondences exist across the expanse of Piazza Maggiore. Although individually each is a virtually symmetrical structure, the relationship between the Palazzo del Podesta and San Petronio crystallizes around an axis that runs between the centre of the palazzo's facade, marked as it is by the tower to its rear, and the right hand portal of the Basilica's facade. In the other direction, the two major openings in the Facciata dei Banchi, corresponding to the existing streets, are loosely aligned with the Orologio and the papal statue in the portal of the Palazzo Comunale. These relationships serve to bind the disparate structures and materials around the piazza into a more coherent ensemble. Vignola's facade subtly unites the adjacent monumental structures,

6.6   Piazza
Maggiore,
Bologna. Detail of
the Facciata dei
Banchi showing
the framing of an
entering street as
a triumphal arch.

its scale and rhythm reinterpreting the earlier medieval portico, but it is the delicacy and relaxed quality of the alignments in plan and section which integrate its exquisitely proportioned surface into the urban ensemble.

In an altogether less significant location (although it was Vasari's home town) the third example, Piazza Grande in Arezzo, has equally disparate romanesque, medieval and renaissance languages around its perimeter, with

Vasari's contribution, the loggia which bears his name defining the northern edge of the square. Topographically, the arcade which is the principal feature of Vasari's intervention acts as a quasi-retaining wall to the park above the town, which was formerly occupied by the Medicean fortress. It serves both to contain one edge of the space of the piazza but also to connect it perpendicularly to the Corso, thereby joining it into the main street network. Its constant rhythm of twenty bays is a simple solution to the demand for a commercial and economical structure. The sobriety and continuity of the loggia provides the necessary element of gravity, horizontality and stability in a space where the other edges are all composed of buildings the verticality of which enables them to accommodate the topographical incline individually. By establishing the level contour of the loggia Vasari enabled it to participate ambiguously in the life of the square, the repetition of the standard bay encouraging the reading of the structure as a banal edge to the space, and suggesting the continuity of the urban fabric, while the prominent position of the vaults allows them to reiterate the theme of the monumental public logge of medieval times.

6.7  Diagram of Piazza Grande, Arezzo, showing the arcade of Vasari's loggia.

The loggia is, however, a product of the political and commercial pressures of the mid-16th century. Arezzo had to readjust to its role as subordinate to Medicean authority, which manifested itself in the strengthening and updating of the fortress. As an attempt to assert revived civic values in the public realm, the Confraternity of the Misericordia had commissioned a commercial development adjacent to their headquarters on Piazza Grande. The rent from the new building would provide income for its charitable

6.8    Piazza
Grande,
Arezzo. Detail
of the facade of
Vasari's loggia.

works as well as being an ornament to the town. Workshops faced the piazza
at ground level under the new arcade, while the upper levels were occupied at
the western end by offices for various civic institutions, connected via a bridge
to the Misericordia, with five houses at the eastern end. The dramatic slope
in the section of the site enabled the office and residential accommodation

to be entered at high level from the rear, with a staircase in the eleventh bay connecting both piazza and rear.

This new loggia was primarily a utilitarian structure where the decorative language was constrained by the need to build within a tight budget. Construction could be phased to meet the availability of funds, and indeed the last bays were not completed till the 1590s, although the project had begun in 1573, the model preserved in Vasari's house serving as a section of a new urban type which Vasari may have seen as having universal applicability. Although the completed design shows several changes, the model accords to the basic form. The facade to the piazza is punctuated by broad flat piers which mark the rhythm of the elevation. The simplicity of the articulation of the twenty bays of the loggia provides the stabilizing point around which the complexities of the other sides are controlled, its spatial effect being to terminate abruptly the disjointed conflicts of its context. The warping of space in plan and section, which results in the importance of a strong spatial diagonal, acts as the virtual axis of the square. This dynamic shifting space is then controlled by Vasari's introduction of that typical mannerist device, the extended and highly articulated shallow surface. As Satkowski points out, 'despite the fact that a three dimensional model of the loggia had been built, Vasari's design is essentially two dimensional in character', the facade being in a sense 'a giant painting where all elements – large and small, receding and protruding, horizontal and vertical – are resolved into a neutral composition' (Satkowski 1979: 128). The shallow pictorial surface of the loggia serves as a compositional screen against which the disparate buildings and the sloping ground on which they sit can be held in balance.

In the three squares described above the ability of the new element to integrate into their contexts is dependent on the clarity of the introduction. Their origins account to some degree for their continued success, allowing them to be read both as continuations of the traditional urban fabric while by their very presence indicating the changes in the method of urban organization. While the Uffizi was designed as a bureaucratic structure, the Portico dei Banchi as a commercial refacing, and the loggia in Arezzo for both uses combined, what all three display is the alliance between different constituencies for the benefit of the public realm. The three examples manifest the adaptability of a prosaic urban element, and its transformation into part of a poetic ensemble. In each case the virtues of the linear form are exploited to enhance different experiences. So the regularity and constancy of rhythm, a base component of the ordering of a repetitive structure, has a different aesthetic result in each case. In Arezzo Vasari created a civic facade but in the process used the arcade to connect the piazza into the urban network. He thereby employed spatial relationships both parallel and perpendicular to the linear block. In Bologna, Vignola's facade continued the form of the previous structure on that site, in emphasizing its function as an urban edge which could be penetrated perpendicularly at triumphally embellished street entrances at Via Pescherie Vecchie and Via Clavature. At the Uffizi, on the contrary, space is extended not through but along Vasari's insertion, emphasizing in pictorial terms not the picture plane but the depth. This dramatic extension into space between the Piazza della Signoria and the street of the Uffizi contrasts with the membrane of the Portico dei Banchi, the screen-like qualities of which are emphasized by the visibility of the streets beyond. At Arezzo, the urban facade controls the flow of space as an abrupt full stop to the emphatic diagonals of the topography. While the recognition of the importance of the surface is necessary for the squares to read as finite places, the articulation of the new surface is also a feature common to all three interventions. The most elaborate is that of Bologna, where Vignola broke the constant rhythm to frame the entry of the two existing streets. The surface of the Facciata dei Banchi is therefore read as a screen through which to enter and to see: *scenae frons* and triumphal arch. The same motif is used by Vasari to terminate the extended void of the Uffizi, and control the view across the Arno. The articulated surfaces of the wing elevations serve to enhance the depth of the space. In Arezzo, in contrast, Vasari again provides a screen, but one which is articulating a change in terrain. All the foregoing examples, however, act as forms of *scaenae frons* for their particular urban theatres.

During the sixteenth century, architectural literature demonstrated the interconnectedness of city and theatre. With the dissemination of the treatise, the design of stage scenery was considered as a form of temporary architecture the rules and conventions of which could be as subject to codification as urban and architectural types. Sebastiano Serlio's famous plates of the tragic and comic scenes expand upon the brief description provided by Vitruvius:

There are three kinds of scenes, one called the tragic, second, the comic, third, the satyric. Their decorations are different and unlike each other in scheme. Tragic scenes are delineated with columns, pediments, statues and other objects suited to kings; comic scenes exhibit private dwellings, with balconies and views representing rows of windows, after the manner of ordinary dwellings; satyric scenes are decorated with trees, caverns, mountains and other rustic objects delineated in a landscape style. (Vitruvius 1914: 150)

The development of perspective, and the visual control of space that it afforded, had its uses and manifestations in both urban and theatrical contexts. The systematization of space and its growth into the method by which space was perceived and understood meant that it was a tool not merely of depiction but also of creation, in short was a device for ensuring that urban harmony prevailed visually, spatially and socially. This discipline existed also in design for the theatre, which could therefore be perceived as a parallel discipline to urban design. In a reflection of Sennett's assertion mentioned at the start of this chapter, both the city and the theatre acted as representations of society, and it is this common representational root, expressed through the technology of perspective, which provided the means for reciprocal influences to be exerted. In Western architectural theory this connection is established as a fundamental premise by Vitruvius, who followed his description of urban space immediately with that of theatres.

6.9   Piazza Grande, Arezzo. A view along Vasari's loggia towards Piazza Grande.

As discussed in Chapter 4, Brunelleschi had demonstrated his control of the representation of space in urban contexts, thereby placing illusionism in a situation which encouraged its theatrical application. The use of public spaces within cities as the arenas of daily and ritual life reinforced the duality of the guises through which they are seen, the square acting as dramatic space, and

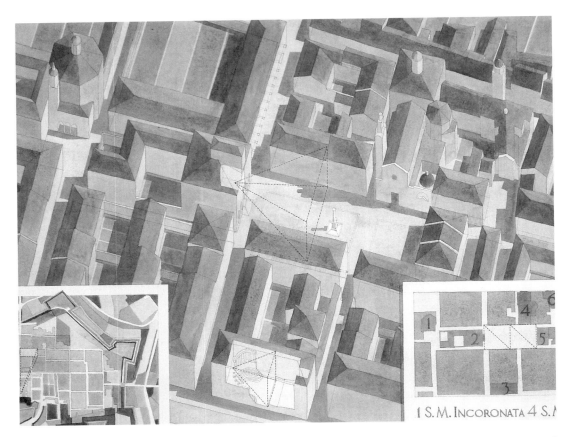

6.10 Diagram of Piazza Ducale, Sabbioneta, showing (from the left) Santa Maria Incoronata, the Palazzo Ducale, the theatre, Santa Maria Assunta, the Palazzo della Ragione and San Rocco.

the stage set explicitly imitating the public realm. Going beyond the limited impact of the previous three substantial examples, in a total urban ensemble such as Sabbioneta, the fourth piazza in this chapter, because of the artificial nature of its construction, these relationships are heightened and their political nature brought into stronger relief. It is one of the few surviving examples of a built renaissance ideal town, and presents a consistent series of themes relating to architecture, urbanism and theatricality at every scale of expression (Forster 1977). Sabbioneta lies in the valley of the Po, roughly equidistant between Mantua and Parma. It was a property of the Gonzagas of Mantua, and was inherited in 1540 by Vespasiano Gonzaga Colonna, who served during the next fifty years as a general and courtier under the Hapsburgs. His personal interest in humanism, architecture and engineering found expression in the design and implementation of his own capital at Sabbioneta. However, upon his death in 1591, Vespasiano's creation lapsed into the obscurity which is still its lot, but which has ensured that his vision of the ideal town has remained unmolested.

Within the gridded network of urban blocks, the Piazza Ducale is formed by subtraction, being merely a missing block and a half. Eight streets lead off the square, subtly indicating the hierarchy of relationships the square embodies. At the westerly end of the space two pairs of streets meeting at

right angles issue from the corners of the space, and frame between them the major monument, the Palazzo Ducale, the seat of ducal authority, centred on the axis of the square. Approximately two-thirds along its length the square is bisected by two streets which enter perpendicularly. On the northern side this street bounds the plot of the church of Santa Maria Assunta, the principal parochial church, while the southern street runs through to meet the town's *cardo*, this junction being the site of the theatre. And, lastly, two further streets lead out along the edges of the square on either flank of the Palazzo della Ragione. The streets therefore connect the piazza intimately into the life of the town, uniting the civic structures into an extended public realm, which reaches beyond the ends of the Piazza Ducale into smaller squares addressing the facades of two minor churches, to the east that of San Rocco, and to the west that of Santa Maria Incoronata which serves as Vespasiano's mausoleum (Canniffe 2001).

6.11   Piazza Ducale, Sabbioneta. The Palazzo Ducale, with Santa Maria Incoronata in the distance – the tragic scene.

The decorum of the square is maintained by the comparative simplicity of the structures which surround it. The edges are lined by three-storeyd buildings, arcaded on the southern side, unremarkable but dignified in proportion. Against this background of largely private structures, then, the monumental buildings are individually treated. Santa Maria Assunta is distinguished by its facade clad in pink and white marble, and the presence of its tall campanile. The Palazzo della Ragione sits almost as a pavilion moored at the eastern end of the square, the wide spacing of its six bay colonnade and its comparatively low eaves line distinguishing it from its context. Finally, the Palazzo Ducale dominates the square, as Vespasiano no doubt intended. Its scale is grander than its context, with five bays, two large storeys and crowned by a central tower which rises from the pyramidal roof. A short flight of steps raises the level of the spacious ground floor arcade, which is faced in rusticated stone work. Above, the stucco of the facade is pierced by five framed and pedimented windows, the central one emphasized by a shallow balcony, from where the duke could address his subjects. This balcony was reached from his private *studiolo*, a room dedicated in its stucco and fresco decoration to his forebears, and crowned on the vault with an image of Phaeton derived from an original image by Giulio Romano in the Palazzo Ducale in Mantua, the principal Gonzaga court. This underscored the connection between Vespasiano's domination of the town and the dynasty's domination of the region, since dynastic myth stated that the overambitious Phaeton had fallen to earth in the valley of the Po.

The foregoing description suggests that Sabbioneta is entirely conventional in its layout as the seat of power of a minor autocrat. What is unusual is its completeness and its date, which places it as contemporaneous with the influence of renaissance urban theorists. The piazza roughly accords with the double square proportion recommended by Alberti. In so far as this scale of application of architectural instruction tends towards the pragmatic, the theoretical origins of the planning of Sabbioneta are perhaps more closely related to the connections between theatrical and urban design, and the last structure to be completed during Vespasiano's life was the theatre, designed by Vincenzo Scamozzi. Although the permanent staging he created has not survived, (unlike the even more elaborate ones he introduced in his completion of Palladio's Teatro Olimpico in Vicenza) the remaining auditorium is itself a significant survival, perhaps the most important single element within the town. For what it eloquently testifies to is the reciprocal relationship between city and theatre, and most especially in Vespasiano's creation of not merely an ideal town, but a representation of *the* ideal town, the renaissance urban paradigm, Rome.

The clue is writ large. Around the three facades of the theatre, perhaps the most richly articulated elevation in the town, is inscribed the repeated legend ROMA QVANTA FVIT IPSA RVINA DOCET which translates as 'How great Rome was, the ruins themselves reveal'. This same tag had also appeared on the frontispiece of Serlio's Third Book (on Antiquity). In the Second Book, Serlio had also illustrated the tragic, comic and satyric scenes of the ancient theatre as recorded by Vitruvius. Despite the lack of sequential publication for the various *libri* Serlio's description of theatre sets, placed between his discussion of perspective construction and his book on antiquity, mediates between the contemporary understanding of human vision and the representation and control of urban space, and the lessons to be gleaned from the study of ancient remains. The tragic and comic scenes represent the theatrical types of public and private urban space, and display an implied hierarchical relationship

6.12   Piazza Ducale, Sabbioneta. View towards Santa Maria Assunta and the Palazzo della Ragione – the comic scene.

between them. Their urban implications form an indication of how decorum was thought to be realized in cities, the tragic being the realm of the major characters both urban and theatrical, and the comic that of the minor ones. Serlio's descriptions are as follows:

Tragic stage scenery is for performing Tragedies. The stage buildings for it should be those of characters of high rank, because disastrous love affairs, unforseen events and violent and gruesome deaths (as far as one reads in ancient tragedies, not to mention modern ones) always occur in the houses of noblemen, Dukes, great Princes or even Kings. Therefore (as I said) in scenery of this sort there should only be buildings that have a certain nobility... (Serlio 1996: 88)

### For the comic scene

The stage buildings for this should be private houses; that is belonging to citizens, merchants, lawyers, parasites and other similar characters. Above all there should be a bawd's house and an Inn. A temple is absolutely essential.

...an open portico through which you can see another building, like this first one whose arches are modern work. The open balconies (which some call pergole, others ringhieri) are very effective on the fore shortened faces. Similarly, some cornices with mouldings projecting from their outside corners which are cut out around and matched with other painted cornices are extremely effective. In the same way, houses that have a great projection work very well indeed – like the 'Moon Inn' here... The most important thing of all is to choose smaller houses and put them to the front so that the other buildings appear above them, as you can see from the bawd's house'. (Serlio 1996: 86)

Although the parallels are not precise, and indeed there is some overlap and blurring between the two definitions, it is not difficult to define the end of the piazza containing the Palazzo Ducale as the tragic scene, and the other end could therefore be designated as the comic scene.

Bisecting the piazza on the line of the streets which enter two-thirds along the length and looking east, we encounter firstly Santa Maria Assunta, which accords with Serlio's reference to the church which 'is absolutely essential'. The building which flanks the church, with its arcade leading out of the square, also has a lower eaves line than is typical of the rest of the square, but the Palazzo della Ragione is the lowest building in the ensemble and its positioning is such that it conforms with the instruction 'to choose smaller houses and put them to the front so that the other buildings appear above them'. Looking west towards the Palazzo Ducale we are presented with 'buildings that have a certain nobility' as befits the tragic scene. The grandeur and symmetry of the Palazzo Ducale and its attendant buildings, fits the general ambience of Serlio's illustration without sharing any specific characteristics, although the funereal presence of the pyramid and obelisk (viewed through the triumphal arch to the rear of the scene), has its parallel in the sight of Vespasiano's mausoleum and its campanile visible to the right hand side of the palazzo. In this theatrical milieu the relationship between actors and spectators is the paramount one, the designation of tragic and comic ends to the same space embodying the political compact between the tyrant and his subjects. As the pinnacle of Sabbioneta's small political hierarchy, it is inevitable that Vespasiano's gaze from his balcony should be downward both physically and socially, towards the rustic and urban mechanicals. These characters in the comic scene, however, have a different unobstructed view, afforded by the wide spacing of the portico of the Palazzo della Ragione, that of the tragic scene and the gladiatorial struggles of the powerful.

This speculative reading of the Piazza Ducale is supported by the decorative evidence of the theatre itself. Kurt Forster has noted the similarity of view between Vespasiano's elevated prospect of the stage, and that of the Piazza from his balcony. Furthermore, in the theatre, the views of the Castel Sant'Angelo and the Campidoglio in Rome, which fill the painted triumphal arches spanning the area between stage and auditorium, have their physical counterparts beyond those painted scenes in the presence of Vespasiano's *rocca* and his own capitol behind their respective painted representations. Not content to merely contemplate the lessons of Rome's lost glory, it would seem reasonable to suggest that Vespasiano sought to recreate that grandeur of contemporary Rome within his own realm (Forster 1977: 81–85). If the theatre frescoes designate the Piazza Ducale as Sabbioneta's Campidoglio then its symmetrical disposition is understandable in relation to Michelangelo's highly theatrical reworking of the ancient site of Roman civic government discussed in the previous chapter. The fresco, and indeed the space itself is focused on the Marcus Aurelius statue. In his own piazza Vespasiano's quasi-imperial ambitions were to be expressed in a bronze statue of the duke by Leone Leoni, seated on a throne rather than Marcus Aurelius's horse, although he is coiffed and clad in the Roman manner and his right hand is raised in the same gesture of benediction. This statue would have marked the epicentre of Vespasiano's domain and now resides in a rather ungainly manner above his tomb in his equally imperial mausoleum.

Despite the uniqueness of its circumstances the Piazza Ducale typifies attitudes to the role of civic life and the exploitation of theatrical methods to maintain political control. The sophisticated artificiality of its situation separates it from more common urban spaces which have a theatrical character, yet it crystallises widespread interpretations of urban life into physical, spatial and temporal creations as ingenious as any drama of the renaissance or baroque. Theatricality as method appealed to the patrons of these developments, of course, because the control exercised could be so great. Cosimo I and Vespasiano Gonzaga, for example, were seeking to enhance the perception of their status as allies of the Hapsburg emperors, and saw the usefulness of these illusionistic constructs. In this autocratic context, as had been true since ancient times, spectacle was necessary as a component in the social contract which established the hierarchy of power. Living within a frozen urban spectacle, the inhabitants as both audience and actors could be expected to comply with stage directions, be they either theatrical or social.

This conscious manipulation of space to enforce social cohesion, albeit in a relatively benign form, was a function of the understanding of spatial organization. These four piazze are direct results of the exploitation of perspective as a controlling mechanism, but they often represent distinct attitudes to pictoriality and sensuality. The theatrical ambiguity between actor and audience which they all exemplify provides a complex web of interpretations which do much to enrich the experience of the spaces for residents and visitors. As Richard Sennett has observed, an acceptance of illusion encourages both an attitude of detachment and assumption of conventional roles. The adoption of perspective as the medium for both theatrical and urban space, as expounded by Serlio, encouraged the design of ideal spaces, validated by their interpretation through antique models. This manipulation is actively participated in by the actor – spectator, so the social control achieved is more the result of co-operation than coercion, the spaces represent models of society where diversity was allowed under the guise of hierarchy, but which was maintained at the behest of those at the summit of the political pyramid. Many were excluded outside these hierarchies, roles within this political performance were largely predetermined and inflexible and the theatrical model of social order would find its fulfillment in the urban configurations of the next century.

# 7

# Baroque: Scale, form and meaning

The political situation which baroque Italy inherited from the sixteenth century was one where display became the means of underscoring through allegory the mediating role of the court. A period of relative peace provided the setting for the most exuberant displays of urbanism, architecture and sculpture, permanent testaments to power which were complemented by the ephemeral festival stagings produced for the usual round of dynastic celebrations, marriages, births, funerals and feats of nepotism. Having its origin in the work of artists and architects gathered in Rome around 1600, the baroque was to dominate European culture until the middle of the eighteenth century (Wittkower 1958). Rome's pre-eminence as the cultural centre of Catholic Europe had been given a contemporary impetus by its replanning during the pontificate of Sixtus V (1585–90), emphasising the city as not only the most significant ancient and Christian city but also the most contemporary in its facilities. The nature of papal government meant that the ruling power was not a continuous dynastic development, such as was broadly represented by the Savoy court in Turin, but rather a periodic assertion of individual family power and influence as popes were elected and died. Their patronage of particular artists and of different religious orders during the devotional revivals of the Counter Reformation provided the impetus for a dynamic constructional and artistic market which formed the aesthetic image of the city until the later years of the nineteenth century. The complexity and invention of form, the continuity of painting, sculpture, interior and exterior architecture, and broader urban design results in the difficulty of analysing baroque urban elements separately from their contexts. To categorize Italian baroque urbanism, therefore, one must interpret its spatial character through an understanding of the morphology of the city, particularly the city of Rome, its ritual narratives and the monuments of its religious and secular communities (Portoghesi 1999).

As has been apparent in the previous three chapters the conditioning mechanism of perspective enabled the totality of spatial experience to be defined by a set of controls which had their point of origin in a single focus, according not with a distant point on the horizon, but on that point occupied

7.1   Piazza
San Pietro,
Rome. View
of the obelisk,
Maderno's facade
of the basilica and
Michelangelo's
dome.

by the privileged viewer, who in the civil structures of baroque Europe
was the prince. However, it would be misleading to suggest that this was a
phenomenon exclusively associated with the representational language of civil
society (Perez-Gomez 1983: 166–95, Vesely 2004: 196–226). The secular life of
the court, performed as a type of extended dramatic spectacle also employed
the characteristic motifs of the baroque to represent political authority as a
mediation between daily experience and the cosmos. It should be remembered
that a product of the period's urbanism such as Piazza San Pietro in Rome had
a spiritual role as a great atrium not only to an apostle's shrine but also to a
significant temporal power. This political dimension will be explored firstly in
an overt example from northern Italy at Venaria Reale outside Turin, and then
in Rome four examples will be considered where the relationship between
the sacred and the secular is more interwoven, the last three smaller spaces
considered in terms of their formal compositional values.

Venaria Reale was a property of the Dukes of Savoy, developed in its
present form in the 1650s, and largely completed within a twenty year
campaign (Canniffe 1998). Its patron was the young duke, Carlo Emanuele
II (1638–75), and his intervention consisted of the orchestration of an existing
town, a palace and a formal garden within a landscape devoted to the courtly
pursuit of the hunt. Its importance as a manifestation of dynastic ambitions
is attested both by the relative speed and extensive nature of its construction,
and by the destruction of the palace by the French forces in both 1693 and 1706,
after which it was extensively refurbished, most notably by Filippo Juvarra.

7.2   Piazza dell' Annunziata, Venaria Reale. View of one of the paired church facades, that of Sant'Uberto, and one of the paired columns, that of the annunciating Angel.

Its creation is, however, only one example of the lavish display produced by the Savoy court both in Turin and in provincial settlements. Power struggles within the house of Savoy and the regency of Cristina di Francia (the Madama Reale) during the infancy of her son, Carlo Emanuele, led both to the growth of rival centres of power and the exploitation of rival cultural influences from France, Spain and Rome with which the various parties were allied, but also to the assertion of a particular Piedmontese identity when the young duke reached his majority. Venaria Reale is indebted to contemporaneous French examples, most notably Versailles, and can therefore be understood to be a product of the particular dynastic connection to the French court through the Madama Reale, who was an aunt of Louis XIV (Cullum 1986).

Piazza dell'Annunziata is the urban focus of the sequence of town, palace and garden, and bears evidence of the cultural nature of the complex. Ostensibly functioning as a recreational centre, as elaborately displayed in the cult of Diana which determined much of the iconography of the palace and the garden, the religious images of the piazza define a specifically catholic identity, both pagan and Christian themes being organized through an axial and processional arrangement which exploits theatrical effects to support a constantly reinforced political absolutism. As Hugh Cullum noted the recent developments in the Savoy capital of Turin provided local precedents for the scheme at Venaria. The extension of the pattern of the Roman grid-plan town with the elongation of a central route from the Piazza Ducale, and the provision of Piazza Reale (now Piazza San Carlo) with its paired churches as a focus to the axis between the Porta Nuova and the palace, provided a typology of successive spaces and incidents organized in perspective space (Pollak 1991). This compositional technique passed from father to son, from Carlo di Castellamonte who was responsible for the completion of Ascanio

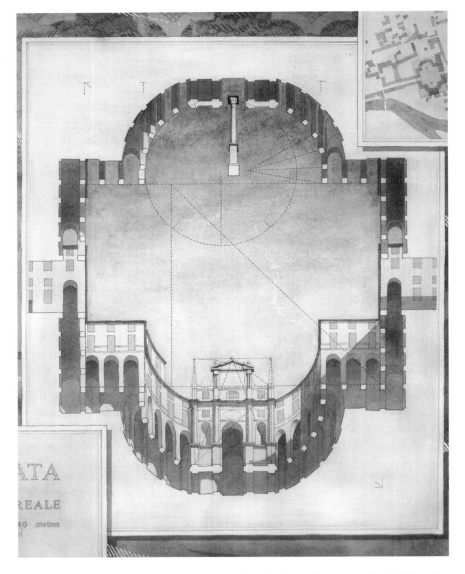

Vitozzi's extension to the city, to Amedeo di Castellamonte (d. 1683), who designed the similar sequence at Venaria.

The architectural character of the scheme, however, was the result of the architect's collaboration with the court rhetorician, as Cullum describes. Emanuel Tesauro had been a servant of the Savoy for most of his life, but his later years were occupied by the devising of the intellectual framework of court entertainments. Venaria, with its emphasis on the hunt, was merely one of the most extreme forms of this activity, providing a permanent and elaborate setting for courtly ritual. While pleasure was the overt purpose of these creations, they were constructed around an instructional intention. It is Cullum's assertion that

Venaria had an explicit purpose: the education of Carlo Emanuele, who was only twenty years old when the idea of the palace first arose, and whose mother continued to govern well after her son's majority. One of the principal themes in a number of contemporary festivals and panegyrics is the Madama Reale's education of her son. The absolute dominion of the palace by the Madama Reale, allegorically presented as the chaste goddess of the hunt, suggests that the ensemble is amongst other things, an instrument for the instruction of the duke, as 'the hunt itself was commonly conceived as a training for warfare, and the Duke's government of the town can similarly be seen as training for his role in the government of the state' (Cullum 1986: 24).

In its original condition the town of Venaria was subservient to the life of the palace, but the depredations and effects of history have served to reverse this relationship, with the town now a suburb of Turin, and the palace remaining a vast neglected complex. To that extent, the linear and axial emphasis which Blaeu portrays in a contemporary image, with the space diminishing towards the palazzo, has been supplanted by the more centralized focus of the confrontation between the two church facades (Blaeu [1692] 1971). The axial approach to the extensive palace passes through the principal piazza, which is organized as a symmetrical entity, with a parish church (dedicated to the patron of the hunt St. Hubert) facing a church dedicated to Santa Maria Assunta paired along a cross-axis marked by twin columns. A rectangular space parallel to the major axis is described, providing the setting for semicircular spaces that imply a counter-axis. Arcading unites these hemicycles which frame the paired facades, establishing the interface between the axis and the space it divides.

The consistently bipartite geometry of the piazza, then, is the result both of the relatively short time scale in which the piazza and the entire ensemble were built, but also of the application of a consistent compositional technique which united town, palace and garden. The axial vistas of baroque perspectivity, intended to layer and define the order of this small cosmos, produces a series of duplications which heighten the theatrical qualities of the space. While the dualism of the two columns, two facades, and two ranges of arcades creates a slightly bewildering experience, the completeness of the whole as an enclosed and defined space oscillates for primacy with the reading of the piazza as a major incident on a processional route that links a sequence of exemplary types. The visual cone of perspective is embodied in the relationship between the foreground of the public realm and the termination of sight lines in the palace, where the landscape is brought under control through the design of the garden, suggesting the means by which the entire territory was mediated through the person of the ruler. As Blaeu portrayed the idealized state of the town the virtually cruciform piazza, with a spiritual axis crossed by a secular one, was intended to provide the antechamber to a realm of pleasure focused on the person of the duke and his retinue. Cullum sees the geometrical piazza of the town as the first space in which the moral narrative is apparent. The twin columns and churches, their association with the Duke's parents, and the shape of the piazza can be seen, as Cullum puts it, 'as an allusion to the Duke's entry into a world whose immanence is ordered and oriented with respect to the celestial realms inhabited by the figures atop the columns. The birth of Christ implied in the theme of the Annunciation can also be seen as a metaphor of the birth of the Duke as the Savoy saviour' (Cullum 1986: 211).

As well as the requirements of internal social control within the state, Venaria Reale spoke also to an external audience, the period of its construction saw turmoil in Northern Italy, bordered as the region was by the rival territorial ambitions of France and the Holy Roman Empire. In this context, the duchy of Savoy was under threat from the attentions of these larger European powers, and therefore had an interest in securing its territory through judicious self-aggrandizement, to which triumphalist ends the display of urban order, consistency and splendour could be usefully applied. While Cullum asserted that the structure and iconography of Venaria Reale was a device for the education of the prince, the cumulative effect of spatial control and dynastic symbolism would be greater on members of the court and citizenry. Although such ensembles were created to fill the gaze of the prince, the paired columns at Venaria were surely intended to inform the lower levels of the social hierarchy, as well as thereby conditioning the ways in which the ruler viewed himself at the centre of his realm, the geometrical order of the entire estate broken down into a series of discrete relationships. The unconscious medium of urban space is superseded by an equally homogenous but clearly artificial spatial realm the hierarchical layers of which are more subtly graded. The balance shifts from surveillance to exposure, with the spaces of the town described so as to support the rituals of the court. The tensions between homogeneity and hierarchy do not resolve themselves, but serve instead to heighten their dramatic qualities. Architectural elements are deployed to promote political cohesion, the duplication of elements for theatrical effect with the consequent reinforcement of the visual and social pyramid. The evident artificiality of these effects does not appear to have undermined their credibility as urban spectacles. This theatricality, as Cullum observes in Venaria, is not itself wholly supportive of an authentic urban life. He characterizes Venaria as 'a pseudo-town...whose animation depends on the intermittent presence of the court, which only accommodates one social stratum'. He sees it as 'an attempt to fabricate the reality of a town within the restricted terms available to the representational system of 'rhetorical space' and conceived, in many respects, as simply an appendage of the palace' (Cullum 1986: 243). At Venaria the exposure of the Duke to the gaze of his subjects produces the public space through which they could observe him in procession either to his church, his palace, his hunting grounds or returning to his capital Turin. He in turn could appropriate a bilaterally symmetrical view of his realm, where the subjects conformed to the geometrical pattern which he had prescribed and of which he was the focus.

If Venaria Reale represents the baroque use of space to support a quasi-religious secular absolutism, Piazza San Pietro in Rome produced during the

same decades can be seen to represent the summit of this use to define the image of the church as a both a spiritual and temporal power (Kitao 1974). Unlike Venaria Reale, the prominence and scale of its location have ensured that it has continued to be regarded as one of the greatest spaces in Europe. The task undertaken by Gianlorenzo Bernini (1598–1680) was to provide a setting for the pilgrims, princes and ambassadors who arrived at the basilica and papal palace. The scale of the space could only be compared with antiquity, but the artist balanced contemporary dynamic effects with an ancient *gravitas*. The idea of the reconfiguration of the square had been implicit since the placing of Sixtus V's obelisk on the axis of the new basilica in 1586 and the completion by Carlo Maderno (1556–1629) of the facade in 1612. By the time Bernini began to work seriously on the task in 1656 he was the most prominent artist of the age, although his employment by Pope Alexander VII (1655–67) was not without risks given the debacle over his bell towers for St. Peter's which had been demolished in 1646 to prevent their collapse (McPhee 2002). This experience, though and the sculptural and decorative work completed inside had given Bernini a familiarity with all aspects of the site, including the problems of changes of alignment and level between the different parts of the huge complex. As it existed the site had two specific aesthetic problems, the asymmetry of the basilica's relationship to the apostolic palace to the

7.4   Piazza San Pietro, Rome. View along the cross axis of the space with the Apostolic Palace to the left.

7.5   Piazza
San Pietro,
Rome. Interior
of Bernini's
colonnades.

north, itself made up of several nonaligned parts, and the facade's masking
of the form of Michelangelo's immense dome. Given the colossal size of the
commission of creating a unified space, the subtlety of Bernini's achievement
is one of its most remarkable features (Krautheimer 1985).

The vast plane of Maderno's facade combined the function of a proportionate
portico to the basilica's cavernous interior, and a site for the benediction loggia
beneath the central pediment. A severe combination of giant order pilasters and
engaged columns, the sobriety of the overall composition contains a unified
composition of many different types of opening. In contrast Bernini's porticoes

which enclose the piazza are a simple device, although the complexity of the geometry from which they are created promoted a high degree of dynamism. The distances between facade and obelisk, and the height differences between their bases meant that great control had to be exercised if the space was to appear as a unified entity. The employment of the elliptical plan for the piazza, after the exploration of circular and rectangular alternatives, provided both a wider setting for the facade and a longitudinal relationship towards the papal palace. This central motif focused on the obelisk was crucially supplemented by the trapezoidal plan of the *piazza retta* between the ellipse and the basilica, the distance between its arms narrowing towards the piazza, and their facades gently distorted to accommodate the change of level. Although replicated on both sides of the facade, the alignment of this space on the north accommodated the entrance to the palace, which would itself be transformed by Bernini into his monumental staircase, the *scala regia* (1663–66). The subtle division of the piazza into these two parts, and the linking of the colonnade's cornice line to an intermediary moulding that forms the springing of the arches which flank the portico of the basilica, creates an ambiguous but strong relationship across the huge distances.

The arms of the porticoes were formed of curves with pavilions that emphasized the cross axis, junctional spaces between the piazza and the *piazza retta*, and the pedimented terminals to the porticoes which echo with the facade pediment in the distant views provided by the clearances undertaken in the creation of Via della Conciliazione from the 1930s. This effect, however, was not the original experience since the extreme contrast was to be effected by emergence from the dark warren of streets in the *borgo*, the urban quarter between the river and the Vatican, into the clear light and space of the piazza. Bernini had planned a curved linking block between the two arms, a 'third arm', and then had proposed moving it back to provide a type of urban vestibule to the new piazza, a plan which had to be abandoned due to the death of Alexander VII in 1667. The gigantic scale of the unadorned columns, providing a tight rhythm of enclosure to the piazza creates different types of space, major routes along the portico roofed by a continuous barrel vault, minor spaces of these routes and stepped areas within the shade of the structure. Framing the piazza, the porticoes also provided a frame through which basilica and papal palace could be viewed, although in edited almost cinematic vertical slices. Bernini's skill was used to effectively mask, through the regularity of the rhythm, the spatial distortions necessary to integrate such an ideal figure into a context with so many contrasts in scale and misalignments in plan. The success of Bernini's design in providing a spatial image for catholicism has proved adaptable to changes in media over three and a half centuries, never more so than during the funeral rites of John Paul II in 2005. In the intervening centuries the piazza would also provide the model for major urban spaces in the capitals of Europe which as Wittkower remarked 'need not be enumerated' (Wittkower 1958: 129).

While monumental spaces such as Venaria Reale and Piazza San Pietro present urban life as part of an overwhelming spectacle, the detailed compositional techniques of form which constitute less prominent baroque spaces can be difficult to identify. There is a complex continuity between different modes and scales of aesthetic practice which integrated different types of flat, shallow and deep space to create all encompassing environments. Each of these types of expression had its own discipline but their combined effects can be seen in the smaller types of urban space which were developed as totalising aesthetic environments from the 1650s to the 1750s. In this period of the urban language of the Roman baroque the categories of flat, shallow and deep spaces can be identified in various examples, such as Piazza Santa Maria della Pace, Piazza Sant'Ignazio and Piazza della Maddalena, all in the Campo Marzio on the other bank of the Tiber from the Vatican. Smaller than the pioneering work of Bernini at St. Peter's, the three much smaller spaces represent a form of urban space where daily spectacle was assimilated into the everyday fabric of the city. Their patrons, Pope Alexander VII at Santa Maria della Pace, the Society of Jesus at Sant'Ignazio and the Camillans at La Maddalena sought to consolidate local property holdings and express distinct identities within the various religious and national communities of the city. Talented architects were employed, respectively Pietro da Cortona (1596–1669) at Santa Maria della Pace, Filippo Raguzzini (c. 1680–1777) at Sant'Ignazio and Giuseppe Sardi (c. 1680–1753) at La Maddalena to provide suitable public settings for the rituals of the individual churches and to create an aesthetic distinctiveness to each of them.

Each church and space had a complex history to work within. The creation of the piazza at Santa Maria della Pace (1656–57) is delicately indicative of developments that were to become commonplace in Rome and other centres in the following decade. The church of Santa Maria was part of a monastic complex in the heart of medieval Rome but had been host to Bramante's essay in ideal geometry in his cloister (1500–04) and choir (1503–09). A century and a half later the tightness of the available dimensions would remain a feature of the locality, creating the conditions for the work of da Cortona. At Sant'Ignazio the piazza (1727–28) as the eventual result of a project to dignify a major new church in the city, also provided its religious community with commercial income in a highly theatrical form. The same commercial motive animated the development of Piazza Santa Maria Maddalena, (c. 1695–1735) although the venerability of its location north of the Pantheon resulted in a more morphologically conventional if stylistically unusual design. Increasingly elaborate in their decoration, in their own turn these notionally devotional works would be succeeded by spaces devoted to urban pleasure.

In baroque architecture, flat space can be defined as the elaboration of the qualities of surface typically involving complex material combinations and the dense layering of architectural members and figures in its use as facade articulation. As a resolutely public surface, flat space expresses a positive statement of materiality where the character of an internal situation reveals

7.6   Piazza Santa Maria della Pace, Rome. Pietro da Cortona's elaborate integration of a small piazza and the church facade.

itself through the exterior. The integration of inscription, symbolic motifs and personifications animate this communicating surface. The combination of explicit character and implicit purpose creates an expression of meaning, which mediates between the perceivable and the invisible. The facades of each example have an explicitly planar quality, albeit at La Maddalena that plane is folded and bent. The overscoring of the superimposed orders, with layer

7.7 Piazza Sant'Ignazio, Rome. A view across the principal space towards the minor entry spaces.

upon layer of pilasters, cornices and pediments provokes the simultaneous effect both of the dematerialization of the wall within its confined space, and the piling up of a series of motifs which reinforce and contradict the message of the essential structure. At Piazza Sant'Ignazio, Raguzzini's facades are characterized by tautness, a membrane stretched across the surface of the buildings and deformed where the space expands. The restraint with which layers are built up on the facades, in the shallowest of low relief inscribed on the surfaces, stands in distinction to the volumetric modelling of the complex spatial structure of the piazza. In the example from which these eighteenth century examples derive, Piazza Santa Maria della Pace, the entire complex is composed of an intense lamination of small incidents which reinforce the effect of the others. The upper register of the facade is composed of convex elements placed against concave planes, their junctions ornamented with linear mouldings and the orthogonal disposition of the architectural members. The horizontal division between upper and lower storeys is extended out on either side of the portico supporting a scrolled wall which counteracts the concave plane behind it from which the facade emerges. The wall then forms a connecting surface between the church and the adjacent houses, with a consequent diminishing of the architectural intensity, the houses covered in modest stucco decoration, and marked by flat pilasters. Text plays its part

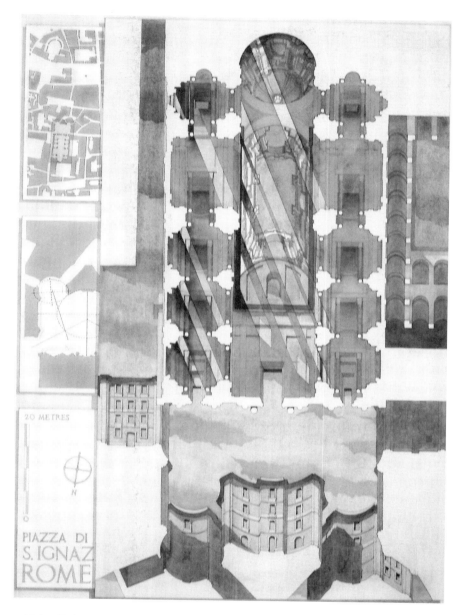

7.8 Diagram of Piazza Sant'Ignazio, Rome. An upward looking view showing the relationship between the piazza and Pozzo's illusionistic ceiling painting.

within all these schemes, either as the inscription which surmounts the portico of Santa Maria della Pace, the direct prayer to the cross over the doorway of the Maddalena, or at Sant'Ignazio the emphatic monumentalism of its dedicatory inscription.

Shallow spaces in baroque urbanism are defined by the sinuous geometrical profiles employed. The surfaces contain the fluid contrasts of concave and convex space, providing a zone of transition between interior and exterior. Shallow space is established by boundaries, but achieves its definition by

7.9   Diagram of Piazza della Maddalena, Rome. An upward looking view showing the facade of Santa Maria Maddalena framed in the footprint of the space and, to the right, the elaborate organ loft adorning the interior of the facade.

the transgression of those boundaries. Therefore the existence of shallow space creates a zone in which a transformation is encouraged, passing from one territory to another in a state of suspension, but being changed by that transition. As the site of exchange the threshold contains its own dynamism, as the three examples demonstrate in their different contexts. This temporal dimension invests shallow space with its own potential. Despite the physical constraints, shallow space affords a vantage point from which neighbouring territories of exterior and interior can be surveyed. The sites of memory and prophecy overlap and contaminate their respective fields. This is nowhere more apparent than at Piazza Santa Maria della Pace where the two storeys of the church facade continue as a screen across adjoining streets that wraps around the piazza, the central void occupied by a semi-elliptical portico, with paired tuscan columns and a shallow half dome (Wittkower 1958: 159–60). The focus is therefore on the threshold between urban and sacred space, a transition represented by the use of idealized form. The portico is the most dramatic gesture within a series of tight spaces, a gesture which gives identity to this small piece of city, but which conceptually is only a transitional space inflated into the principal motif. At Piazza Sant'Ignazio the concave facade of the central building, and those of the two minor buildings visible either side of it suggest the moulding of the space of the piazza into a positive urban entity which orchestrates views and experiences. Entering the piazza from the labyrinth of streets which Raguzzini adapted, the eye is focused on oblique views of the flanking buildings, until one enters the narrow cylinders of space carved out of the corners. These serve as thresholds from which to take in the clearest view of the church facade (Connors 1989). Arriving in the piazza proper and looking back at one's point of entry, it appears to have been swallowed up by the animated profiles of the apartment houses, now arrayed in symmetrical disposition like a group of attentive courtiers. To consider another threshold, the concavity of the Maddalena's facade, linked to the geometry of the elliptical nave and mediating the misalignment between piazza and church provides a space of reflection. Approaching the piazza from either north or south a tower of space is defined by the billowing facade, as if a heavy veil was suspended across the boundary between piazza and church. This fabric-like character is an illusion which contrasts with the solidity of the facade's members. The free-standing columns of the portal mark the central boundary of the outer limits of this zone of shallow space which is strongly framed, at the edges by the built up layers of pilasters and above by the superimposed rhythms of pediments and cornices.

The last of the three thematic categories, that of deep space, presents the effect of a sensual assault. In contrast to the tangibility of enclosure, the language of celestial distance and immensity is revealed. This immersion in deep space forms the site for the meeting of the subject with the full drama of the interior. In place of the close attention to the surface in flat space, or the limited horizon afforded by shallow space, the eye is immediately thrown to the furthest realm of the space, as an ideal is offered, creating a dynamic sense of movement which is generally upward. Physical mass follows the view, lifting the effect of centredness upwards. Pushed into this new context, the body finds its opposite in the recessive folds of the interior. Through this conjunction a relationship is formed which is physical and therefore spatial. Deep space becomes the outer envelope which contains the body, giving it its sense of place and meaning. At Santa Maria della Pace, the facade of the church itself became the backdrop from which a series of layers eddy out to create a small urban space, its extreme depth taking the form of an elongated vista from a major thoroughfare, coupled with the connections to narrow minor streets. This result is achieved within an environment where the ensemble of the piazza appears as a sudden vision of ideal architecture within an apparently disordered context. The continuity with which these devices are treated then serves to distract the viewer from the asymmetrical disposition of the streets adjacent to the church. These streets were too narrow for carriage traffic, and therefore the piazza's functional origins in the widening of the street allowed for traffic to turn around having delivered or retrieved important visitors to the church. This theatrical construction thus had a role in the practicality of the city's daily life, but sought to transform the mundane realities into an exquisite urban experience. Similarly operating on both the prosaic and ideal planes, at La Maddalena the unexpected moulding of the church's nave from the conventional rectangular and symmetrical space into an ellipse with its implied vertical pole transforms the principal sensation from onwards to upwards (Mallory 1977). This is supplemented by the superimposed layers of organ loft, nave cornice and choir gallery, which represent the collapsing of distances, while their increase in size as they ascend telescopes the space visible out from the centred viewer. However, should the viewer ascend in to the gilded realm of the organ and choir loft, it is revealed not to be constructed of numinous celestial forms, but the timber and plaster armatures of illusionistic baroque theatricality.

In contrast at Sant'Ignazio, entering the piazza and losing oneself within it signifies a moment of arrival, reiterated on entry into the church, and recognition of the space from which the impulse for movement sprang. The sight of Andrea Pozzo's painted vault confirms the sense of boundless space within the immense interior. The anamorphic constructions required to create these celestial depictions raise the issue of how illusion and reality were both perceived and understood during the baroque (Pozzo [1693] 1989). Such ceiling decorations were constructed to convincingly deceive the eyes of the congregation in the nave. In the highly theatrical worship of the Counter Reformation the priests were beyond the proscenium arch, actors who were participants in a divinely sanctioned drama, and therefore adepts of the secret knowledge of the manifested numinous (Wittkower and Jaffe 1972). For the clergy, largely occupying the apse beyond the crossing, the fictional nature of these heavenly mansions is revealed to them by the high degree of distortion used. Following the famous Jesuit dictum of ends justifying means, the confirmation of faith by aesthetic means which the Council of Trent had encouraged was worth the illusionistic skill of an artist and priest such as Pozzo.

These three Roman sites provide a tool through which the complexities of the different spatial sensations of the period can be studied, but the question remains as to what their particular motifs signify? It should be apparent that the devices employed are intended to embody the transcendent within the everyday. Geometries are compressed and extended to destabilize the viewer's sense of the ordinary. Archetypes are manipulated to evoke the recollection of other sacred sites and times. Forms are excavated to project the viewer into a celestial future. The mundane urban situation was to be understood as containing within it the space of the marvellous. However, from the viewpoint

7.10   Trevi Fountain, Rome. An example of civic display in a baroque city.

of subsequent urban history that ecstatic vision of urbanism was a delusion. Within half a century, industrial processes were to call into question the ethos of the city as anything other than a commodity. The tradition of the city as a representation of the heavens, traceable back to ancient civilizations, can be seen to terminate in the sensual spaces of the baroque. Devoid of any significant spiritual meaning, that urban sensuality would also find its greatest secular demonstrations in eighteenth century Rome, with the dramatic cascade of the steps and terraces of the Spanish Steps (1723–6) by Francesco de Sanctis (see Figure 14.6) and the Trevi Fountain (1732–62) by Nicola Salvi. In both instances a single gesture comes to dominate the space in which its stands, a dominance still so unusual in urban form as to maintain those spaces' importance in the tourist experience which grew up around them from the time of their construction. The examples of spaces of purely aesthetic effect were amplified to an urban scale, without the claims to the representation of cosmic order through geometrical and harmonic composition which had been explored in the earlier examples. While transcendent intentions had been extrapolated as a continuity between urban exterior and public interior famously depicted in Nolli's 1748 plan of Rome, the spiritual impulse of such techniques of the composition of space gave way to the scientific paradigm of the enlightenment, a direction which had been prefigured in the previous century (Bevilacqua 2004). For example, at Venaria Reale the piazza so elegantly delineated, is automatically undermined by the scale of the processional axis which splits it in two identical pieces. The creation of the vista invites direct movement, the consequence of which can only be destructive of the tradition of enclosed urban space. In *Flesh and Stone*, Richard Sennett remarks that 'as the desire to move freely has triumphed over the sensory claims of the space through which the body moves, the modern mobile individual has suffered a kind of tactile crisis'; in Sennett's view 'motion has helped desensitise the body' and this general principle is now realized in cities filled with neutral spaces, cities that have succumbed to the dominant value of circulation (Sennett 1994: 256). The utilitarian attitude to urban space which followed would, however, be obscured by the charms of historicism and the rhetoric of Italian national identity, issues which will be explored in the next section.

# PART III

# THE CITY AND NATIONAL CONSCIOUSNESS

# 8

# Neo-Classicism: Style and political ideology

Italy's role as the cultural lodestone of European architecture and urbanism would undergo a subtle transformation during the period from about 1750. Travel to the peninsula would become a phenomenon not only for those intent on a career in the arts, but also for those who sought to be discerning patrons. In a sceptical age such cultural travelling would eclipse the previous phenomenon of pilgrimage but would also make the Italy of the Grand Tour an ongoing series of encounters for the sharing and development of ideas which would dominate Western taste for the next two centuries (Wilton and Bignamini 1996; Scott 2003). The influx of visitors, with their patronage and connoisseurship, would stimulate the Italian situation as it was exposed to external assessment, in regard to both the preservation of its heritage and the quality of its public realm, these two fields initially under the direct supervision of the various absolutist states.

Produced through the spread of the printed treatise, the consensus which had seen renaissance architectural theory (and its mannerist and baroque descendants) recognized as the prevailing architectural language throughout Europe began to disintegrate under various pressures. The scientific revolution which began in the seventeenth century placed any received doctrine under threat. In architectural terms this would undermine the enigmatic forms of the baroque with a preference for more rational forms of construction, theorized by Laugier in France and Lodoli in Italy. Conversely, direct experience of ancient sites available through the Grand Tour developed a scepticism about the treatises of Alberti, Serlio and Palladio and their attempts to create universal systems. The reality of ancient monuments was more fragmentary, their forms less geometrically complete than had been suggested in the treatises. Archaeology's pragmatic uses were numerous. Initially it could be a source of income to the state through the trade in antiquities. Then it could be an instrument of patronage through the use of newly discovered motifs in the developing manufacturing industries of textiles and ceramics. The less directly pecuniary forms of prestige associated with culture through both the arts and sciences could be fostered with the opening up of sites to investigators and the publication of their findings, and an eclectic, essentially picturesque sensibility would develop from the appreciation of the juxtaposition of the ancient remains and the modern world. Ultimately the dramatic increase in archaeological activity during the mid-eighteenth century would present a series of new inspirations to artists, architects and designers in their pursuit of new urban forms. The excavations of Herculaneum from 1707, at Pompeii from 1748, and Paestum from the 1750s, although unsystematic, would provide the forms for an aesthetic revolution which would prefigure the political upheavals which sprang from the events of 1789.

The political models on offer to Italians were limited. Republicanism as demonstrated by Venice, would by the eighteenth century be associated with decadence and corruption and the republic's dramatic collapse at the end of the century did not suggest that it was an abiding form of government. Conversely the monarchical system available under Hapsburg, Savoy and Bourbon rulers offered an implication of stability, even after the dynastic changes which characterized the diplomatic world of Europe in the early eighteenth century. The increasing tendency of the monarchs to identify their rule with rational philosophy rather than divine sanction would erode the previous iconographic language of rulership in favour of the claims to endurance supported by the conscious appropriation of historical architectural languages. Within this political context, the archaeological discoveries of ancient sites in southern Italy provided great impetus for urban reform throughout the peninsula, and through the agency of Grand Tourists, throughout Europe (Salmon 2000). Although the aesthetic of the new discoveries was difficult for an essentially rococo sensibility to digest, debate was provoked between the adherents of contemporary style and those who sought ancient justification for what would later be regarded as rational (Rykwert 1980). While ornament, in the form of ceramics, wall-painting, mosaic and sculpture would furnish the trade in antiquities, the brute forms of the surviving architecture supplied not only a sublime *memento mori* for a vanished urban culture but also laid bare the infrastructure and engineering which had enabled those cities to flourish.

Architectural transformations would develop in parallel with changes in the political and dynastic situation. In the south the arrival in Naples, after over two centuries of regencies, of a royal family and court would bring new opportunities for patronage to the largest city in Italy. Charles of Bourbon had previously enjoyed his Farnese inheritance as Duke of Parma before relocating to Naples in 1734, establishing a court which was to survive, including a Bonapartist interlude, until 1860. In Florence, the Medici dynasty died out and were replaced by the recently united Hapsburg-Lorraine, to add to their existing control of Lombardy. The Savoy court in Turin, with brief acquisitions of Sicily and Sardinia would establish its monarchical aspirations with the Kingdom of Piedmont. However, the French invasion of Italy in 1797 would lead to the definitive destruction of the Republic of Venice, and the temporary removal of papal authority. Napoleon's subsequent distribution of territories to the families of his brothers and sisters, and his establishment of a Kingdom of Italy in 1805 would attempt a new dynastic system but following his fall from power in 1814 only the court of his Hapsburg widow as Duchess of Parma would survive until 1847. In each of these situations, the political change would be marked by renovations and creations of public works where the neoclassical taste was used to denote the cultural aspirations of benevolent despotism, the purity of revolutionary fervour, the imperial pretensions of Bonaparte and the continuity of the old dynasties upon their restoration. What characterises the examples to be discussed in this chapter is the independence of aesthetic motifs as definers of the public realm, as screens designed to contain and provide meaning, but without any substantial purpose beyond urban beautification.

If the political divisions of this period were sharp, the aesthetic ones were equally divisive, although polemical stances would tend not to be easily categorizable in built work. For example, the connoisseur Winckelmann's assertion of the superiority of Greek over Roman art, coinciding with the publication of the Greek temples at Paestum, would appear to define a decisive break with the work of previous decades from the 1750s. However, a convinced advocate of Roman achievements in art, architecture and engineering such as Giovanni Battista Piranesi (1720–78) would be able to exploit the fashionability of archaeology and proceed in his various activities on a path which showed a high degree of continuity with the baroque. His only surviving built work, the church of Santa Maria del Priorato and its attendant Piazza dei Cavalieri di Malta in Rome (1764–66) aptly illustrates the ambiguities of the period (Jatta 1998). These qualities can also be discerned in the professional sphere, with Piranesi's career a series of overlaps between the roles of architect and archaeologist, antiquarian and artist. In his drawn, built and written work he sought to resist the rationalization of the urban experience in favour of a dramatic exploration of symbol and allegory, aesthetic experience and historical memory. Distinguishing itself from the typical urbanity of the baroque, especially those Roman examples discussed in the previous chapter, at Santa Maria del Priorato a more attenuated space is defined which attempts not so much to enfold as to narrate. The layered images of the piazza and church facades create a backdrop against which ritual actions could proceed, with a space projected out from the accumulated images in which the action can be caught.

Piranesi was born in Venice, and initially was trained in scenography before establishing his studio in Rome. His career is famous for his publication of views and surveys of antiquities of the city which catered for the collecting market of the Grand Tour. He had hopes of more permanent patronage with the election in 1758 of a fellow Venetian as Pope Clement XIII, and he would be employed by the pope's nephew, Cardinal Giovanni Battista Rezzonico, in his role as Grand Prior of the Order of the Knights of Malta. The crusading order, officially that of St. John of Jerusalem, had relocated several times as they retreated from the expanding Ottoman forces. Their headquarters in Rome was on the Aventine Hill, in a situation which remains relatively suburban, but which afforded the knights a good view of the major port of

8.1    Piazza dei Cavalieri di Malta, Rome. On the right is the entrance screen into the estate of the Knights of St. John.

the city, the Ripa Grande. An existing medieval church was given over to them and Piranesi's task was not only to provide a new facade and redecorate the interior, but also create a more public face to the order in the form of a new gateway and ceremonial space which together form what remains one of the most unusual spaces in the city (Wilton-Ely 1993).

The piazza, in the suburban context of the Aventine, is defined by the gateway into the knights' estate (today a sovereign territory within the Republic of Italy), and walls on two other sides. A spy hole in its doorway offers the excluded a famous and much viewed image of the dome of St. Peter's basilica framed in a garden avenue. The motifs employed by Piranesi have a funereal sobriety in their organization, creating an atmosphere of regularity and order, but any sense of convention is overturned when the detail of the forms is examined closely. Paired obelisks sit atop the stucco walls with a series of panels crammed with iconography providing clues to the inquisitive. The motif of the order, the eight-pointed maltese cross, and the heraldic symbols of the Rezzonico family, the castellated turret and the double headed eagle, are used as decorative items. These symbols are then accompanied by representations of shields, cannons, bows and quivers of arrows, swords, daggers and military standards. Perhaps incongruously garlands, medals, lyres and pan-pipes are also portrayed in low relief in the architectural frames which Piranesi provided. They imitate the type of *capricci* of fragmentary archaeological remains which he often produced in his engravings, with particular reference to the ancient carved representations of

militaria from the base of the Column of Trajan and the trophies of Marius. The decorative use of the severed heads of Turkish captives referred to the specific military history of the order, but as John Wilton-Ely has observed the exploitation of this iconography had a longer history since it referred to the ancient Roman ceremony of the *armilustrium* which brought the fighting season to a close and had taken place on the Aventine (Wilton Ely 1993: 117). This history imbued the site, as it was developed by Piranesi, with the *mise en scene* for its elegiac and melancholy atmosphere. Those actions or at least the historical echo of past rituals, have been petrified into a series of permanent theatrical props. Marked by its obelisks and memorial tablets the piazza presents a form of anticipatory space, the messages of which prepared the viewer for the sepulchral qualities of the church facade.

8.2   Piazza dei Cavalieri di Malta, Rome. Elements of Piranesi's screen to the piazza showing the decorative use of militaria.

Facing out across the Tiber, the new facade repeats the combination of conventional overall form and extraordinary detail, its laminations of a piece both with the interior of the church itself and the frozen scenography of the piazza. Both then employ a full iconographic repertoire to portray their respective narratives, but the facade is the most constrained element of the sequence, because of the accommodation of the existing doorway and oculus, and the employment of paired pilasters and a pediment which create a restrained image of authority. The decorative motifs are more exclusively military in character, swords displayed attached to the pilasters, standards flanking the doorway, shields and armour in the pediment and, masquerading

8.3    Diagram of elements from Piazza dei Cavalieri di Malta, Rome, showing the facade of the church, a detail of the screen wall and the relationship between the church (facade and altar) and screen walls to the piazza.

as volutes, a pair of serpents which refer, as a symbol of the god Aesculapius, to the medical activities of the Knights Hospitaller. However, as the central motif, the emblematic character of the image of the reeded sarcophagus under which one enters the church arrests the journey in space and time. The strangeness of the combinations of military and naval, genealogical and religious symbols serves to define a place which is as removed in time as it is delimited in space, an effect of distance which remains tangible to the contemporary visitor.

The interior continues the allegorical themes, with a low relief decorative scheme on the ceiling vault and a huge sculptural form at the high altar. The ceiling panel consists of more militaria, including Constantinian *vexilla*, with a knight's tunic and a representation of an armed ship to refer to the order's former naval prowess. The high altar again employs the motif of an abstracted ship, resting on the huge form of a reliquary sarcophagus and supporting a representation of the globe from which rises, borne aloft by angels, the figure of Saint Basil of Capadoccia in a state of apotheosis. Although the silhouetting of the altar against the light adds to its initial effect of animation, a legacy of Piranesi's scenographic training, the monochrome pallor of the entire ensemble of the interior retards any feeling of movement or action. This atmosphere of stillness provides the place for an encounter with architecture as constructed of meaning and the fulfilment of a spatial desire which had been anticipated in the piazza and in the facade. As discussed in the previous chapter, the retardation of movement that characterises shallow space in the baroque is here succeeded by the apparent inertia of suspended time. This in turn gives way to an acceptance of the atmosphere of calm, as the impetus to movement falls away, along with the surface detail that bleeds out on the rear of the altar (Tafuri 1987: 47–50). The apotheosis of Saint Basil represented above contains within it the conventional language of celestial distance and immensity, but behind the typical view of the military community, the infinite is embodied in the purity of abstract forms and the sublime power they convey, as the rear of the altar discards the decorative surface to reveal the pure geometry of the sphere, the motif *par excellence* of enlightenment architecture. Through the employment of a more speculative language for traditional architectural figures Piranesi introduced an abstract series of motifs which appealed to those who found his work irrational, but admired his ability to imagine an idealized world. As displayed on the Aventine, Piranesi's urbanism of the motif, an architectural language attempting direct communication, could be seen as the end of the tradition of the baroque. The same ideas, as represented in the plan of his 1762 *Campus Martius* volume, would provide a visionary proposal for the consumption of those who sought to project ideal space in the modern city. Although this utopian ambition was indebted to the speculative imagination on the past, it would indicate the direction of the development of urban space.

A similar sense of urban beautification would be the inspiration in Padua for the architectural theorist Andrea Memmo (1729–93), a student of Carlo Lodoli (1690–1761), in his renovation of the Prato della Valle dating from 1775–76. Memmo's contribution to theory was his *Elementi dell'architettura Lodoliana* published in 1786, which promoted his mentor's desire for the removal of ornament. However, Memmo's official position as *provvenditore* (provider) of the Republic of Venice made him a significant patron and he sought to reclaim a large area of swampy marshland for use as a market place and pleasure gardens. He commissioned the Vicentine architect Domenico Cerato (1715–92) to provide a plan which used the figure of a large ellipse with crossing paths to create a regular figure within the roughly triangular space, a figure which evoked the form of an ancient water theatre or *naumachia*, as had been illustrated by Piranesi in the *Campus Martius*. During the excavation of the site, to drain the area and connect it to the existing canal network, the remains of the ancient city's Roman theatre were discovered, thus providing an archaeological justification for the modern development. Memmo's idea was to create an urban space in the form of a didactic landscape and ideal form was introduced into the city as an example of the enlightenment ethos, the typically baroque form of the ellipse reinvigorated with new meaning. The long tradition of Italian garden design is brought to bear on the urban space, a site of relatively relaxed civic pleasure. Precedents include the adjacent but much smaller and circular *Orto Botanico* founded in 1545 and the *isolotto* at the Boboli gardens in Florence (1630–37), the latter example an elliptical island sitting within water within densely planted woods. If the former was essentially a scientific environment and the latter one dedicated to aristocratic pleasure, at Padua the instructional and the diverting are combined. The water takes the form of monumental canals, lined with statues and obelisks surrounding a central island called after its founder the *isola memmia*, but the context being a vast space with views of urban monuments, particularly the basilica of Santa Giustina, and the more distant domes of Sant'Antonio. The programme of statuary comprises numerous figures from history associated with the city and the Veneto, including Padua's mythical Trojan founder, four popes of Venetian origin (including the recently deceased Clement XIII), Galileo and in a later addition the great neoclassical sculptor Antonio Canova. In early versions of the project, the island was to serve as a market space, with stalls surrounding the space or arranged on one half of the ellipse. However, the island was eventually preserved as a garden space, planted with trees and serves as an urban oasis, and one of the last significant demonstrations of public patronage by the Republic of Venice. Memmo's attempt to inculcate noble values amongst the decadence of a social system which had been in decline for centuries was to fail in the face of political changes which were to come from beyond the Alps, and which after the brief period of Napoleonic rule would put the Veneto under Austrian occupation until 1866. The first urbanistic signs of these political changes in Padua were the removal by the French occupiers and their collaborators of the statues of some doges from the sides of the canals and the erection of a Tree of Liberty on the *isola memmia*.

The presence of French control throughout Italy would produce many proposed changes to urban form, although not all would be implemented. Ephemeral festival architecture would play its part in providing new aesthetic models as, for example, Piazza San Pietro in Rome played host to revolutionary fetes celebrating the city's incorporation as part of the French state (Kirk 2005a: 86–88). Following the establishment of the Napoleonic kingdom of Italy in 1804 Piazza San Marco in Venice was the site of one of the most enduring constructions of the period, the creation of a royal palace under the viceroy Eugene de Beauharnais at the western end of the square. The church of San Geminiano was demolished and a new wing added, eventually completed by Giuseppe Maria Soli (1745–1822) which continued the arcades between the Procuratie Vecchie and the Procuratie Nuove and created a series

of grand salons above with the best views in the city (Plant 2002: 65–71). In Milan, which was the capital of the new kingdom and where Napoleon was crowned in the cathedral with the iron crown of Lombardy, the plans were more extensive but their only partial realization was to be long delayed. To the north west of the city centre the 'Foro Bonaparte' was proposed by Giovanni Antonio Antolini (1756–1841) as a new business centre in the form of a vast circular enclosure to the Castello Sforzesco. The purity of its geometry, made possible by the expropriation of clerical property which had begun under the Hapsburgs, presented in a single dramatic gesture the project of the modern city to use open space as a means to isolate monuments, treating them as compositional devices and historical relics and surrounded by new, rationally planned urban structures and city blocks (Rossi 1982: 144–46).

As has already been mentioned Bonaparte's attempt to establish territories for a dynasty meant the replacement of the existing rulers, and in Naples this would lead to the creation of one of the foremost spaces of the period. The dramatic neoclassical space of Piazza del Plebiscito has its origins in the *largo* adjacent to the Palazzo Reale where festivals were held by the Spanish viceroys during the sixteenth and seventeenth centuries. However, following the establishment of the Bourbon court under Charles III the city gained enhanced status as a royal capital, with a court, its attendant bureaucracy and the activity of public works which went with it, although the most notable construction project of the period was the Reggia at Caserta many miles from the city with its combination of a vast palace in an immense ordered

8.4  Prato della Valle, Padua. View of one of the surrounding canals during the restoration of the statuary.

8.5   Piazza del Plebiscito, Naples. View of the portico and dome of the church of San Francesco di Paola.

landscape. As has been mentioned previously, archaeological enterprises had encouraged the development of neoclassical taste at the Naples court and a desire to emulate antiquity inspired the eventual design of the piazza, or *foro* as it was initially termed, in front of the Naples palace. Its design (and to a greater extent its nomenclature) would reflect the seismic political events which affected Europe in the wake of the French Revolution. The expulsion of the Bourbon king Ferdinand IV in 1806, his replacement by Bonapartist kings (initially Joseph, Napoleon's elder brother and then their brother-in-law Joachim Murat) and eventually the Bourbon restoration (as Ferdinand I of the Two Sicilies) in 1815 would both delay work, and encourage a renewed impetus as each successive regime sought to emphasise their hold on power in a space directly outside their palace windows (Ossanna Cavadini 1995).

Despite this political turmoil however, the issue of architectural language was remarkably consistent, so pervasive was the archaeological taste. The initial project from 1808 for the 'Foro Murat' designed by Leopoldo Laperuta was for the palace facade to be confronted by a hemicycle of corinthian columns, recalling in a truncated form the design of Piazza San Pietro in Rome. Pairs of subsidiary buildings for the municipal authorities were designed to occupy the sides of the space between the palace and new colonnade. However, following the restoration Ferdinand held a new competition, for the 'Foro Ferdinandeo', in which the Rome-based architect Pietro Bianchi (1787–1849) triumphed. His project used the existing foundations to create a doric colonnade (more *à la mode*) and a circular church, San Francesco di Paola, as a votive offering of thanks for the restoration of the throne to the Bourbon dynasty. Paired equestrian statues of kings Charles and Ferdinand reinforced the dynastic message of continuity. The church is directly based on the ultimate neoclassical precedent, the Pantheon in Rome, but with significant adaptations. For example the ionic portico was required to combine with the lower side doric colonnades, and with pairs of small domes as side chapels helping make the transition between the colonnades and the great central dome. The ensemble was therefore firmly allied to archaeological motifs, but with the complexity of its pure volumes and sober lines was also convincingly modern. The interior continues the imitative manner with the employment of a corinthian order. Externally the 'roman' dome and the 'greek' colonnade were complemented by 'egyptian' lions, but the urbanistic effect was to complement the severe facade of the Palazzo Reale (later ornamented with a series of statues representing the roll call of dynasties who had held Naples), and frame to either side a view towards the Teatro San Carlo (Charles III's great cultural contribution to the city founded in 1737) and the later Galleria Umberto I (1885–92), and on the other side out to the Bay of Naples. Completed in 1846, the piazza's name would change again following the final expulsion of the notoriously despotic Bourbons in 1860, and the plebiscite with which the Kingdom of the Two Sicilies joined the Kingdom of Italy.

The final example from this period, Piazza del Popolo in Rome, was a space which had developed since medieval times but which reached its definitive form during this period of political change. The piazza's design was the result of a gradual accumulation of gestures which culminated in the space's amplification and completion by Giuseppe Valadier (1762–1839) to a series of designs produced between 1794 and 1824, a timespan that is indicative of the continuity which underlay the changes of government (see Figure 0.4). The piazza, growing at the point where the Via Flaminia entered the city of Rome through Bernini's gate in the Aurelian Wall was a site where significant visitors to the city would come to be feted, adjacent to the church of Santa Maria del Popolo. The trident of roads which developed either side of Via del Corso, the present Via del Babuino and Via di Ripetta, had its focus marked by the obelisk placed in the centre of the space by Sixtus V in 1589. This single intervention tied the piazza into the network of the city, which would become emblematic of baroque urbanism, and provided the impetus for the theatrically paired churches inserted between the roads. Designed by Carlo Rainaldi (1611–1691) the churches, on the east Santa Maria di Monte Sacro (1662–75) and Santa Maria de'Miracoli (1675–79) on the west, were intended to create the impression of symmetrical identity, although the sites were not identical so that Rainaldi's strategy was to employ respectively an ellipse and a circle for the composition of the domes. They were constructed with the purpose of emphasizing the city's threshold, and the paired domes and paired

8.6   Diagram of Piazza del Popolo, Rome, showing (from the left) the gate into the city, the facade of Santa Maria del Popolo, the obelisk, the paired churches of Santa Maria di Monte Sacro and Santa Maria de'Miracoli and the trident of streets. The cross axis is formed by Valadier's terraces, screen walls and fountains.

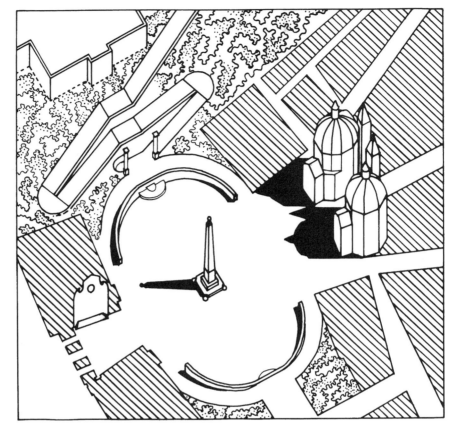

campanili were complemented by paired pedimented temple fronts which prefigured the taste of the eighteenth century (Ciucci 1974).

Thus far the development of the piazza had been pursued at the leisurely pace with which the nepotistic papal administration conducted its affairs. Valadier's intervention in the space was initiated in 1794 when as a young architect he presented a project for the piazza's redefinition to Pope Pius VI, and its effective militarization by the erection of paired colonnaded barracks (Kirk 2005a: 115–20). With the French occupation of Rome in 1798 the architect redesigned his project as an urban garden space, associated with an adjacent public garden on the Pincian Hill, and introduced a cross axis centred on the obelisk. The elliptical garden space which was thus defined had its Roman origins in Bernini's work at Piazza San Pietro but transformed for the neoclassical taste, and perhaps also the more recent example of Prato della Valle in Padua. A series of transformations would follow as the urban character of the space was emphasized and the civil engineering difficulties associated with the hill were resolved. In the centre of the piazza the obelisk was given a new base and surrounded by fountains featuring 'egyptian' lions. Low screen walls, ornamented with sphinxes formed the hemicycles with a

fountain of Neptune towards the Tiber, and a fountain of Mars backed by a series of terraces, rostral columns and cascades against the Pincian. The culminating feature was a three arched loggia supporting the final terrace where an elevated view towards the dome of Saint Peter's was provided, an entirely appropriate change of directional emphasis once Pius VII returned to the city following the abdication of Napoleon in 1814. The papal administration was content to continue with Valadier's project, with four substantial building elements created in an animated neoclassical language, a new flank wall to the church of Santa Maria del Popolo and a small barracks building framing the view of the Porta del Popolo, and a pair of commercial buildings framing Rainaldi's churches. The archaeological taste is evidenced by the piling up of motifs, including the statuary, the placing of another obelisk on the summit of the Pincian Hill and the decorative panels of militaria (similar to those on the Aventine) set within a romantic landscape which is designed to contrast dramatically with its urban context. The eclectic architectural language favoured by Piranesi had found an expression on a civic scale.

The historical coincidence that this intense rediscovery of the classical world should occur at the same time as the onset of industrialization amplified the effect which occurred three hundred years earlier with the conjunction of the renaissance and the invention of printing. Huge new unadorned structures,

8.7   Piazza del Popolo, Rome. The Fountain of Neptune.

such as institutions for social control, harbours and other works of civil engineering could be created which emulated the scale of archaeological discoveries, a regularity emphasized by the general restraint of ornament. In a counter movement the collections being amassed in Naples and Rome, and gradually being put on display for the public good, suggested juxtapositions of artefacts from different sources and hands which exercised the ingenuity of architects and designers in the creation of palace interiors, either for new residences or the developing phenomenon of the public museum. This contrast of austerity of form, and accumulation of ornament, rooted simultaneously in the archaeology of the past and the rational 'enlightened' present supplies a fork in the path of the development of urban spaces. In contrast to the continuity expressed in baroque culture, between the cosmic and the urban, the exterior and the public interior, we see a self-conscious separation and an enhancement of the difference of effect in the viewer, with a principal role in secular scenarios less likely to be that of the prince, and in religious ones a more rational supreme being celebrated in forms unencumbered with the emotional exaggeration of the Counter-Reformation.

The social changes which occurred in this period would have a profound effect on the representational character of urban space in Italy. The position of the aristocracy would begin to decline as new wealth began to be more influential in property ownership and development. Courts in Turin, Florence, Rome and Naples would continue to plan and build, but generally for more utilitarian purposes than absolutist display. Venice, after the fall of the republic would lose its independent impetus, and enter a process of physical and material decline. The growth of anticlericalism and the reaction to it would have long-lasting effects. The confiscation of church property, commencing under the enlightened despots, but accelerated during the revolutionary era, would erode the church's standing in temporal matters, although the scepticism of the eighteenth century would give way to an official public piety. This would become a source of conflict when the movements towards national unification would meet papal opposition, leading to the beginnings of a divide between political and ecclesiastical spheres. Although the church would still exercise enormous patronage, the work it commissioned from the early nineteenth century onwards would cease to be as culturally significant as hitherto had been the case. Secularism would become the defining frame of reference and even in situations where substantial churches were integrated into new urban projects, as with those of the Gran Madre di Dio in Turin (1818–31) by Ferdinando Bonsignore and San Carlo al Corso in Milan (1836–47) by Carlo Amati (see Figure 14.3), their archaeological character formed a bypass around the Christian past to an era of ancient civic magnificence. The similar, Pantheon-inspired, form of the Bourbon temple in Piazza del Plebiscito in Naples though represented a more reactionary agenda.

The social and political upheavals of the century between 1750 and 1850 had more immediately dramatic consequences in the cities of northern Europe through the growth of industrialization and the explosion of urban populations. In the very different economic state of the Italian peninsula

8.8   Caffe Pedrocchi, Padua, showing the eclectic historicism of the original neo-classical building on the right and the gothic extension.

industrialization was not such an issue, cities were governed and designed by the same flux of dynastic aggrandisement, the temporal claims of the papacy and the exposure to the direct influence and control of foreign powers. While one strand of this situation would portray the Italians as unable to control their political destiny (in Metternich's famous phrase, Italy was nothing more than 'a geographical expression') she was also a storehouse of form for the elaboration of civic complexes throughout Europe, the colonies and newly independent states in the Americas. The consolidation of the number of Italian states agreed at the Congress of Vienna, the growth of secular ideologies and the widely perceived backwardness of the restored Bourbon monarchy helped cultivate the desire for national unification which was associated with the idealizing form of the Caffe Pedrocchi in Padua (1816–42) with its contrasting neoclassical and gothic architectural languages designed by Giuseppe Japelli (Meeks 1966: 124–29). The civic traditions of northern and central Italy would be expressed after the *Risorgimento* and the unification of Italy in the plaques erected in every city to record the presence of Garibaldi or Vittorio Emanuele II, and the voting figures in the plebiscites with which they acceded to the new Kingdom of Italy. In urbanism a more middling taste would prevail than that recorded in this chapter, with an emphasis less on an idealization of the past than on the pragmatic expression of the efficiency of the new state. In that process a certain spirit evaporated from urban spaces, a sense of individuality and intellectual vigour which the previous examples each expressed. Italy's course in the century between 1850 and 1950 would see unprecedented urban development and an often self-conscious expression of political motive, but the relatively small number of eighteenth century Grand Tourists would be succeeded by increasing numbers brought by the developing rail network to see the cities which had hosted pre-industrial civilization. The romantic taste for ruination and picturesque decay, and the attempts to create a new type of urban space on its aesthetic principles would give way to a more pragmatic language as the cities of the new nation state expanded, and adjusted to their unfamiliar role as provincial centres.

# 9

# *Risorgimento*: The formation of a national urban space

With the defeat of the Austrian army in Lombardy and the victory of Garibaldi's forces against those of the Bourbon monarchy in the south, Vittorio Emanuele II of Savoy was declared king of a united Italy in 1861. This achievement of national unification proceeded during the 1860s as other provinces were assembled, culminating with the seizure of Rome in 1870, and the changed situation presented the country's unique and widely admired urban culture with two specific challenges. Firstly there was the desire to function as a modern European nation state (the motive, along with the desire to end extra-territorial domination, which had driven the various political, military and diplomatic strategies of Mazzini, Garibaldi and Cavour) and to rank with Britain, France and the similarly recently unified Germany. This process was to be manifested urbanistically in the drive for the efficiency and hygiene with which modern cities and a nation were organized. Secondly, in the rival cities of the Italian peninsula, each embodying their regional and historical differences, it was felt important to express a form of national identity in architectural and urban form. These two currents would combine to create a specific genus of piazza, often named after the heroes of the *Risorgimento*, which expressed the confidence of a bourgeoisie content with the compromises of a liberal constitutional monarchy and the new political settlement.

However the issue of the appropriate architectural language for these new urban developments would be an important part of the national debate. In the field of the Italian language the Tuscan dialect, the language of Dante, would be given preference over those from other regions, becoming the official language of the state. Similarly, in the field of architecture there were several candidates from Italian architectural history, and an authority such as the writer and architect Camillo Boito (1836–1914) favoured the Lombard romanesque as being suitable for a variety of modern civic functions. More conventional tastes prevailed, however, and a neo-renaissance style became the common language for new developments, an architectural language which suited the preference for symmetrical urban layouts. Despite the dominance of these urbanistic strategies, the appreciation of irregular city spaces had its adherents, following on from the appreciation of urban form created by the eighteenth century *vedutisti*. The Austrian architect Camillo Sitte (1843–1903) conducted the first systematic survey of northern Italian spaces (Collins and Collins 1986). His methods, aided by the ease of travel by rail from Vienna, were based on direct observation of the spaces, preferably from nearby high towers, this experience being abstracted through plan diagrams which generally removed the tendency towards picturesque values, an aesthetic form in any case now supplied by the increasing availability of photographic views. Sitte's comparative studies emphasized the importance of the quality of enclosure, and saw in the irregularity of the spaces not the imperfections of aesthetically inferior taste but pragmatic systems for the efficient flow of traffic, induced by the non-alignment of streets entering spaces. He contrasted this unfavourably with the contemporary tendency to create larger spaces and axial routes which he regarded as responsible for the phenomenon of agoraphobia. He also saw that the placement of monuments in axial positions deprived them of aesthetic values which had been characteristic of earlier periods when advantage was taken of buildings as backdrops to statuary. Again this had pragmatic value in not creating obstacles to traffic flow, and his combination of the practical and aesthetic would be recognized after its initial publication as *Der Stadtebau* (1889) through the translation of his work into French and English in the following decades. The Sittesque method was to be influential on the young Charles-Edouard Jeanneret in his early studies of urban space, before (following his transformation into the modernist Le Corbusier) he would disavow Sitte's approach as 'the donkey's way'. Within Italy Marcello Piacentini, the son of the eminent architect Pio Piacentini, would be one of the early practitioners of Sitte's principles, as will be discussed in the next chapter (Etlin 1991: 124–28, 225–54).

The audience to which the new urban developments in Italy were addressed were twofold, an internal one and an external one. Like the practice of conscripted military service in a distant part of the new kingdom, national urban identity was initially created by the importation of Piedmontese models further south, as the Savoy monarchy's civil and military apparatus expanded its control. Conformity to this new political identity developed in a relatively passive manner. The external audience of northern European visitors were also intended to be impressed by the signs of modernity in territories previously regarded as backward, but there was a dissenting view. Sitte in the field of urban form, and the English critic John Ruskin in the field of architecture and its social impact, were promoters and idealizers of historic Italian urban culture as a model for emulation in industrialized societies, and were among those dismayed by the impact of modernity on the slowly decaying cities they so admired. In an urban environment where industrialization had yet to make any significant impact, the scale and regularity of the new interventions presented significant discontinuities within densely occupied city centres (Plant 2002: 131–33). The losses of traditional buildings as new boulevards and embankments were constructed, however, could be documented by photography which presented new perspectives for both the proponents of progress and the regretful harbingers of urban doom. While the *risanamento* process, the renewal of urban environments, affected many cities, the forces of preservation also sought to marshall their often nostalgic desires into a more scientific form. In 1883 the *carta del restauro* initiated by Boito was the first document to produce principles to govern the conservation of architectural monuments, emphasizing the importance of historical integrity and the role of the craftsman to produce work in the spirit of the original rather than a mechanical copy. Although drawn up in an era which favoured the replication of historical styles, the immediate significance of this position was hard to discern, its impact on the authentic preservation of historic environments would become apparent when those historical styles fell from use (Kirk 2005a: 176–83).

The form in which these new developments were created had a strongly distanced relationship to the host situation. Although there were significant examples of major interventions, the principal cities had grown organically, layer upon historical layer, so that they presented dense accumulations of settlements and historical monuments. While this charmed many visitors it was a source of shame to those imbued with a reforming spirit which, following on from unification, wanted to create a modern image for the new state. If the contemporary model to emulate was Haussmann's Paris, the compositional strategy of straight boulevards connecting significant urban monuments was itself derived from Sixtus V's replanning of Rome. The scale of the new boulevards, to accommodate increased horse drawn road traffic and the provision of sophisticated sewage systems led to an increase in architectural scale which suited the representational ambitions of civic authorities. Conveniently blaming the delays in the modernization of several cities on the lassitude of the previous regimes, the vigour of young Italy would be demonstrated in projects which demonstrated their embrace of modernity. Yet in its final phase, the previous political settlement had embarked on benign and advanced urban reforms. For example in Rome Pius IX's rule, notorious for its opposition to the project of Italian unification, had sought to embrace the modern world in architectural and urban form through the removal of baroque accretions from early Christian basilicas in the city. Conversely the modern habit of tobacco use would be given a relatively grand urban presence in Trastevere through the construction of the Manifattura dei Tabacchi (1859–63). The large complex (built on the grounds of the church of Santa Maria dell'Orto to which Vignola had supplied the facade) featured a grand pedimented neo-classical front by Antonio Sarti (1797–1880) with engaged tuscan columns above a rusticated ground floor. The forcefulness of this public presence was framed by an area of workers' housing designed by Andrea Busiri-Vici (1817–1911) and called the Quartiere Mastai after the pope's family name. The buildings centre on a circular piazza in front of the factory's temple front, the Piazza Mastai, and were executed in a sober architectural language. The ameliorative nature of this benevolent social provision was not, however, enough to prevent the fall of the papal states and city's eventual submission by the new kingdom of Italy.

While the territory of the new state was being accumulated, the question of the nation's capital remained fluid. During the brief period when Florence was capital of the new kingdom from 1866–70 Giuseppe Poggi (1811–1901) undertook a master plan which brought contemporary urban development to the city. This consisted of the creation of a boulevard in the contemporary manner, along the line of the city's fortifications, and a dramatic viewpoint, the Piazzale Michelangelo on the Oltrarno, as a terrace approached by a winding but monumental route in the manner of Valadier's work on the Pincian in Rome. The centre of the terrace was ornamented with a bronze copy of Michelangelo's David (a twin to the marble copy placed in the Piazza della Signoria following the original sculpture's removal to the Galleria dell'Accademia in 1872). However, the most radical project in which he was involved, less dependent for its effect on the unique topography of the city, was the clearing of the Mercato Vecchio to create Piazza Vittorio Emanuele (now Piazza della Repubblica) which would prove a more typical work in the period, a project on which Poggi collaborated with Mariano Falcini (1804–85). The site was of historic importance because of its continuous occupation since Roman times as the commercial heart of the city. The city's newly enhanced status, and the construction of a modern covered market (designed by Giuseppe Mengoni in 1874), condemned the site to clearance in the hope of evoking the spirit of the Roman forum which had once stood on site. The new buildings significantly inflated the scale of architecture in this part of the city, and included a triumphal arch spanning over the western side of the square completed between 1893–95. Such gestures generally met with a negative response, especially in the following century, when critical opinion focused on what had been lost in the creation of an image of modernity (Meeks 1966: 307–12).

Elsewhere in Italy, the completion by Carlo Amati of the facade of Milan cathedral under the period of Napoleonic rule had provoked a desire to complement the *duomo* with a suitably dignified piazza. An unformed space existed, to the west a roughly rectangular space was available, with existing market structures, although compositionally it was not aligned with the new facade. Towards the south another larger space served as a forecourt to the Palazzo Reale, which had been redesigned in 1773 by Giuseppe Piermarini, but again this space was at an oblique angle to the side of the cathedral and did not align with the other space either. With the holding of a competition in 1860, the year following Lombardy's liberation from Austrian rule, the city authorities decided to resolve these aesthetic problems by promoting a new project to be funded by a lottery. The prevailing taste dictated a huge rectangular space aligned with the facade and fitting into the street network. However to the north of the space there was a specific desire, approved of by the new king, to connect the proposed square to that existing between the Teatro alla Scala and the Palazzo Marino, the seat of civic government. Different elements of this strategy had been the subject of numerous studies, which had sought to resolve the geometrical and visual problems by creating an ample piazza, but (although the novel means of funding by lottery failed)

a competition resulted in the project designed by the Bolognese architect Giuseppe Mengoni (1829–77). His first project from 1863 was remarkable in emphasizing the spaces which would form the new relationships between the urban elements. The facade of the *duomo* was to be faced axially by a new palazzo, an element of the masterplan which was never constructed. Crossing this major axis was a longer route which stretched from the Piazza della Scala through a symmetrical street with a central octagon. This new path entered the piazza between paired theatres, for comedy and comic opera respectively, with its axis terminating on the other side of the square by a royal loggia attached to the Palazzo Reale and forming a junction with its separate piazza (Geist 1983: 371–401). From this comprehensive idea the project developed, with the addition of a cruciform plan to the streets introduced, fulfilling the implication of the previously planned octagon, and the decision to glaze over the public passages of what was developing into a substantial commercial structure. While Milan already had glazed commercial arcades in imitation of French examples, the popular impact of the glazed structure of the Crystal Palace for the Great Exhibition in London in 1851 would also have had some bearing, especially as the project was now to be financed by an English company with the requisite technical knowledge. However, Mengoni had

9.1  Piazza della Repubblica, Florence. To the left is the Colonna dell'Abbondanza which survived the nineteenth century demolitions.

9.2   Piazza Duomo, Milan. The northern edge of the space was defined by new commercial structures and the entrance to the Galleria Vittorio Emanuele.

subtly maintained its Italian origins by designing the central octagonal space to equal the diameter of Michelangelo's dome of St. Peter's in Rome.

What Mengoni achieved was the creation of the Galleria Vittorio Emanuele eventually completed in 1878, creating a huge commercial arcade which is the definitive example of this nineteenth century building type. The typology of the piazza was also transformed, with the Piazza Duomo combining religious, regal and popular elements in a balanced composition. The Galleria itself, replete with its abundant iconography was obviously intended to be regarded as more than merely a glazed street between the two urban spaces. Made possible by the exploitation of glass and cast-iron technology, the introduction of the shorter cross arm provided the opportunity for the great domed crossing, which effectively presented Italy with a new form of public open space. But if its form was intended to evoke the heights of Italian architectural achievement, there were those who also thought that this modern marvel symbolically represented the national destiny, as to citizens of a nationalistic mindset the plan bore a striking similarity to the cross on the coat of arms of the house of Savoy. A personal echo of the good fortune the Galleria was deemed to represent for the nation survives in the encouragement of visitors to spin on their heel on the genitals of the bull depicted on the floor of the

9.3 Piazza Duomo, Milan. Galleria Vittorio Emanuele showing Mengoni's triumphal treatment of the facade. (Compare with Figure 6.6).

octagon, in this instance the heraldic symbol of the city of Turin, Milan's rival but also the city historically associated with the Savoy.

The facade to the Piazza Duomo, long delayed in its completion, featured a triumphal arch and was intended to be surmounted by a *quadriga*, matching another on the unbuilt royal loggia opposite on the other side of the square. Continuous arcades were designed to line the piazza, motifs which with their perpendicular relationship to the duomo facade recalled the similar relationship of Vignola's Facciata dei Banchi with San Petronio in Mengoni's native city of Bologna, discussed in Chapter 6. Shortly before the unveiling of the triumphal arch with its dedication to the king, Mengoni fell to his death from the scaffolding in December 1877. His plans for the piazza remained incomplete, the cross axis eventually being completed in the following century by the *arengario* planned by Giovanni Muzio between 1937–42 (Irace 1994: 124–32). Despite the Galleria's traditional representational motifs, artificial lighting ensured that the goods on display through its plate glass windows would provide new forms of urban diversion. This work alone, designed in a flamboyant neo-renaissance manner, signalled the arrival of a modern bourgeois democratic state on the European scene, and it remains one of the major public spaces of Italy's financial and industrial centre. Its influence would be felt throughout Europe and North America, but

9.4 Galleria
Umberto I,
Naples. A
reworking of the
new commercial
space of united
Italy, imported
from Milan to
the south.

within Italy its immediate progeny would be the Galleria Umberto I in Naples (by Ernesto di Mauro and Emanuele Rocco 1887–91) which imitated Mengoni's original closely and the Galleria Colonna in Rome which had a tortuous planning history and was not completed until 1922 (Geist 1983: 428–37, 543–49). However, the commercial character of such projects became less novel as they became commonplace and the demand grew for a more conventionally representational monumental language for public spaces.

Rome's status as capital of the kingdom from 1870, its expansion and replanning would be spurs to an urban design campaign which compared itself self-consciously to the remains of antiquity and the products of the renaissance and baroque periods which the following further two examples, Piazza dell'Esedra and Piazza Venezia, demonstrate. Outside the city's remaining papal enclave at the Vatican, Rome's centre and edges would undergo dramatic transformation. The Tiber embankments would be designed to control flooding, and new bridges created to carry a series of boulevards. Agricultural land within the walls would be occupied by new development, especially for new ministries, planned on a modern grid iron system, but generally respectful of the historic patterns of straight streets leading to significant monuments (Kirk 2005a: 222–259). The period of the *Risorgimento* had coincided with the arrival in Rome of the most modern means of transport in the form of the railway. The creation of the Stazione Roma Termini between 1866 and 1874 would lead to increased development in the north eastern section of the city. The name of the station was derived from its proximity to the remains of the *Terme di Diocleziano* (the Baths of Diocletian) and the fragment of the whole complex which had been converted by Michelangelo from 1561 onwards into the church of Santa Maria degli Angeli. With the entry into Rome of Italian forces through the nearby Porta Pia (also designed by Michelangelo 1561–64) and the city's declaration as national capital, property developments which had already been initiated during the last years of papal control, such as the Via Nuova planned by Archbishop Frederic de Merode, were appropriated by the new state as an opportunity to create a grand Parisian boulevard where ministries could be sited, the route now designated as Via Nazionale. Heading westward towards the remains of the Forum of Trajan, the eastern end of the boulevard terminated on the facade of Santa Maria degli Angeli, but within sight of the new station. It was therefore appropriate that a new piazza should be planned which could act as a gateway for visitors to the new capital and its adjacent ministries as well as introduce them to the archaeological remains of the ancient city. The well tried strategy of the hemicycle was again adapted, for which there were ancient precedents *in situ* in the form of the outerworks of the Baths complex. The archaeological remains were stripped of most of their later external accretions (in the best new archaeological and conservation practice as promoted by Boito) and opposite the newly cleaned ruins a pair of grand quadrant buildings framed the view down to the centre of the city.

The buildings which defined the new piazza were the work (1888–89) of Gaetano Koch (1849–1910), the pre-eminent Roman architect of the period and exhibited his neo-renaissance stylistic preferences. Carroll L.V. Meeks refers with approval to 'the semi-anonymous manner' with which Koch created new buildings which complemented in a reticent manner the existing background buildings of the city (Meeks 1966: 376–86). He refers to the facades of Koch's buildings as largely falling into three formulas which were well designed but sought not to draw attention, and that the examples of his work at Piazza dell'Esedra are an unusual combination of one formula dependent on pedimented windows and another dependent on the use of pilasters.

Generally such elevational systems are flat, but the untypical situation at Piazza dell'Esedra (now della Repubblica), with the facades dramatically curving offered the architect a new opportunity. The form of Koch's buildings, especially the hemicycle and arcade was influenced by the archaeological context but also by Paul-Henri Nenot's prize-winning project for the first competition (1881) for a memorial to Vittorio Emanuele II (following the king's death in 1878), although without the triumphal arch positioned to span the opening of Via Nazionale. In his completed project Koch's elevations are relatively sober in comparison to other Roman buildings of a similar date. The ends of the curved sections are marked by more decorated pavilions, which showed the influence of Charles Garnier's Paris Opera, and the straight sections contrast with this arrangement having their central pavilions emphasized. However, the grandeur of the conception was noteworthy for the generous ground floor arcades dramatically transforming Bernini's famous precedent for commercial uses, and elevated half a level up from the increasingly busy roadway by flights of steps.

As its most flamboyant feature the centre of the piazza was ornamented with a grand new fountain inaugurated eventually in 1901. This fountain had a subtle political resonance as it had been reconstructed from the fountain erected in 1870 by Pius IX outside the new railway station as his last work of urban beautification. The fountain's waters were provided by the Acqua Pia Marcia, the first aqueduct constructed in Rome since the beginning of the seventeenth century. Its sculptures are the work of Mario Rutelli, the central figure of *Glaucis* wrestling with a spouting dolphin was only installed in 1911 for the fiftieth anniversary of the kingdom, and surrounded by a quartet of playful nymphs representative of the *belle époque* and considered rather scandalous in their day (Morton 1966: 234–36). The political significance of the space had been further reinforced by the celebrations for the marriage of the heir to the throne (the future Vittorio Emanuele III) which took place in the church in 1896, and provided an example of the new piazza's appropriateness for the nation state's recently developed grand ceremonial.

By this date, however, work had already commenced on the largest and most significant monumental urban space to be associated with the constitutional monarchy, planned around a structure the silhouette of which still dominates the skyline of the city, the Monument to Vittorio Emanuele II. Piazza Venezia, as the termination of Via del Corso in the heart of the city at the foot of the Capitoline hill was eventually chosen as the site to commemorate the country's first king. The site's central position in Rome ensured its visibility from all points throughout the city, and the replanning of the city with routes radiating out from it further reinforced its importance. The iconography of monarchical commemoration was a phenomenon which had to be reinvented in Rome since all the immediately available precedents were papal, and therefore associated with national disunity. There was also a general dismay at the prosaic quality of the bureaucratic structures which were springing up around the city for various ministries, such as the huge Ministry of Finance built with relative

9.5   Diagram of Piazza dell'Esedra, Rome, showing the relationship between the new structures and the footprint of the Baths of Diocletian, including Michelangelo's church of Santa Maria degli Angeli.

speed on Via Nazionale between 1870–77. The desire to reify the state in a way which downplayed utilititarian necessities, and concentrated all available energies on rhetoric would become known, in honour of the new king, as the *stile Umberto,* but forever associated with the monument to his father (Meeks 1966: 287–403).

Following the second competition for the monument in 1882 (in the search for an Italian winner) the young architect Giuseppe Sacconi (1854–1905) was declared victorious, having fulfilled the criteria of placing an equestrian statue before a monumental screen backing on to the Capitoline hill. The project required substantial demolition of medieval and renaissance buildings and its height would tower over venerable existing monuments such as the Roman Forum, the medieval Santa Maria in Aracoeli and the renaissance Campidoglio. Openly mocked by subsequent generations, the vast structure constructed between 1885 and 1911 defined Italy's desire to be seen as a substantial imperial power in the modern world, through a fanciful confection of largely purposeless steps, platforms, colonnades and dramatic iconography. In some respects Sacconi's design was a model of sobriety in comparison to many other of the competition entries, which combined architectural motifs on a huge scale

9.6   Piazza Venezia, Rome. The Monument to Vittorio Emanuele, presiding over the amplified and symmetrically ordered space. To the right is the Column of Trajan standing in the ruins of his forum.

and in unprecedented ways to attempt to express the relatively new concept of Italian national identity. The preferred design referred in an inventive way to ancient precedents, such as the ruins of the Temple of Fortuna Primigenia at Praeneste outside Rome, and other, hellenistic, temple complexes in Asia Minor. The archaeological taste was most evident in the structure's similarity to the type of ideal reconstructions of ancient sites produced by the holders of the *Prix de Rome* at the national academies in the city, an educational process which emphasized facility in architectonic composition in its purest form (Kirk 2005a: 231–39).

Sacconi's monument, the original footprint of which had to be widened for structural reasons, is composed of three layers which increase in height as they ascend. The base with its flight of steps opening to the north is relatively solid, but is itself carefully controlled so as not to obscure the upward gaze towards the immense equestrian statue of the king. He sits on a huge podium rising from a central rostrum on the intermediate level, where most of the allegorical sculptural decoration is displayed. The final level consists of a gently curving stoa as a screen wall with an immense corinthian colonnade. Critical opinion has generally been negative, although in his survey of Italian eighteenth and nineteenth centuries Meeks was rather more generous about its qualities.

It is breathtaking in its rich intricacy and variety of form, thus testifying in an inescapable manner to the least artistic passer-by the vast wealth lavished cheerfully on such a supremely non-utilitarian building. It is a triumphant statement of faith in a material future. A memorable image has been created. The form is unique. Rarely has so tremendous an artificial hill been constructed to support a temple. No traditional theme could have had equal power; no temple, dome, or triumphal arch could have been contrived on this scale, only a ziggurat or a pyramid. But neither of them would have the stamp of the nineteenth century so markedly. Artists and students have often dreamed such fantasies, but they have remained on paper. It is an astonishing achievement to have realized in three dimensions. (Meeks 1966: 346–7)

The scale of the structure allowed the *quadrigae* terminating either end of the screen wall to be seen from across the city, while at closer range, the Piazza Venezia itself was reconfigured to extend the monument's symmetrical totality. The axial relationship of the monument and Via del Corso, and the internal symmetry of the monument, were the starting points for further demolitions to create a precinct around the *Vittoriano* to Sacconi's revised plans from 1897. The ninth century basilica of San Marco and the fifteenth century Palazzo Venezia were regarded as venerable structures worthy of preservation. However the smaller Palazzetto Venezia was deemd an obstacle to appreciation of the new monument and was demolished and rebuilt further west in 1910–11, while the Palazzo Torlonia, remodelled by Valadier, had been completely removed in 1906–07 and a new building, the Palazzo delle Assicurazione Generale constructed as a pair to the Palazzo Venezia, on the other side of the axis (Reed 1950). Intended as a cenotaph for the king (who had been buried in the Pantheon) the body which was eventually interred at the foot of his statue was that of the Unknown Soldier of the Great War, his presence confirming the sacred character of the structure, the *Altare della Patria*, signalled by the permanent attention of a guard of honour for the eternal flame. That conflict's association with the completion of Italian territorial integrity through victory over the Central Powers meant that a few years later its signification of victory through sacrifice, with the *Risorgimento* conflated with the Great War, would acquire the presence of a new and ambitious political power.

In 1929 Benito Mussolini moved the head of government's office to the Palazzo Venezia, so that his view from the balcony during speeches would include this abstract embodiment of nationhood. The square continued to be amplified to accommodate the crowds fascism demanded, and the attachment of the space to a supposed imperial destiny was reinforced by the construction of the Via del Mare heading towards the coast, and of Via del Impero (Kostof 1973: 56–58). Inaugurated in 1932 to commemorate the tenth anniversary of Mussolini's assumption of office, its path provided a straight military parade route from the Colosseum on a line to Mussolini's balcony in the Palazzo Venezia across the excavated archaeological remains of the imperial fora. The deadening symmetry of the original arrangement was therefore overlaid with a diagonal relationship which suggested the new regime's aspirations to action. Given the complexity of the site, a central traffic interchange where routes across the city from all directions met, and the desire to expose archaeological and historical sites such as the Capitoline hill itself in the presence of a monument to the relatively young state, what results is an exaggerated placelessness where a vast structure dominates an enormous vacancy in the heart of the city. Despite its appropriations of antique dress, the Piazza Venezia represents all the symptomatic conditions of the modern city, dominated by traffic, reliant on the effects of the tourist spectacle and generally disorienting and unappealing to the citizen.

Whatever the rhetorical confidence of these new spectacular urban spaces, with grand figurative sculptures, artificial lighting and in their commercial areas plate glazing presenting significant opportunities for material display, Italy faced specific problems which were masked by these stage sets. The political situation was one of frustration and apparent stasis, with national destiny converging on territorial expansion overseas to create a colonial empire, ambitions which had led to foreign adventures in Abyssinia which resulted in humiliation in 1898, and then the annexation of Libya in 1911, from a weakened Ottoman Empire. Domestically anarchism was responsible for a number of provocations and outrages not the least the assassination of the king Umberto I at Monza in 1900, a flash point in the tensions between property owners and the growing ranks of the impoverished industrial class. The new spaces of the developing Italian cities provided arenas in which these rival groups could encounter one another, where class divisions became explicit in civic spaces in which the spiritual presence of the church had no role because of the *froideur* between the kingdom of Italy and the Papacy, and economic and social status was the ultimate signifier in the secularized city.

Against this luxurious but inequitable and disaffected urban environment the city to come was to announce itself at the end of the first decade of the new century with the cultural provocations of the Futurists. They were dismayed by the aesthetic stagnation that they identified with Italy's obsession with historic architecture. Dispensing with the constraints of tradition and convention the Futurists proposed that an aesthetic should be formed from the new urban sensations of noise and dissonance, speed and size. If the city in itself was to continue to be valued it was to find its worth not in its columns, arcades, plazas and flights of stairs appreciated by the discerning pedestrian but in the ironwork and glazing, elevations and piling up of floors visible through the windscreen of a speeding motor car. In one specific performance in 1910 the Futurist leader, Filippo Tommaso Marinetti ascended the Clock Tower in Piazza San Marco in Venice and denounced the city's decay and dependence on tourist income, ensuring his message was understandable to the visitors by throwing down leaflets produced in several languages. Marinetti proposed that the decaying *palazzi* of the city be demolished and used to fill in the canals, but his implicit target was across the piazza. The campanile in Piazza San Marco had collapsed in 1902 and its replica was nearing completion. Above all the new campanile demonstrated the policy of *com'era, dov'era*, 'as it was, where it was', which sought to preserve the Italian urban landscape as an historical environment (Plant 2002: 261–64). The aesthetic violence to traditional civic values which the Futurist scenario envisaged, however, was nothing to the social and political threat which would be unleashed with the Great War, and which the Futurists would see as the fulfilment of their ambitions.

While political turmoil was a feature of many competing nation states at the beginning of the twentieth century, architectural and urban projects in Italy had specific significance because the country's unrivalled cultural heritage. It was a field in which the country was identified as a leader, and about which her many visitors felt they could voice an opinion. In the Italian situation, the intimacy of the context was especially complex, since the architectural forms and political precedents which other nation states exploited were often Italian in origin. The achievement of national unification had created the first opportunity in modern times for the manifestation of an Italian national consciousness which represented an independent state, but it had also drawn attention to the specific meanings of their architectural and urban forms. The eclecticism of the new architecture, often presented within sight of authentic examples of the past, was seen as either fulfilling the idea of inevitable progress towards national self-fulfillment, or as demonstrating the superficiality of an inauthentic contemporary political settlement. This intellectual division between the emotional pull of tradition and the aspiration to modernity would continue to characterise Italian attitudes to the city throughout the twentieth century. While the redevelopment of Rome as capital of the kingdom of Italy had been generally recognized to be problematic and unnecessarily destructive, the energy of the new state could be directed both towards the systematic preservation of its heritage, and the remaking of its cities in a manner which reflected its economic growth. Fresh impetus would be given to this dual process after World War One, and Mussolini's accession to power following the ensuing political crisis. The parallel developments of state archaeology and urban scenography were then combined in the service of a concerted campaign of totalitarian propaganda.

# 10

# Fascism: The urban language of authoritarianism

The kingdom of Italy's entry into the Great War in 1915 produced several results. Victory over the Central Powers, most especially the old antagonist Austria-Hungary, placed Italy at the top table as the borders of Europe were redrawn at the peace conference at Versailles. But expectations had been raised which could not be fulfilled and which would lead to civil disorder between rival paramilitary political groupings. On the Left, the Russian Revolution of 1917 offered the prospect of a similar overthrow of church and monarchy in Italy in the cause of the equalization of society. On the Right, the territorial expansion brought about at enormous loss of life on the Alpine front would lead to the enhancement of nationalist attitudes. The unemployment that followed the mass demobilization, and the inability of weak governments to provide effective remedies produced the situation in which the rising demagogue Benito Mussolini would be invited by the king to form a government. From 1922 until its initial collapse in 1943, Mussolini's government, through its murderous removal of its opponents, its control of the media, its provision of employment through self-glorifying public works, its foreign adventurism and its pursuit of racial policies would embed the term fascism in popular usage.

The rhetoric of fascism found its most persistent form in architectural works, where every Italian city shared in the creation of an image of a new Italy which was less indebted to overt historicism than that favoured by the despised bourgeois democracy, was radical in its use of modern materials and forms, but which none the less was required to express national identity in accordance with the regime's cultural policies (Etlin 1991). Fascism was, of course, deeply ambivalent about its position in relation to culture. Roman and Italian heritage, insofar as it represented previous periods of political power, was useful as a fig leaf to cover exposed political might, but contemporary art with its rival avant-garde groupings did not provide the same service of cultural certainties from the past. The Futurists, with their emphasis on physical action and sensation could have been calculated to appeal to a regime famous for its thuggery, indeed Marinetti would become a leading cultural figure within the regime. With a more culturally conservative agenda, the Milan based *Novocento* (Twentieth Century) group captured a more subtle form of urban disquiet, but ultimately neither they nor the Futurists were entirely satisfactory as organs for the promotion of fascism. Mussolini's delusion as his regime retained power was to see himself not as solely the revolutionary man of action, but also as the heir to the imperial Roman mantle, wielding his pick axe to construct *autostrade* and to expose antiquities (Kostof 1978).

Mussolini's general policy for the state was to increase the population and improve its health, with a view to creating a martial spirit that would support his international ambitions. At one level this could have benign effects for the individual, but his or her ideological worth was of importance only in the mass. As Mussolini put it

Anti-individualistic, the Fascist conception of life stresses the importance of the State and accepts the individual only insofar as his interests coincide with those of the state, which stands for the conscience and the universal will of man as a historic entity. (Mussolini 1936: 12)

The body of the fascist therefore had an historical destiny which would be seen as the creation of an empire, especially once Mussolini's fantasies would begin to be outstripped by the maniacal ambitions of his northern European rival Hitler. In Italy the appeal to a renewed Roman cultural *imperium* would increasingly feature as public projects became more megalomaniac, but even relatively early in the regime, the exploitation of Roman typologies and forms could serve to suggest the inevitable validity of the regime as part of an historical continuity. The requirement for propaganda to represent scenes of progress, however, meant that the relationship to the past could only be highly selective, if not sometimes deliberately falsified. Periods such as the middle ages, when the Italian political scene was marked by foreign domination and civil war, would not be deemed suitable for emulation despite their great cultural achievements. Urban environments deemed to embody cultural decadence, for example the quarter around the mausoleum of Augustus and the densely built up area adjoining the imperial fora in Rome could be swept away to reveal the powerful ancient ruins beneath. The production of urban spaces during this period, therefore, took place in two different contexts which underline the simultaneously forward and backward looking attitudes, firstly the introduction into existing situations of fascist environments and secondly their creation *ex novo*, and an example of each will be explored in detail.

The first space which exposes many of the issues introduced above is in Brescia, Piazza della Vittoria, and is another example of that city's hosting of emblematic urban spaces. An analysis of the principal fascist intervention can be used to expose aspects of the false memory of the city (Canniffe 1997). One significance of the squares in Brescia, which Piazza della Vittoria brings into sharp focus is the continuity of tradition by which each of the medieval, renaissance and fascist examples reflected the Roman precedent by a creative misinterpretation. The urban type of a rectangular space dominated by a principal monumental building or complex went through a series of transformations, with a longitudinal axial arrangement of the medieval piazza

10.1    Piazza Augusto Imperatore, Rome. To the left the excavated remains of the Mausoleum of Augustus and to the right one of the buildings framing the new space.

and the cross axial plan of the renaissance square. Geometries can be identified so that the framework of the spaces and their interconnections can be mapped, and an order be discerned for the distribution of historical fragments and forms. However, Piazza della Vittoria was not built up like Piazza del Duomo by layers of continuous construction, although that illusion was attempted, nor could fascism allow any multiplicity of rival iconographies as Piazza della Loggia had witnessed. This duality culminated in a situation where not only the new fascist piazza referred iconographically to the Roman era, but the genuine remains of that period were refabricated to underscore the connection to the present. As an exercise in urban and political design, it evoked memories

10.2   Diagram of Piazza della Vittoria, Brescia showing the *torrione*, the portico of the post and telegraph office, the *aregno*, and the tower 'of the revolution'.

and connections to Brescia's historic spaces, but Piazza della Vittoria has a unsettling quality. In both cases a rectangular space running north–south was delineated, with the principal public structure aligned axially at the northern end. The lumpen character of Marcello Piacentini's architecture forms subtle connections with the existing urban fabric and the spaces beyond, the new piazza attempting in its geometry and iconography to bring to summation Brescian urban development (Lupano 1991: 108–11). Visual connections to medieval and renaissance spaces were allied to an orientation and formal typology having their explicit source in the remains of the Roman town of

10.3  Piazza della Vittoria, Brescia. The: tower 'of the revolution' viewed from the base of the *torrione*. The blank frame originally contained an equestrian portrait of Mussolini.

Brixia. As has been referred to in the last chapter, Piacentini (1881–1960) was originally a disciple of Sitte. A picturesque attitude to geometry, the clear definition of public space, the exploitation of specific vistas and connections with other spaces characterize the Sittesque influence, while the architectural language is much more generic.

Piazza della Vittoria, completed between 1929–32, was itself the final result of a large planning exercise to improve the functioning of the city, a

rationalization which was abandoned due to expense in favour of the rhetorical monumentalization of an area of the historic centre, medieval in date and deemed an obstacle to progress. However, functional planning was suspended in favour of a more overtly representational scheme, though the immediate reason for the site of the new piazza was the demolition of an existing unhygienic quarter. The new public space thus created glorified Mussolini directly, being completed to celebrate his tenth anniversary in power, but the variety of its profile and materiality attempted to obscure the fact that it was entirely constructed within a few years. Paradoxically, despite the attempt to portray an organic but deceptive history, each element is treated as an individual monument, with peripheral connections through ground floor arcades used to form the enclosed civic realm that had been favoured by Sitte. The purpose of a public forum was signalled by the honorific position provided for the modern mean's of communication, the post, telegraph and telephone office, but also by the placing of an orator's podium or *aregno* decorated with scenes of Brescian progress up to fascism, and standing at the foot of a small tower ('of the revolution') which was originally adorned with a portrait relief of Mussolini on horseback. Diagonally opposite the *aregno*, a 12-storey office tower, the *torrione*, provided the largest single element in the piazza while a figurative connection to this symbol of urban progress was established through the siting of a colossal naked male statue at its base, Arturo Dazzi's *The Fascist Age*. The statue's presence was intended to evoke the same form of heroism associated with Michelangelo's *David* in Piazza della Signoria in Florence from four centuries earlier, although its sculptural quality was far below the level of that model.

The diagrammatic quality of this ornamentation and the simplicity of the overall planning strategy is ameliorated by the picturesque massing of the elements. The axial view towards the post office is varied by the asymmetrical pairing of the tower of the revolution in marble and the brick mass of the office tower. These three elements then frame and dominate the views of the square, the *torrione* suggesting a certain aggressive power, the tower of the revolution rather unsubtly in conflict with the dome of the baroque cathedral beyond in Piazza del Duomo, and the post office portico producing a dull echo of the Roman *capitolium*. It has also been suggested by Richard Etlin that the early version of Piacentini's post office had referred to precedent in the three bayed form of the renaissance Palazzo della Loggia, the barrel vaulted roof of which was visible in profile behind the post office in the neighbouring Piazza della Loggia (Etlin 1991: 418–26).

All the major piazze in Brescia can be seen to follow the pattern established by the Roman forum, but far from imitating that origin, the elements of Piazza della Vittoria subvert their antique precedents. For example the portico of the *capitolium* can be seen to have its contemporary parallel in the facade of the post office. The corinthian order of the original, however, was too feminine for this robust example of state patronage, and instead Piacentini reduced the members to a blunt banded pier the profile of which vaguely resembled a *fasces*, a less obvious form than the literal use of an eagle-headed axe *fasces* that Piacentini had previously employed in his triumphal arch at Bolzano of 1928. The bronze statue of the personification of Victory discovered in the early nineteenth century, after whom the new square was named, was herself too delicate in scale and form for the new environment. She was replaced as the

10.5   Piazza della Vittoria, Brescia. The post and telegraph office, the piers of which take the form of emblematic representations of *fasces*.

presiding figure by the hulking form of Dazzi's *The Fascist Age* with its clenched right fist echoing the architectural raised fist of the *torrione*. Antonio Maraini's historical panels on the *aregno* below the tower of the revolution unwind the thread of the city's history as the blackshirts are shown as the inheritors of Brescian and Roman culture. This flow of time becomes a complete cycle as

10.6   Piazza della Vittoria, Brescia. Detail of the *aregno*, where the relief shows contemporary fascists giving the Roman salute, and ancient Romans with the statue of Victory.

the Roman soldiers worship a representation of the Victory, and fascists greet each other with the Roman salute and both modern and ancient figures grasp the *fasces* (Piacentini 1932).

Historical reference can create rich urban experiences over time, as both Piazza del Duomo and Piazza della Loggia demonstrate, but Piacentini sought to overcome two thousand years by a thin veneer of allusion. Although the insertion of the new piazza into the existing fabric owes its origin to the an interpretation of the Sittesque phenomenological method, the publication of the square on its completion in 1932 revealed the attempt to recast the scheme in the manner of a technological advance. Piacentini's work enabled authoritarian power to be validated through the appeal to specific urban memories, resting on foundations which were archaeologically speculative, reconstructed for propagandistic purposes. Such memories were themselves simultaneously invalidated by the representation of this cultural excavation as itself progressive and advanced, when it systematically subsumed the future to a highly selective interpretation of the past. Genuine Roman archaeological remains, uncovered during the clearing of the densely built-up medieval quarter, and therefore an authentic urban memory, were not allowed to disturb Piacentini's chill reinterpretation of an atrium for the tower of the revolution. Similarly the organic process of historical decay in Piazza del Foro could not be allowed to give witness to the true fate of empires, as was discussed in Chapter 1. Instead history had to be reversed and a false memory constructed as a more theatrical ruin. However, with the inevitable irony which historical events provide, ruination came to Piazza della Vittoria in 1945 with destruction caused by the Royal Air Force bombardment (Galli 1975). After subsequent repair and the removal of the more obvious fascist insignia it too is now only a simulacrum of its original state.

The self-conscious referencing of historical precedent reached its present crisis in the early twentieth century because of the divorce between architectural clothing and contemporary engineering. Piacentini's response to that dilemma in architecture had been to reduce the complexity of traditional architectural languages to the bluntly emblematic, while blurring the connections into the existing urban fabric. In the politico-cultural sphere, when he inaugurated the square, Mussolini was on the point of abandoning the trappings of aesthetic revolution in favour of a wholesale self-identification with the legacy of Augustus and his empire. The representation of the regime would then largely employ a traditional language, even when it was representing tanks, armoured cars and aeroplanes in marble mosaic pavements, as will be described in relation to the next example the Piazzale del Impero at the Foro Mussolini (now Foro Italico) in Rome constructed in 1937. The Foro Italico in Rome remains one of the most evocative spaces created under Mussolini because of the directness of its political propaganda and its completeness as an example of fascist urbanism. Dedicated to the training of the body, its stadia and gymnasia remain in active use for the highest levels of national and international sport set against a background of persistent fascist iconography that barely acknowledges the national ignominy in which the regime resulted. Ostensibly this imagery from seventy years ago is as harmless as that of Roman antiquity, arcane in its references to lost empires. There is a curiously kitsch quality to the modern sporting apparatus that adorns the heroically naked statues, yet the regular slogan DUCE A NOI might as easily be written in contemporary spray paint as in ageless mosaic. Providing the central distributive artery for the complex, Piazzale del Impero is the most

10.7 Piazzale del Impero, Foro Italico, Rome. A view along the central spine towards the obelisk dedicated to Mussolini, with in the foreground a mosaic of Apollo holding a laurel wreath and the *fasces*.

didactic essay in the ideology of the regime, where its unambiguous purpose is portrayed in words and images. The Rome of Augustus served as the model for the iconography of this space (Greco 1991).

Foro Mussolini was developed in the late 1920s, on vacant land to the north of the city beneath Monte Mario, a site which was resonant with fascist mythology. Here the blackshirts had camped before the 'march on Rome', the

10.8   *Stadio dei Marmi*, Foro Italico, Rome. This figure, poised with his football, represents the southern city of Bari.

post-rationalized 'revolutionary' event which brought Mussolini to power. It was therefore deemed a potent situation in which to train Italian youth under the auspices of the *Opera Nazionale Balilla*. Although the site's initial development was piecemeal, the rural surroundings provided echoes of the gymnasia of antiquity, and classical iconography was to come to dominate the site (Ferrero

2004: 34–55). Enrico del Debbio was initially the architect in charge of the project, creating the Academy of Physical Education as an arched symmetrical block with applied *Novocento* details that faced the Tiber and led through to the *Stadio dei Marmi* with its sixty male nude statues. A further axis between the river and the larger stadium, the *Stadio dei Cipressi*, was developed with a covered swimming pool as a pair to the original academy building. Between them and adjacent to the river Costantino Costantini erected an obelisk of a single piece of Carrara marble which remains inscribed to Mussolini. Closer to the *Stadio dei Cipressi* a fountain in the form of a sunken marble sphere was designed by Mario Paniconi and Giulio Pediconi. The axial space between the sphere and the obelisk was to become the Piazzale del Impero, the most significant ceremonial space of the complex, under Luigi Moretti (1907–73). Moretti had risen to early prominence as a young architect through his astute social connections. His work was characterized by a smooth clarity of form, exemplified by the design of the *Palestra del Duce*, within the new swimming complex at Foro Mussolini. Here the literal embodiment of the state in the form of Mussolini's torso (so often exposed for the harvesting of crops and the digging of tunnels) was to be exercised in a veined marble hall and tanned on a discreetly screened sunbed. In a similarly luxurious architectural language, Moretti's design of the fencing school, the *Accademia di Scherma*, this language was extended to a marble clad building expressive of the internal gymnastic volumes, and terminating the southern part of the Foro Mussolini (Bucci and Mulazzani 2000: 53–63, 68–69).

The urban landscape which Moretti produced at the Piazzale del Impero had to unite a group of routes and monuments which had developed during the previous decade. His compositional strategy was one of imposing a strong control on the form of the space as already defined, and has a muted palette of white marble and white and black mosaic. The central axis between the fountain and obelisk is treated as a raised spine flanked by lower mosaic pavements in rectangular frames. Mosaics also surround the circular space around the fountain where several routes crossed. These featured, between panels of fascist slogans, images of ancient and contemporary sports and military feats. Maps of ancient and contemporary Rome reinforced the connection between past and present, while large marble monoliths defined the edges tapering towards the obelisk, each dedicated to a significant event from the *Risorgimento*, the kingdom of Italy's participation in the Great War, and the rise of Fascism. This culminated in a large block reproducing the text of Mussolini's declaration of the Italian Empire in 1937.

As was referred to earlier, these imperial aspirations had featured in fascist ideology from early days, fuelled by resentment at the colonial possessions of the other Great Powers, a humiliation at the hands of the Abyssinians in an earlier attempt at colonization, and a lack of total satisfaction with the settlement of the Treaty of Versailles. Mussolini looked back to a time when the most powerful capital city in the world was not London, Paris or Washington but Rome and wrote

The Fascist State expresses the will to exercise power and to command. Here the Roman tradition is embodied in a conception of strength. Imperial power, as understood by the Fascist doctrine, is not only territorial, or military, or commercial: it is also spiritual and ethical. An imperial nation, that is to say a nation which directly or indirectly is a leader of others, can exist without the need of conquering a single square mile of territory. Fascism sees in the imperialistic spirit – i.e. in the tendency of nations to expand – a manifestation of their vitality. (Mussolini 1936: 45)

Despite the denial of any aspiration for territorial expansion, the invocation of antiquity in the form and scale of structures such as those at Foro Italico represented the imperial direction to which the regime increasingly looked. Aspiring to an innovatory, indeed revolutionary character, the regime found inspiration in the attitudes and achievements of the past. As a result of material shortages brought about by international sanctions imposed after the invasion of Abyssinia in 1935, technological progress needed to be harnessed within a specifically Italian context, and the glorification of Augustus provided a surrogate for that of Mussolini. Every means of propaganda could be exploited to this purpose, but architecture provided a considerable degree of the requisite permanence, and indeed in their unadorned form bore a close similarity to the built but ruined memories of Augustus which survived into the twentieth century. Diane Favro's description of the Augustan Campus Martius might serve as a description of Mussolini's intentions for the Forum which bore his name.

...the entire district could be conceptualised as a vestibule for Rome. Visitors to the city experienced a huge district of grand marble structures laid out with Hellenistic orthogonal precision. A few Republican buildings and sculptures, notably those transferred from the Capitoline, established the venerable heritage of the city, yet the predominant message projected by this district was about Augustus and his impressive achievements. Vitruvius argued that a great house needed an impressive forecourt (Vitr. 5.2). So did a great city. The Augustan Campus Martius served this purpose admirably. (Favro 1996: 207–08)

In creating a symbolic landscape for fascism, Moretti chose an iconographic language which worked with temporal and corporal references. The images of the mosaic pavement blurred antiquity and modernity, with sport identified as a training for war, culminating in sanitized episodes from the Abyssinian campaign. The Augustan image of Mussolini finds its spatial realization in the delineation of Piazzale del Impero as a vast abstracted torso, where the urban scale of the complex focuses collective attention on the image of the body of the martial athlete. The ancient image of Rome as having the form of a lion, illustrated in the pavement, was superseded by that of the new city being remade literally in the image of the dictator. Mussolini's self-identification with the figure and legacy of Augustus provided the regime's propagandists (including architects and designers) with ready sources for iconography with which to represent the leader. Augustus himself had consciously refined the images with which political power was represented, dispensing with the Egyptian references which had characterized the years around Caesar's assassination, and reviving distinctively Roman imagery, albeit often derived from hellenistic sources. While the image of Augustus had become the mode with which to represent imperial aspirations, Mussolini's architectural campaigns in Rome itself, and his military campaigns in pursuit of an empire, explicitly echoed Augustus's activities. Through this exploitation of the cult of Augustus, Mussolini sought to emulate not merely his political success, but also the divine status which Augustus assumed through proxy via the imperial family cult. Despite the expediency of the Lateran Treaty and the rapprochement between church and state in 1929, fascism continued to aspire to a status beyond a mere political affiliation. Through the exploitation and fabrication of martyrs a sacrificial aspect was introduced to party buildings which confirmed the self-image of a cult. Mussolini was both the principal minister of such a cult and its chief object of worship. His image, formed increasingly in imitation of Augustus took on a multilayered significance as a quasi-mythical being. A key image in this regard was the statue *Augustus of Prima Porta* which was replicated for example during Mussolini's clearing of the imperial fora and the creation of Via del Impero. The significance of this image in antiquity was immense, as Paul Zanker has observed.

The princeps who wears this new image of victory on his breast plate becomes the representative of divine providence and the will of the gods. It is not a question of heroic deeds; through his very existence, the offspring of the gods guarantees world order. The harmony between the state and the gods guarantees the world order. Inspite of the glamorous appeal of this statue, it is not incompatible with the many images of the togate Augustus with veiled head. He had no need to present himself as military victor in a series of new and spectacular exploits, for he possessed this quality permanently by virtue of his close relationship to the gods. (Zanker 1988: 192)

Spiro Kostof has identified elements of this image in the mosaic panels decorating another Fascist urban intervention, that around the Mausoleum of Augustus. (Kostof 1978: 304) This image of Augustus, propagandized relentlessly by Mussolini (especially in celebration on the 2000th anniversary of his birth in 1937) was itself sedimented with references to the representation of heroes in the pre-Roman world. John Pollini has noted

For a Roman, ...the statue of Augustus from Prima Porta would have surpassed ideologically its polykleitan prototype and any other heroic Greek model, especially Alexander the Great. ...In Roman thinking, Augustus, who brought peace through victory to the world, far outstripped any Greek hero and is therefore represented in the Prima Porta statue as the vir sanctus et gravis, fortis et sapiens, as well as saviour, benefactor, and inaugurator of a new Golden Age. Above all, Augustus is presented as the new archetypal hero of a true world state. (Pollini 1995).

In his campaign to be seen as such a figure, Mussolini adopted not only the imperial image of Augustus, but also the naked heroism of the archetypes which Augustus himself invoked implicitly through the creation of an iconography of power. The undecorated forms of speech favoured by fascism, the stripped forms of the architecture employed and the cult of the martial

10.9   Piazzale del Impero, Foro Italico, Rome. The fountain in the form of a sunken marble sphere.

body created an environment of propaganda from which buildings and spaces are the most enduring remnants (Falasca-Zamponi 1997). To return to consideration of the Foro Italico in the situation of the partially completed monumental complex which Moretti had to address, the distances involved, and the individual characteristics of the buildings and stadia required the introduction of a strong unifying spatial element. In contrast to the sort of dense urban situation which might have been encountered closer to the historic centre (in the projects for the Mausoleum of Augustus, which will be referred to further in Chapter 14, and the imperial fora where the figural space would have appeared as a negative entity carved from the surrounding built volumes) at the Foro Mussolini a positive spatial gesture had to be employed, figurally representing the body of the dictator. This situation parodies the christian iconography of the cruciform church, dually representing the body of Christ and the primary instrument of his passion, but also is an echo of Dinocrates's proposal to recast Mount Athos as a statue of Alexander the Great, as relayed by Vitruvius in his second book (McEwen 2003: 92–102). Symbolism of a very direct sort featured in the propaganda of fascism, from blackshirts spelling out the word DUCE in a crowd, to monumentalizations of the capital letter M. Given Moretti's interest in form, is it too much to suggest that the anthropomorphic qualities of the Piazzale del Impero might be more than just a coincidence of axial planning and convenience of circulation?

An anthropomorphic reading of the space would feature the circular fountain as the head, with the central platform as the spine, the monolithic inscribed blocks as the ribs, and the obelisk as the penis. Echoing the ithyphallic representations of antiquity, the image of Mussolinian space draws power from that of Augustus, with the conjunction of obelisk, pavement and circular mausoleum at the Horologium Augusti referred to in Chapter 1. This anthropomorphic tracing reflected that of an antique hero, but it also aspired to represent a contemporary superman. John Pollini observes of Mussolini's ancient model that

The image of Augustus, as transmitted in the Prima Porta statue as a whole, is both retrospective and prospective: retrospective in that it invites comparison with the prototypical ideal of the Classical past; prospective in that it reflects the optimism of the Augustan Principate and transforms Augustus into the new model of the heroic ideal. A new model could be established only if it superseded some old archetypes(s). (Pollini 1995: 272)

However, far from its physical presence as a neutral marble image, contemporary observers, such as Simonetta Falasca-Zamponi, perceive the image of Mussolini as animated especially in regard to its relationship with the masses. The impulse to sportsmanship which the dictator propagated echoed the Augustan patronage of athleticism and the games, but the accelerated possibilities of propaganda in the twentieth century allowed the icon to be vivid, and Mussolini in particular to be seen as an active man

...in the totalitarian politics of fascism, there was only one focus of desire, only one object of pleasure: the regime anthropomorphically embodied in the public persona of the Duce, Mussolini. Living in a different constellation than film actors did, but still a star, Mussolini attracted interest and admiration; he projected aura and awe. And the regime seemed to count on the spectacular nature of his political trajectory in order to satisfy the consuming needs of the population. The image of Mussolini sold well, whether in postcards or soap bars or as a model of style. Records and radio diffused his words, the cinema propagated his icon, posters and calendars commemorated his deeds. Political publicity exalted the figure of Mussolini as the link between the people and the nation, the expression of fascist principles. The "gendered mass" was supposed to adhere to the regime and place authority in the hands of the state through its faith in Mussolini. The Duce would then be able to capitalise on this love and turn the female mass into a virile army whose spiritual attributes overcame material predispositions. A loving body of admirers was only conceived as depersonalized and desensitized integration of the body politic. (Falasca-Zamponi 1997: 144–45)

The fascist emphasis on the cult of the leader and of the body had its denouement in the display of Mussolini's mutilated corpse in Milan in the aftermath of the liberation in 1945. In an architectural parallel to the eventual treatment of his body, during his fall from power Mussolini's image was removed from thousands of public buildings throughout Italy, along with other symbols of his regime. Yet in Rome, at the renamed Foro Italico, a massive marble obelisk still bears his name and his vainglorious proclamations still frame the Piazzale del Impero.

10.10 Piazzale del Impero, Foro Italico, Rome. The durable mosaic pavement features much overt fascist iconography.

In other examples of urban design under fascism the references which architects employed were either essentially historicist in their allusions to Roman exemplars, or were rationalist in structure if not in execution. At Foro Mussolini, the overwhelming conception of fascism was neither nostalgic nor futuristic but instead converged on the moment of action. In its insistent iconography of the athletic body, in mosaic, in statuary, but above all in the flesh of the athletes, the fundamental unit out of which the corporate state was consructed was represented. The exemplar for such bodies was that of the *duce*, and the plan symbolism which Moretti employed for Piazzale del Impero therefore took the emblematic form of his body. This identification with its leader had echoes to the cult of Augustus which Mussolini propagated, but in terms of antiquity also echoed Augustus's self-identification with the human ideal, either divine or heroic, as represented by the Doryphoros, the canon of Polyklites. The descent of this ideal image into kitsch under fascism, as interpreted through the marble footballers and skiers of the *Stadio dei Marmi*, or mosaic depictions of bathing suits, only serves to underline the delusions of the regime and its leader. Notwithstanding Kostof's query regarding the successfulness of political propaganda as urban design, these troubling images remain powerful (Kostof 1978: 322).

The impact of fascist urbanism was, of course, much more extensive than these two monumental examples of the genre. The autocratic impulse of fascism provided the political cause for large scale urban interventions and extensions. Every city had its fascist structures, either directly associated

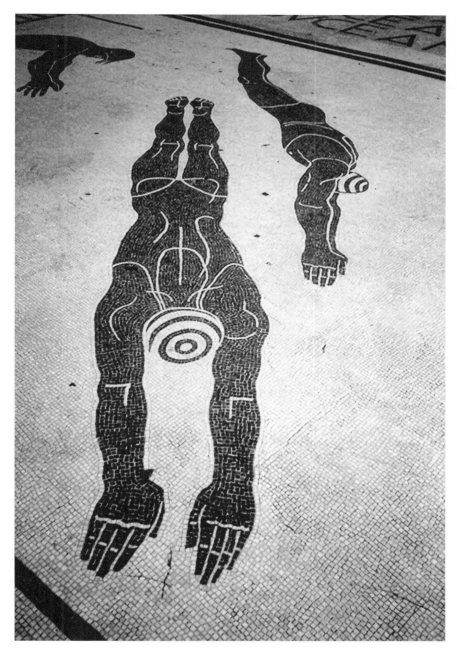

10.11  Piazzale del Impero, Foro Italico, Rome. The ancient technique of mosaic is also used to represent contemporary athletes.

with the party, or a product of one of the arms of the corporate state, such as collective housing. While the historical reference has been emphasized in the above examples, programmes of completely new construction and settlement, as in the towns created in the drained Pontine marshes, such as Sabaudia, Littoria (now Latina) and Aprilia, and those created in Italy's

10.12 Piazza Roma, Aprilia. The church of San Michele Arcangelo rebuilt after destruction during the Second World War.

colonies, presented the opportunity to be more forward looking, but they featured traditionally defined honorific public spaces (Besana, Carli, Devoti and Prisco 2002). South of the capital, a new Rome was planned in the later 1930s for a projected exposition in 1942, a suburb of the city now called E.U.R. Planned under the aegis of Piacentini, the symmetrical clarity of baroque precedents were exploited by the team working under Giovanni Muzio in the design of the Porta Imperiale. The principal axial route around which the settlement is planned is punctuated by a pair of columned exedra which bound a large space bisected by the main road from Rome. This division made it impossible for the enclosed area to be regarded as a unified space, the inflated colonnades reduced to monumental scenography for speeding cars (Irace 1994: 46). The survival of these barely established environments after the onset of war suggests that beneath the veneer of fascist symbolism the urban structures were appropriate and based on enduring principles. In the postwar period, with the regime overthrown and the country suffering from serious deprivation, the highly dubious certainties represented by these examples would be replaced by a more experimental method which eschewed the rhetorical use of urban space that defined the public face of fascism, but also dispensed with the traditional spatial hierarchies of Italian architecture and urbanism.

# PART IV

# URBAN EXPRESSION IN AN AGE OF UNCERTAINTY

# 11

# Neo-Realism: Urban form and *la dolce vita*

Italy's entry into the Second World War in 1940, her surrender to the Allies in 1943, German occupation and the civil war which would follow before eventual liberation in 1945 punctured the self-confidence of the cultural and political elite. Mussolini's adventurism had destroyed the economy and left large numbers of the surviving population suffering penury and disease. However, reconstruction would be entered into urgently because of the tense political situation of the start of the Cold War. As a frontline state in the new ideological conflict, bordering both Communist controlled Yugoslavia and Soviet-occupied Austria Italy would benefit from American aid as her industrial base was re-established and the post-fascist constitution was designed, with the monarchy ended by plebiscite in 1946 (the first occasion on which the franchise was extended to women), and an Italian Republic declared. Civil war had produced a highly fractured political order which would be exacerbated by the onset of superpower tensions between the former Allies. The elections of 1948 were dominated by the divisions among the former resistance comrades and the spectre of Soviet domination through the agency of the Italian Communist Party, but were won by the Christian Democrats. Backed by the church and the United States they were to remain an almost permanent feature of Italy's numerous short-lived post-war governments for the next five decades.

Fascist patronage had tainted all construction for two decades, and architects and planners therefore had to start from a position of degree zero in their proposals for the reconstruction. The former regime had been associated not only with ponderously rhetorical public work, but also with Italian modernism, and the leading figures in the profession expressed a degree of ambiguity in their recreation of architectural languages after 1945, indulging in a form of amnesia which attempted to cleanse pre-war Italian modernism of its now unpalatable fascist associations. The demise of totalitarianism and its overt appropriation of history would bring with it a rupture in the continuous tradition of defined urban space as an organic and unconscious reflection of the political order. The manipulative force with which fascism had exploited historical forms for party propaganda, dispensing with its early adherence to modernity, meant that in the initial post-war period any attachment to historical forms would be regarded as politically suspicious. Therefore this period of post-war reconstruction provided a pause for reflection in the matter of urban space, an understandable reaction to the negative use of the rhetoric of the piazza under fascism. If fascist spaces, and the fascist use of spaces, had created a monologue of public expression, the political pluralism of the new era would occupy these same spaces with a noisy visual battle of rival party posters. The messages of the parties, increasing in number and impact during elections and referenda, would also have to compete for attention with commercial images and illuminated signage, as well as the more local, customary and transitory black bordered death notices. The evening passegiata, the collective stroll through streets and squares, would only be relaxing if one ignored the cacophonous rival claims to party or brand loyalty (Cheles 2001).

Within the architectural field, with the destruction of other European cities presenting a form of *tabula rasa* to urban designers, the Italian situation was something of a paradox. There had been massive bombardment mainly at the behest of the Allies, with the Germans attempting to salvage a reputation for *kultur* by minimizing the loss of historic environments. Damage to urban centres caused by the struggle for territorial control meant that their reconstruction was a priority, although Italy's housing problems in 1945 were extremely serious. The level of destruction in centres such as Florence, where Giovanni Michelucci (1891–1990) supervised the reconstruction of the city quarters adjacent to both ends of the Ponte Vecchio spared by the Germans, led to a renewed interest in the actuality of historical models, free from the propagandistic purposes to which urban heritage had been put under the former regime. As well as its cultural value, there was a recognition of the potential for tourism which carefully restored and promoted historical environments could attract. Eventually a significant school of urban conservation would spring from this research. But most immediately pressing was the need to improve the living conditions of the poor, which would lead to a concentration on the part of architects and planning authorities on the provision of housing, the best examples of which combined innovative and vernacular technologies to produce new types of popular environment, labelled subsequently by the term neo-realism (Rowe 1997: 100–16).

The combination of Italy's reduced circumstances and the desire by different cultural groups to expose the actuality of the experience of war resulted in the exploration of neo-realism in a number of cultural forms. Although applied to literature and the visual arts, its most famous products were films, especially *Rome, Open City* (1946) by Roberto Rossellini and *The Bicycle Thieves* (1948) by Vittorio de Sica (Seavitt 1998: 129–31). Popular and critical successes, the films portrayed aspects of Roman life during the struggle for liberation and its economic consequences through the integration of documentary techniques and the use of non-actors which reflected experience back to their audiences, rather than offering them distracting spectacles. Although, with their depiction of the

11.1 Oltrarno, Florence. A detail of Giuseppe Michelucci's contextual postwar reconstruction adjacent to the Ponte Vecchio.

direct brutalities of fascism and the deprivations of post-war unemployment the films presented a politically engaged position, they were commercial products which were responding to the popular mood. As a genre neo-realist cinema also dealt with peasant themes, but it was the urban context which featured in these definitive examples. The city depicted, though, was not that of central places, the

11.2   Diagram of Piazza dei Cinquecento and Stazione Termini, Rome, showing the relationship with the remains of the ancient Servian Wall.

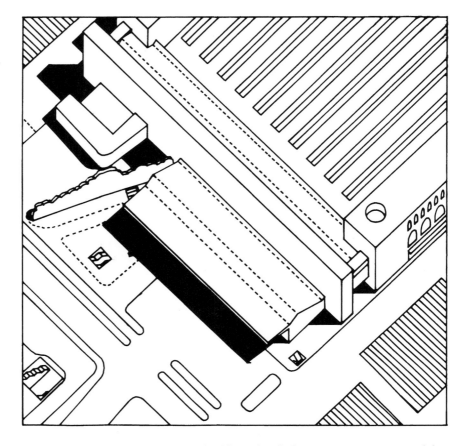

piazze where the former dictator had been lauded or tourists congregated, but the marginal spaces of the city where the poor lived in decaying properties or anonymous new blocks on the periphery. Traditional urban space lapsed from view, except where used to underscore contemporary miseries, a disappearance paralleled in the field of urbanism by the architectural concentration on the formal design of housing (Tafuri 1989: 3–48).

In the professional sphere the legacy of the civil war and the post-war settlement would be a form of clientelism where the major political parties, the Christian Democrats, the Socialists and the Italian Communist Party (the biggest in western Europe) directly or indirectly controlled different aspects of the construction market, commercial office development, public buildings and housing, and bribes were expected for the allocation of contracts. This was cut across by an academic system where positions in schools of architecture depended on nepotistic connections and political allegiance, which sometimes manifested itself in the ideological confrontations that characterized architectural debate, reflected also in the editorship of the principal journals and reviews. Early in the post-war period these political debates were characterized as attempts to create a divide between organic and functional architecture within the modern movement. Despite the changes in architectural language before and after 1945, and the removal of the most rhetorical motifs after that date these divisions continued, under different guises, the disputes between traditionalists and modernists, and within modernism, which had developed in the late 1920s.

Few significant new urban spaces date from this post-war period, although one major example would be the square and facade of the Stazione Termini in Rome, completed for the Holy Year of 1950. The original project was implemented by Angiolo Mazzoni from 1938–42, and the station was completed between 1947–50 by teams working under Eugenio Montouri and Annibale Vitellozzi. In *Italy Builds*, it is the one contemporary exception to the series of contextless object buildings, and with regard to its exploitation of its major contextual feature Kidder Smith gushes

This fourth-century-B.C. wall in the very midst of this startling modernity emphasizes as nothing else could to the traveller the roots and never-dying cultural contribution of the most fascinating city in the world. (Kidder Smith 1955: 232)

In the completed project a great glazed hall communicated directly with the piazza outside. The sense of contemporaneity this scheme produced was modified by two elements, the presence of a section of the Servian Wall which passed through the facade at an oblique angle and formed one boundary to the space, and the attachment of the new hall with its over sailing roof to the rather more monotonous forms of the station beyond designed during the fascist period (Ferrero 2004: 94–104). The asymmetrical vault of the main roof reflected the profile of the Servian Wall so that its silhouette could be appreciated by waiting passengers. The cantilevered roof and canopy were offset compositionally by the wall of office accommodation behind it, with ribbons of continuous windows coursing across the travertine facade which acted as a modern screen to the arcuated forms of the station side buildings. The cross galleria, open at either end and connecting into the street network of the city was identified as serving as a mid-twentieth century equivalent to Milan's Galleria Vittorio Emanuele, if without that structure's enduring glamour. The axial arrangement of the earlier designs survives in the disposition of ticket hall and restaurant either side of the main through route, and the station can therefore be seen to represent the political situation of the country as an open, modern, democratic veneer was placed over a substantial fascist legacy. The openness of the new facade helped disperse passengers along the elevation to the Piazza dei Cinquecento, although the original intended relationship to the public space has not survived the increase in road traffic at this important urban node. The Stazione Termini demonstrated that skill in the design of the public realm had not disappeared with fascism, and that new architectural languages could be used to create significant contemporary places. But the urban forms which modernism favoured throughout the developed and developing world would prove inimical to the traditional urban environments which provided the context for most architectural work in Italy. The clearances of dense urban areas and the creation of unformed voids invited direct movement, the consequence of which could only be destructive of traditional urban space. This formal context, freed from its associations with the immediate historical past would return to exert an influence two decades after the end of the war when modernism's promise was seen to have failed and a distant perspective on early twentieth century architectural history had been gained.

Many significant architectural figures who had been prominent under the regime, such as Moretti and the aged Piacentini, continued their careers, although their former political affiliations caused them some professional problems (Kirk 2005b: 149–53). However, in this period there were two central architectural figures who came to the fore, Bruno Zevi (1918–2000) and Ernesto Rogers (1909–69). Zevi's championing of organic architecture continued battles with academicism that were already fifty years old, but his attempt to recast architecture was to promote the appreciation of space as fundamentally an architectonic rather than an urban phenomenon. The internal logic of a building was seen to have primacy over its external appearance, indeed in Zevi's *Architecture as Space: How to look at architecture* the Vittorio Emanuele Monument in Rome was specifically condemned because it had no internal rationale and consisted exclusively of external rhetorical motifs (Zevi [1957] 1974: 33) The implicit political message was one of complete rejection of what the monument represented, indeed of the representational qualities of architecture *per se*. In contrast an architecture which grew organically from its interior uses was proposed, with the urban form left as the organic by-product of internal architecture. The logic of this course was for buildings to express individual identity rather than any reciprocity, and in application the resulting urban space would simply fall victim to the motor car which was beginning to dominate the urban scene. Architecture retreated into itself, into internal necessities and away from any duty to the collective experience of the city.

In contrast, the position of Rogers was more dependent on creating a continuity of experience of design ' from the spoon to the city', where rational processes of organization and manufacture would be harnessed to fulfill social needs (Branzi 1984: 8). For Rogers, the principal CIAM correspondent in Italy, his position was quite nuanced, with the editorship of *Casabella* providing him the opportunity to promote a reflective debate about architecture and the city. Rogers, one of whose professional partners, Gian Luigi Banfi, had died in the last days of the Second World War at the Nazi concentration camp at Mauthausen, was prepared to acknowledge in a form of *apologia* Italian modernism's debt to fascism as a focus of youthful idealism, marking also disillusion with the regime, and the names of other significant architectural figures who had died at the hands of the fascists or their allies. In the introduction to *Italy Builds* he remarked on how the congruence of Italy's experience under fascism and the development of modernism in architecture lent it a unique perspective (Kidder Smith 1955: 9–14). The language of the international style had already been formulated in Germany and France before the young Italian architects, the *Gruppo Sette*, announced their adherence to its ideals in 1927 (Etlin 1991: 225–38). The enforced adoption of conventional materials due to

11.3   Torre Velasca, Milan, viewed from the roof of the *duomo*.

the international embargo on steel during the late 1930s, had also given Italian modernists the spur to explore traditional forms to extend the language of the new architecture. This particular history gave post-war architects a distance from the normative language of modernism, but also limited their abilities to create new urban spaces, since wholesale urban planning had been a feature of the former regime. The new context against which such experiences were to be employed was rampant commercial redevelopment, often of a hostile nature, with little regard for a devalued historic environment seen now as a locus for mass tourism. In contrast the professional and academic reevaluation of traditional urban form for its typological value which emerged as a concept during this period became allied with an economically pragmatic concentration on existing situations and a scientific approach to the analysis of urban forms. In Milan, Rogers would transform the work of his practice BBPR from the cool abstraction of the open cube memorial to the deportees in the Cimitero Monumentale in Milan (1945–55) to the super-medievalism of the Torre Velasca (1958). One of the most controversial products of the more established urban design process, the structure adopted an expressive form in its provision of new office and residential accommodation. Critically this evocative image avoided the need for any traditional form of urban space by concentrating its energies on its dramatically jettied silhouette (Kirk 2005b: 170–74). The building's upper storeys suggested that this leading modernist practice had adopted a conservative stance in relation to urbanism and indeed the circle of younger architects around them (such as Aldo Rossi who will be the subject of the next chapter) were like their contemporaries in Team 10, keen to expose the failings of modernist urbanism as experienced in the new developments.

While Italian architects were concerned with internal debates and with the many social problems of their country it was left to others to reassess the qualities of Italian urban space and identify its unique characteristics. In contrast to the internal debates, this external scrutiny (in the train of the occupying armies, both the Germans and the Allies, and the assessors of cultural value before, during and after the war) came initially in the form of a series of publications which attempted to analyse both the historical and contemporary situations, and which sought to define some clarity within a confused situation. The first publication was the article *The Third Sack* by Henry Hope Reed in *The Architectural Review*. On the pretext of informing the numbers of pilgrims who would be drawn to Rome for the Holy Year of 1950, Reed placed recent developments against the historical context of the renaissance and baroque city. The rearrangement of Piazza Venezia received particularly unfavourable coverage, as an example where a significant historical space had been turned into a hostile stream of traffic. It was quite a strong indictment of the trends in modern urban planning as evidenced in one city, and its lack of any positive contemporary examples indicated the gap which had already opened up between the past and the present (Reed 1950).

The second publication, which has already been mentioned, was *Italy Builds: Its Modern Architecture and Native Inheritance* by the American critic G.E. Kidder Smith, a survey of contemporary Italian architecture published in 1955 where the division between the historic and the modern was again quite marked. The book's two sections, dealing with contextual matters and recent building reinforced the implied lack of continuity between past and present. The traditional images which are referred to as exemplary subjects are explicitly urban, showing the importance of the piazza in relation to the design of the building. In contrast the contemporary examples are (with the one exception already noted) isolated, the urban context absent, or at least cropped out of the photograph. Published bilingually in English and Italian the implicit message of this book was that the new forms presented in the second half of the book were, despite their use of modern materials and non-traditional forms, as dependent on the territorial and climatic context of the Italian peninsula as the historical examples in the first section although the connections were hard to discern (Kidder Smith 1955).

The last publication, which did not appear until 1963, was a product of a specifically British sensibility, townscape, which as well as surveying the grand manner of urban composition was adept at identifying the secondary order of signage, decoration, street furniture and daily usage which vivified an urban environment, especially in the hands of its greatest exponent Gordon Cullen (Cullen 1961). *The Architectural Review* had promoted townscape and it was the journal's publisher H. de Cronin Hastings who under the pseudonym Ivor de Wolfe produced *The Italian Townscape* as a compendium of photographs, descriptions and diagrams which sought to account for the phenomenon in a comprehensive manner. Townscape in origin had grown out of the romantic picturesque perception developed in the ruined cityscape of Second World War London. It spoke of a national consciousness of survival in the face of military attack, and might therefore be deemed appropriate to the fragile state of Italian consciousness, but townscape was essentially content to concern itself with the optimistic sun-filled images which appealed to aficionados from colder climates, the surface dressing of urban space rather than its substance, its gaze firmly averted from the huge new developments which characterized Italian urbanization in this period.

This research and observation on the Italian scene was divided between those who concentrated on appearance and those who claimed to see beyond that to the underlying structure. In the first group the proponents of townscape identified techniques which would appeal to a sense of Anglo-Saxon pragmatism to modify the already recognized hostile effects of the application of architectural modernism. Against this context, the international visitors who came to the modernist CIAM conferences in Bergamo in 1949 and Venice in 1950 were presented with a country where the projects being produced by the younger generation of architects were firmly within orthodox modernist models, even if they did make some acknowledgement of vernacular precedent in their use of materials. However, the universal models favoured by the older generation of modernists, and the intuitive approach of townscape would be critiqued by those who claimed a more thorough appreciation. Such an attempted critique would be produced by the adherents of Team 10 (named after the tenth CIAM conference in Dubrovnik) in their analysis of urban form influenced by contemporary anthropological research. As with townscape, the gaze which conditioned their work was essentially that of the outsider (with the exception of their Italian member Giancarlo de Carlo) with the organic nature of traditional environments standing as a representation of a more authentic life than that available in the contemporary planned world. However, an ambivalence about traditional architectural form would require that the pattern beneath the surface appearance be invoked, an analytical method which itself began to disintegrate when its forms became models which were much emulated and its products directly applied as solutions to new problems. If its great archetype was the Italian hilltown, free of association with planned propaganda, redolent of an urban life which emphasized community rather than order, the work of de Carlo (1919–2005) in producing the masterplan for Urbino between 1958–64 was its most successful demonstration, a study which initiated a long series of architectural interventions in the city and its outskirts (de Carlo 1970).

De Carlo's role, despite his relative isolation, was a pivotal one, as a figure who was well connected in the leading international architecture networks of his day principally through Team 10 and his earlier connection to Rogers with whom he had collaborated in the international fora of CIAM. Yet the uniqueness of his position in these arenas was matched by his detached position in Italian politico-architectural culture, since (if one accepts the paradox) his affiliation to anarchism meant that he had a distanced attitude to the aesthetics of the traditional city. On the one hand his study of Urbino was an exemplary demonstration of the validity of urban conservation policies during an era of wholesale redevelopment. Yet at the same time the exposure of the great Mercatale ramp, constructed by Francesco di Giorgio, which was concealed under the 18th century theatre was the most publically visible intervention. The university buildings introduced into the fabric of the city, most notably the Magistero, concealed their novel architectural forms behind relatively anonymous exteriors, as if afraid to be seen intruding on the form of the renaissance city (Zucchi 1992; Blundell Jones and Canniffe 2007: 165–76). The self-effacement of such a strategy deprived the urban network of a public face for a major institution, abdicating the provision of the public realm to the historical past, a gesture that might be regarded as radical only in its modesty.

This humanistic aversion to the recognisability of the expression of public function through the presence of public space was rooted in a position which would leave de Carlo remote from the ideological positioning of other Italian architects. His architectural and urban intentions, beyond the interest in conservation, would fail to communicate outside the group of fellow professionals with whom he collaborated. Even within Team 10 his position was isolated, since his highly individualistic work stood apart from that of others in the group, by terms banal or mechanistic. The attempt by this circle to abstract the rules of social patterns from traditional architectural form, while simultaneously denying themselves the comfort of those forms and their characteristic materials undermined the faith in a modern urbanism from within the architectural profession at exactly the same time as the utopian project of modernism was under attack from without. However the aesthetic attention lavished on the Italian urban environment in pursuit of an ultimately elusive humanistic modernism would provide material with which a younger generation of architects, both Italian and foreign, could reconstruct the idea of the European urban tradition and within it the significance of the legibly public space.

The hiatus in the development of the piazza represented by the this post-war period, uniquely devoid in the historical scope of this book of significant examples of the genre, owes much to the architectural object fixation of modern architecture. Open space had little value in comparison to the value of buildings, and once property speculation became a commonplace element in the planning system it was unlikely to gain any value. Policies which foresaw a use for traditional urban forms would have a surprising origin in those pursued in communist controlled Bologna (Benedetti 1973). For ideological purposes the city council were keen to frustrate commercial development, as a means of protecting the interests of the working class quarters which occupied the city centre. These mutually supportive motives could therefore be used to create an image of the city which was based firmly on its past, but which would come to be regarded and internationally acclaimed as startlingly progressive. The values first successfully implemented in Bologna would then be adopted by other major Italian cities which had already experienced some degree of destructive improvement. Policies for the conservation of historic centres had been codified in the Gubbio Charter of 1960 and these were to influence the study commissioned by the Bologna city council from Leonardo Benevolo between 1962–65. This study brought together the typological studies developed by Saverio Muratori with proposals for how the essentially medieval city form could be helped to function more efficiently in the very changed circumstances of the late twentieth century. The careful quasi-scientific basis with which such typological researches could be pursued, the concern for authenticity leading to the removal of subsequent historical layers which obscured the original state would also lead to a tendency to try to preserve the original dimensions in height and width, militating against the agglomeration of small units into larger plots. The limits thereby placed on use encouraged the maintenance of residential quarters in historic city centres, preserving the signs of daily life which would prove attractive in that most unscientific market of cultural tourism. The pedestrianization of Piazza Maggiore in Bologna in 1968 presented itself as a political signal in favour of equality, against the prioritization of private car ownership, the appropriation of what would come to be seen as 'green' urban policies and the validation of the aesthetics of the traditional urban environment. With the widespread political unrest which developed in 1968, and the slow down in construction brought about in the wake of the energy crisis of 1973 the urban stage was set for the values demonstrated in Bologna to be exported to other European centres. The social value of defined urban space, indeed its value as a component of the architectural project would return to prominence, and would contrast unfavourably with the work of the recent past (de Pieri and Scrivano 2004).

With Federico Fellini's *La Dolce Vita* (1960), a new Italy was presented in film which was intent on hedonism, and which had abandoned its traditional values, although the urban spaces acted as a form of code for social audacity. Although more bourgeois and materially comfortable than those depicted in neo-realist cinema the peripheries of the city are still presented as bleak, in contrast to the glamour of the central spaces of Rome, and in particular the allure of the Trevi fountain where Anita Ekberg frolics in the waters and seduces the hero Marcello. Public space is reappropriated after the self-denial of the post-war years. The economic miracle which Italy was witnessing had renewed confidence in public display, both at the level of the family, with the growth of car ownership, and at that of the nation, with Italy's hosting of the Olympic Games in 1960, the fascist context of most of the sporting venues being politely ignored. But in *La Dolce Vita* the reenvisioned historic public space was similarly shorn of any direct political meaning, signification which might refer to the unpalatable political circumstances ignored, and replaced with the aesthetic of sensation. Spaces which had previously been intended to evoke historical memory, and the endurance of various particular values were now to be regarded as backdrops for the spectacular moment, a disposable and interchangeable element, sometimes in cinematic techniques artificially replicated or simulated by back projection (Bass 1997). The availability of such sites for tourists, increasing in numbers and global reach, especially for the major centres of Rome, Florence and Venice, undermined the sense that they might be authentic manifestations of Italy's urban culture. Prosperity brought in its train disaffection with the *status quo* and the desire to break through the beautiful surface image Italian cities presented to the world.

In this scenario, the appearance of another avant-garde, Superstudio, a group of architects based in Florence in the late 1960s, brought together two particular aspects of urban culture in that period. Firstly, there was the critique of consumerism represented by the Italian post-war economic miracle and the favouring of radical solutions to social and political problems. Secondly, the vulnerability of the historic urban environment revealed by the flooding of Florence and Venice in 1966, suggested the possibility of liberation from the constraints of architectural and urban conservation. This conjunction allowed Superstudio to envision a new type of urban existence which did not indulge in the technological obsessions of their equivalents in other developed countries groups, nor the slow retreat into historicism of the post-modernists and advocates of the vernacular (Lang and Menking 2003). Instead they proposed an environment which dispensed with notions of property division, of good design as commodification, and above all the traditional restrictions of place. Superstudio thereby established a distinct Florentine architectural culture, less historically and politically driven than the schools of Rome, Milan and Venice. Despite the beginnings of political unrest and violence, this was a time of optimism where the possibilities of economic growth and social change seemed limitless.

Dispensing with the diversity of urban traditions, Superstudio predicted a future where accelerated technological progress and miniaturization could liberate mankind from inequalities by creating a uniform environment. In the spread of their projected *continuous monument* even the corporate skyscrapers of Manhattan were reduced to museum objects, their individual architectural expressions now redundant. Applied across cities and wildernesses, its elemental forms were intended to solve the problem of human habitat by spanning the globe with a single environment which liberated the rest of the earth's surface to nature. What distinguished Superstudio from their contemporaries was the totality of their vision. Although always keen to provoke, they adopted an architectural language which they applied to the design of objects, buildings and cities. Exemplified by the project 'histograms', the cartesian forms managed to suggest both the rationalism of contemporary corporate forms and the global mysticism of the counter-culture. A good deal of professional skill was required to span this division, through an easily identifiable production which had learnt the graphic lessons of Pop Art. The critical position of Superstudio in relation to the consumer culture on which they depended encouraged them to work on urban projects so vast and provocative that they could not be commodified as easily as furniture and even buildings, a strategy which had similar ambitions to contemporary land art. As one of their collaborators commented

The most important development to which we wished draw attention was the profound change that the very concept of a city had undergone. For some time the modern metropolis had ceased to be a place and had become a condition; it was this state of being that was uniformly circulated throughout society by consumer goods. Living in a city no longer means inhabiting a fixed place or urban street, but rather adopting a certain mode of behaviour, comprising language, clothing and both printed and electronically transmitted information; the city stretches as far as the reach of these media. (Branzi 1984: 63–66)

Against this optimistic utopian prospect, the energy crisis and subsequent economic downturn of the early seventies would bring to the fore a more equivocal vision of Italian urbanity.

# 12

# Neo-Rationalism: Aldo Rossi and the rediscovery of typology

The period of reconstruction had specific effects on several Italian cities. For example Milan's expansion during the economic miracle, with the displacement of populations which went along with it, had exposed new discontinuities in the formerly coherent Italian urban situation (Foot 2001). At the same time, throughout the developed world the generalized disregard for urban context in the architectural proposals of the 1960s and 1970s provoked a reaction in which the issue of memory as physical and poetic content came to the fore, nowhere more so than in Italy. By the 1960s, historical forms free of their recent fascist taint again became the subject of serious research by Ernesto Rogers and his collaborators not only in the field of anonymous urban fabric, the morphological approach favoured by Saverio Muratori, but also in the form of monumental structures. The group which had gathered around Rogers during his editorship of *Casabella* had explored these historical issues as well as critiques of contemporary design through the pages of the magazine, and from this combination emerged a scepticism about the functionalist claims of orthodox modernism and the local individualism of Team 10. In this search for architectural and urban authenticity this grouping favoured the typological approach (Kirk 2005b: 182–85). This new avant-garde movement (referred to variously as *la Tendenza* or neo-rationalism) presented their proposals in boldly geometric forms, and from this circle Aldo Rossi (1931–97) was to emerge firstly as a significant urban theorist, and then as the creator of potent architectural images in drawn and built form. For Rossi the political context of this focus was the type of authenticity which intellectuals often ascribed to working class life rather than a romanticization of the previous social conditions, but from his early career his work was to be suggestive of nostalgia. However, in a period marked by considerable social unrest, Rossi's position on the political Left was to lead to him being banned from teaching in Italian universities by the government, and the pursuit of an academic career outside Italy.

The continuous process of urban history was a theme which was developed in Rossi's *The Architecture of the City*. Published in Italian in 1966 and translated

12.1 Piazza Anfiteatro, Lucca. Housing built within the remains of the Roman amphitheatre, an example of Aldo Rossi's theory of permanences.

into English in 1982, the book presented a tough critique of the modernist city, but used marxism to argue for an almost fatalistic adherence to the *zeitgeist*. Rossi proposed that architecture stood outside the fluid tide of history, dependent for its power on the qualities of its geometry and accumulation of patina through its survival over time. This placed great emphasis on the collective experience of the city, and consequently reduced the individualizing tendencies of the unique monument, creating a significant focus in this analysis on the issue of permanence in architectural typology. Historical examples cited by Rossi such as the Palazzo della Ragione in Padua (referred to in Chapter 3) and Piazza Anfiteatro in Lucca evoked the power of a form to support different uses and interpretations over centuries, a phenomenon which contradicted the monofunctionalism advocated by orthodox modernists. Rossi's text distinguished surface appearance from context, the atmosphere of a city being apparently replicable without any comprehension of the typology from which it was built, although this division would be a phenomenon which would bedevil the broader reception of his own work that was decades in the future. Mistrustful of the subjectivity of proponents of contextualism, his rationalism sought an architecture and urbanism which was less apologetic about its presence, but which acknowledged that time would transform it, that it would, as it were, domesticate the urban intervention through use. The ambiguity of this position in relation to the temporal dimension contrasts with the fixity with which contextualists appropriated a past point in history (Rossi 1982).

The poetic content of *The Architecture of the City* breaks out from the quasi-scientific tone it adopts as a cover. Influenced by the left leaning utilitarianism of contemporary architectural theory, it moved beyond the common explanation of vernacular typology to the then unfashionable study of monuments. The political and the formal tendencies found a common precedent in the so-called revolutionary architects of the eighteenth century, particularly Etienne-Louis Boullée, and the development of didactic architectural visionary projects. The traces of that impetus on the city of Milan, marks of French occupation under Napoleon, also proved influential since they existed at the junction between utopian planning and the physical character of the city. The Foro Bonaparte (referred to in Chapter 8), the massive encircling of the Castello Sforzesco only partially realized, was a tangible example of the persistence of powerful geometric architectural forms. It was but a fragment of a much more extensive project which had a functional intention, in terms of easing circulation through the city, but which employed compositional methods to create memorable civic vistas. Rossi wrote of the designs

Ultimately they took into consideration and respected the artistic buildings and historical memories of the city; the monuments were seen as the seat and testimony of municipal history, and placed as backdrops to the straight streets and the centers of piazzas, almost as constitutive elements of that larger plan of construction and of ordering which history forms over time and in which cities come to be mirrored. (Rossi 1982: 193)

Characteristic of its origins during the high period of international style modernism, Rossi's book concentrated on buildings rather than spaces. However one passage deals with the Roman Forum and uses that space as an example which fulfils many themes, the relationship between topography and place, between the planned and the organic, between history and the present. His reference to its timeless qualities is explicit in not depending on the counter intuitive meaning of separation by history, but rather on the contemporaneity of its historical existence. He considered the life of the forum in the following terms.

People passed by without having any specific purpose, without doing anything: it was like the modern city, where the man in the crowd, the idler, participates in the mechanism of the city without knowing it, sharing only in its image. The Roman Forum was thus an urban artefact of extraordinary modernity; in it was everything that is inexpressible in the modern city. ...

What tied the idler to the Forum, why did he intimately participate in this world, why did he become identified in the city through the city itself? This is the mystery that urban artefacts arouse in us. The Roman Forum constitutes one of the most illustrative urban artefacts that we can know: bound up as it is with the origins of the city; extremely, almost unbelievably, transformed over time but always growing upon itself; parallel to the history of Rome as it is documented in every historical stone and legend, from the Lapis Niger to the Dioscuri; ultimately reaching us today through its strikingly clear and splendid signs. (Rossi 1982: 120)

For Rossi, the forum as an urban artefact embodied the essence of the city of Rome, displaying the layers of its history, its point of origin and its contemporary centre. It is a space and context which could not be replicated elsewhere, only evoked through analogy. Its history represented the type of metamorphosis which Rossi implied would be the desired fate of his own buildings, their regularity and geometry eroded by inhabitation and use, but accommodating that change and persisting through time, accreting memory.

While the significance of the collective and of typological fitness were characteristics Rossi's theory shared with modernist urbanism, he reached back beyond the development of industrial functionalism to the classificatory forms created by Jean-Nicolas-Louis Durand at the start of the nineteenth century. Yet, although an imitation of historic forms might be unsuccessful, the forms of the historic city remain worthy of study to disinter their meanings for the society which created them. Rossi's study raised three challenges. Foremost among them, and which is the subject of this book, was the extent to which certain aspects of physical urbanism are related to the manifestation of political structures and fictions. There was also the issue of the precise methods of representation of attitudes to citizenship and the ability of architecture to provide an adequate and expressive urban language. And thirdly there was the question of what the analysis of historical types revealed about the application of similar spatial techniques to contemporary situations. However, typology in Rossi's design work was a poetic rather than a scientific category, and he applied a few forms in different combinations and contexts to paradoxically create a highly recognizable and individual language of architecture. The relationship to construction can also be thought to provide a problematic dimension to the reception of the work. Although his fame gave Rossi the opportunity to use a rich palette of materials in later projects, the tendency was to envision the projects in ordinary materials, steel, concrete, brick, stucco. In realization these often seem crude, a perception which has two sources. On the one hand the disengagement between design and execution meant that supervision was sometimes patchy. While this experience had some echoes of modernist attitudes to materiality, it is also connected to the specifically Italian attitudes of neo-realism discussed in the previous chapter and the concurrent fine art movement of *arte povera* (Flood and Morris 2001). If the latter placed an aesthetic value on material simplicity as an evocation of conceptual depth, the former placed ordinariness and actuality in a privileged position, as a direct contrast to the falsehoods and delusions which had supported fascism.

Within this intellectual milieu, Rossi's early substantial projects approached the issue of urban space in a stealthy manner, as if to break cover would impede the success of his strategy to recover urban values in architecture. The housing Rossi designed between 1969–70 at Gallaratese on the outskirts of Milan revealed the particular characteristics of his evocative use of typology. Carlo Aymonino was the master planner of this megastructural project, but Rossi's project is subtly distinguished from the formal rules of this new context by its

use of colour, scale and the interpretation of tradition. Aymonino's blocks are large scale, and have a red crag-like appearance with the exterior formed to express interior functions. In contrast, Rossi's block is more modestly scaled, reticent in its modeling and faced in white stucco. The principal public feature is the portico which runs the length of the block, providing a portico to the development on two related levels, the junction of which is negotiated by a monumental set of steps and four overscaled cylindrical columns (Moschini 1979: 52–57). The daunting abstraction of this space is ameliorated by the delicate use of scale, with the endless colonnade made of frequently spaced fin walls, their dimensions related to the distance between the hands of an outstretched figure. The regularity of its form reflected its origins in traditional types of Lombard housing, but its refusal to articulate the uses to which its public element could be put meant that it was regarded as heartlessly oppressive and interpreted as a late flowering of fascism. Rossi's principal references, historical tradition and the experience of the modern, were shared with fascist architecture. But he was working in a context where historical form had been mistrusted and modernity had become an internalized search for novelty. Rossi had no embarrassment about the context in which he had been formed, and was concerned to step outside the futile search for the contemporary, in the manner of his great hero, the early twentieth century Viennese architect Adolf Loos.

12.2   Gallaratese housing, Milan. Aldo Rossi's use of public space in the form of a colonnade beneath the apartments.

An allegorical invocation of the city also features in Rossi's most celebrated project, the New Cemetery of San Cataldo in Modena designed between 1971–78 and still incomplete (Blundell Jones and Canniffe 2007: 189–200). Rossi won the 1971 competition to design an extension to the neoclassical cemetery, originally created by Cesare Costa between 1858 and 1876. The phased construction of the extension project did not begin until the early 1980s, but the extensive publication it received has ensured that the haunting images of the drawings and photographs capture the quintessence of Rossi's work (Barbieri and Ferlenga 1987: 46–53). However, it is not a space but an object which provided the literal structure of the new cemetery, the figure of the skeleton. Taking its cue from the high walled and colonnaded rectangular layout of the original 19th century cemetery, Rossi delineated a new precinct of roughly equal dimensions. In the original the graceful stoas of columbaria provide complete enclosure with chapels situated in the main ranges, the centre being left for burial. Rossi, however, reversed this arrangement, occupying the centre with a monumental complex around which the meanings of the new cemetery are focused. In this one gesture alone his critical attitude to the relationship between past and present is revealed, but he also evoked the work of his own immediate predecessors and recent history. In an echo of the open cube of BBPR's memorial to the deportees in Milan, at the centre of the project there is the sanctuary, a hollow cube open to the sky and punctured with regularly spaced square openings. It has the appearance of an abandoned construction site, of an incomplete project. While occupying space in a modernist manner, the cube of the Modena Cemetery takes as its motif the necropolis of the eighteenth century, an especial debt to Piranesi and his transhistorical architecture. Here it represents the transitory nature of contemporary life in a fugue on the collective housing unit (Eisenman 1979). The abandoned house or the deserted factory are among the urban images which Rossi exploits for the elegiac qualities they evoke, yet there are other meanings and echoes, indicative of a broader historical perspective. Although they feature colonnades similar to that at the Gallaratese housing, the barracks-like quality of the columbaria of the new cemetery distil the memory of the barracks of the camp at Fossoli, built outside the nearby town of Carpi and the site of deportation for all the victims of the nazi occupation of Northern Italy. Less than 20 kilometres apart, the same train line to the north passes the new cemetery and Fossoli. With his sensitivity to the resonances of banal forms and their echo of the horrors of the twentieth century, the ambiguities of Rossi's aesthetic choices are apparent. They express a context which is not only related to a common culture but, at close proximity to such a significant site, were also local and historical. As had been the case with Costa's cemetery, the geometrical configuration of Rossi's work attempted to create order on the disordered urban periphery. The ultimate collective experience is exploited to inform the contemporary city about recently lost urban space, and a nostalgic atmosphere appeared to have replaced faith in technological and social progress.

The representational aspects of Rossi's work bring the observer up against the disillusionments of contemporary existence, irrespective of the uses these

works were intended to house, but the publication of a city of the dead only made the issues of representation and language more resonant. The work of architects such as Rossi, and others of *la Tendenza* such as Giorgio Grassi, presented many paradoxes in relation to urban design (Crespi and Dego 2004). The curious power of an essentially personal vision as a repository of public expression compounds the mismatch between Rossi's influential writing and his widely published design work, and also the differences between the drawn and constructed work and the relationship between intention and realization. The combination of the rational and the visionary, the mundane and the monumental would pervade Rossi's theoretical work and the building projects which followed, although this dual nature was perhaps best captured in the drawings, both visionary sketches around persistent architectural themes and project drawings. The graphic language of the images is so energetic as to suggest an urban world independent of the experience of the building. Partly this could be accounted for in the pragmatic uncertainties between design and construction which many of Rossi's projects experienced. The drawings might be the only realization and therefore had to contain the full quality of the ideas which the project embodied but in the restricted sensual appropriation available through vision (Adjmi and Bertolotto 1993). Within the limited world of the page, the drawings themselves contained many enigmatic elements which stretch beyond the similarities to early twentieth century *pittura metafisica*. The conventions of orthographic projection are often manipulated to project an

12.3   Cemetery of San Cataldo, Modena. Aldo Rossi's cubic sanctuary occupies the central space of the projected complex.

12.4   La
Nuova Piazza,
Fontivegge. View
of the approach
from the station
towards Rossi's
raised piazza.

initially objective form into a subjective vision. Plans, their elements composed
with geometric logic, are much more than the distribution of building parts,
with the implicit suggestion that they are representational, of a body or a city,
in an extension of revolutionary *architecture parlante*. Elevations too, perhaps
paradoxically, through their quality of human absence evoke the passage along
colonnades and the pensive figure at the window. Sections especially when
heavily shadowed reveal the 'intimate immensity' of the interior, and often in

the drawings these architectural conventions are used to frame fragments of detail and atmosphere. The rigidity of the plan as frame might therefore be read as a metaphor for the framing of daily urban life which Rossi's buildings were designed to accommodate. The drawings, especially the carefully composed panels of images, act as windows into the world of the project.

As Rossi's career progressed his commissions offered the opportunity to deal with more conventional public commissions, and create the type of public space which he had studied as a young man. The major example was La Nuova Piazza, at Fontivegge, Perugia, a development on former industrial land (Rossi 1984: 37–74). The outskirts of Perugia present a sad prospect when contrasted with the beauty of the historic centre of the town, discussed in Chapter 3. The steepness of the topography and the piecemeal nature of the industrial, commercial and residential developments had produced a chaotic and formless peripheral area. Leaving the railway station and beginning the steep ascent to the city, the visitor encounters the new piazza. Between a department store and the prominent corner column of an apartment building one ascends a flight of steps up to the sloping surface of the piazza. A central fountain stands between the incomplete spine of an apartment building and a confidently expressed public building raised on its podium. Primitively defined elements of colonnade, portico and repetitive rectangular windows create this demonstration project for the new Italian city space of the late twentieth century, evoking its 'bureaucratic inertia'.

As yet incomplete, Rossi's project consisted of a *broletto* or public building, a residential block, a theatre building and a commercial block arranged around a piazza which spans over the road connecting to the station. The decision to accommodate car parking as a basement deck allowed for a new ground plane to be established which would be free of traffic, but followed the sloping terrain typical of traditional piazze in the region, such as Piazza IV Novembre in the same city. But far from integrating itself into the dramatic topography of Perugia, the new piazza sought to re-establish the centre at a lower and more accessible altitude, even to the extent of imitating the positioning of the individual elements of the city core. So as the piazza rises the centrally placed fountain is flanked on the left by a public building and on the right by the dense urban wall or residential element, with the as yet to be constructed theatre closing the progression. This apparent contextualism is subverted by the realization that the ground on which the new piazza stands is an artificial topography, the 'authenticity' of the plan form, its historical grounding, not extending to the section. The individuality of the elements that Rossi designed for Fontivegge suggests that his analysis of traditional urban forms found expression in the design of the new urban components yet, as he had asserted in 1966, an imitation of these forms would not itself ensure success (Rossi 1982: 123). His new buildings are dumb structures awaiting the accretion of meaning which only the layering of history can provide. In the meantime the vacancy of their forms requires appropriation by the citizens whose attitude is one of apparent indifference to the surroundings, or at least a complete

12.5   La
Nuova Piazza,
Fontivegge.
The fountain
and *broletto*.

acceptance of them as organic parts of their lives, the buildings and piazza
providing the surfaces against which daily and ritual activities are set.

The commercial element of the project is a largely blank object with
entrances at the piazza and street levels, axially placed at the lower end of the

piazza. The office building, containing regional government administration, is formed by a seven storey range of offices on three sides of a raised courtyard open to the piazza on the fourth side. This court is then bisected by a central wing supported on a quadruple height colonnade, the blank facade of this wing being crowned by a primitive pediment and the familiar Rossian motif of the clock. The office complex is a simple cubic form clad in two types of skin, square proportioned glazed screens, or square punctured openings in the panelled stucco wall. Relief from this regularity is provided by the rusticated masonry of the podium arcades, and the copper-clad cornice level. The severity of these elevations provides the backdrop to the significant features of the entrance element and the industrial chimney preserved to the north of the building. But this *broletto*, a name which places the building in the tradition of northern Italian communal palaces, is a paradoxical construction poised between the taut architectural language which has become most identified with Rossi and his followers, and elements which suggest the continuing influence of Viennese *Sezessionstil* architects, although the irony has to noted that Rossi clothed new his public structure in a language associated with a period of hollow rhetoric and imperial decay.

While the residential building was intended to have a certain amount of variety in its modelling and fenestration, the sheer size of this single largest building in the development will, perhaps, tend to defeat its architect's attempt to introduce rhythm into the elevations. The sloping ground plane produced difficulties in the composition and proportioning of the facades. To the road leading to the station, the rusticated base of the residential block was intended to be split centrally, but to the piazza the rustication would run through as a constant, producing in effect a four storey height podium at the lower end. The public scale of this termination, acting as a sign to the nearest public thoroughfare and the railway station, was further accentuated by an eight storey high corner column, which in early sketches addressed the road rather than the piazza. In a different arrangement the split block and monumental column had featured as urban elements in Rossi's Gallaratese housing block, so that the Perugia housing served as a self-referential sign.

In the designs for the unbuilt theatre the building is itself divided into the auditorium below the ground plane and the public hall above, held between rectangular gable walls, fronted by a large conical structure, Rossi's sign of collective memory which was to serve both as the theatre building's foyer and as the principal civic symbol in the space. Its form is an echo of both the preserved chimney already on the site, therefore implicitly referring to the memory of the site, and in personal terms to the similarly shaped form of the communal grave proposed in Rossi's project for the Modena cemetery. Rossi's sketches in particular place great emphasis on the importance of the conical form of the theatre entrance, the sketches indicating the desired scale of this element as an object in the piazza, although the models indicate that its proposed size was relatively small. It was, of course, a conscious feature of Rossi's architectural language that the scalelessness of his forms had the result

12.6   La Nuova Piazza, Fontivegge. The exaggerated portico of the *broletto* seen from beneath the colonnade of the apartment block. The facade features Rossi's familiar motif of the clock.

of producing a disjointed character in the environment he proposed, but the eventual intention would appear to be to centre attention on the most public element of the project. In another demonstration of a personal memory placed in the public realm, the fountain which sits in the centre of the piazza recalls the form of the *Monument to the Partisans* designed and built by Rossi for the town of Segrate in 1965 (Moschini 1979: 44–45). The elements of the fountain, the walls and stair, are simplified, but here they were clad in travertine rather than the exposed concrete of the original. Its positioning establishes the focus of the new piazza and compensates for the irregularity of its shape and the varying degrees of enclosure around its perimeter, as the very different Fontana Maggiore does in Piazza IV Novembre.

The last example of Rossi's urban work to be considered is more modest in scale and complete in execution. The Piazzetta Croce Rossa, completed in 1988, is a small urban space in the centre of Milan, on the major thoroughfare of Via Manzoni, and adjacent to the opening of Via Montenapoleone, and therefore in the middle of what has become the fashion quarter of the city, and one of the most important centres in this global industry, the so called *quadrilatero d'oro,* the golden block (Ferlenga 1999: 206–07). The urban space sits above the Montenapoleone Metro station with entries and exits to and from the station disposed around the space, but the centre is focused on a symmetrically arranged space, lined with two rows of trees, benches and street lights. On the axis sits the *Monument to Sandro Pertini* (named for the President of the Italian Republic 1978–85), in the form of a cubic block faced in the same pink and grey Candoglia marble as is used on the *duomo* of Milan. Ten metres square the cube is blank on two sides, with the third featuring a bronze clad water spout in the form of an equilateral triangle, with a long horizontal slot in the facade above. The fourth side, which faces towards the opening of Via Montenapoleone, is open and consists of a set of oversized steps up to a viewing platform. The monument's elements refer to a number of examples of Rossi's personal iconography, and therefore to his general typological collection of forms as expressed in previous works. So the cube in Milan refers to the cubic sanctuary at the Modena cemetery, and its conjunction with steps within the form to his competition design for the *Monument to the Resistance* at Cuneo (1962). The triangular fountain was another familiar motif, first used in the courtyard of the De Amicis school at Broni in 1969–70. The oversized steps, as a form of auditorium had been used in the courtyard of the elementary school at Fagnano Olona of 1972 (Moschini 1979: 37–39, 58–60, 68–76). Most users of this space would be unfamiliar with these works, but would be familiar with the conventional, everyday sources in the cityscape from which Rossi himself distilled his preferred forms. The monumental flight of marble steps, however, would be familiar to most Italians as the compositional basis of the Vittorio Emanuele Monument in Rome, the national shrine but also the spectre that haunted the country's twentieth century architecture. Its offspring sits in miniature in Milan, denuded of its iconography and its steps or seats awaiting the unfolding of a more quotidian urban drama.

Growing out from the specific context of post-fascist Italian architecture, Rossi invoked the 'rational' classificatory procedures of the Enlightenment but combined this approach with a distinctive graphic language and these two aspects appealed to two different audiences. While Rossi was taking the researches of the Italian school of urban morphologists and defining a series of architectural types, his images also evoked a series of urban atmospheres where scale disjunctions attempted to link the domestic and the urban. Rossi's career subsequent to the publication of *The Architecture of the City* was determined in particular by the initial dissemination of his drawings and then later by his writings, since the English translation of the book did not appear for a decade and a half. His buildings, given the complex nature of the Italian construction industry, took even longer to appear although international commissions were to play an enhanced role in the latter phase of his career. His drawings with their intense shadows, violent juxtapositions of scale and bright colours presented a much more immediate and evocative experience, and generally an urban one, of familiar elements in unfamiliar combinations. Intriguing and easy on the eye, their superficial appropriation as exemplars of Milanese design culture and their association with postmodernism meant that many of Rossi's theoretical positions remained obscured. Despite the extent of their reproduction, and the banality of their subject matter perhaps this is a testament to the fact that images retain their power even when they are defiled through overfamiliarity.

Although mistaken for its superficial similarity to fascist architecture, in Rossi's deliberate use of barely resolved junctions between concrete, stucco and steel are echoes instead of the industrial landscape which was redefining Italian urban form during these years. Their rhetoric was based on the typical left-leaning technique of the heroization of working life and environment, a utopia of the ordinary, ostensibly devoid of fashion and materialism which Rossi had witnessed in the Soviet Union. Philosophically, this evocation does not suggest a policy of anything goes, but rather that a tolerant attitude to variety might best be accommodated in a self-effacing and robust frame with an enigmatic presence. At Fontivegge, for example, Rossi's familiar forms of colonnade, steps, corner column and monumental clock are combined to create a disquieting space, but these preferred forms create an interference with the transmission of his ideas, reducing the impact of the space to a sterile replication of the historical spaces Rossi so admired. Yet Rossi's research in typology took place in a context as much physical as it was cultural and it was here that the deftness of touch came to the fore. In a contemporary milieu which placed value on the precision of detail the issue of place would be seen as a distraction. The stained concrete and cracked plaster, the scale which is redundantly or perhaps significantly oversized, the metal stairs and grilles, are the elements of the typical environment from which an architectural and urban typology might be deemed to arise. Its very banality is a sign both of its ubiquity and its comprehensibility. Although it should be acknowledged that the formation of the new piazza took place in an immediate context

with little to recommend it, Rossi's attempt, however futile, is one which endeavours to retrieve some defined public space from the surrounding chaos. Ultimately Rossi's effort to create a piazza at Perugia remains unsatisfactory because its indifference is too studied, this indifference taking the curious form of suggesting that architecture alone is required to produce a public space. This fallacy has been a commonplace of urban thinking at least since the Enlightenment, and is most evident in the autonomous architecture of modernism (where a general *tabula rasa* was presumed), because the tendency to treat architecture as an inclusive discipline is misleading. Architecture's requirements for coherence in its form and detail tends to exclude diversity and variety of expression. Rossi's exploitation of a familiar but highly personal language would seem to deny the possibility of the buildings representing the aspirations of the citizens, while his avowed skill as an analyst of urban types did not prevent him from choosing an indigenous but perhaps inappropriate precedent. Despite the power of these historic forms they are able to support any function which might be housed within them. The ambiguities which make a space inhabitable in a number of different ways are virtually impossible to prescribe, so the ambiguities which Rossi provides are only visual ones, disjointed use of scale or the application of constant rhythms, for example.

12.7 Piazzetta Croce Rossa, Milan. Aldo Rossi's signature cubic form is here used as the *Monument to Sandro Pertini* in the creation of this small urban space.

Despite his declaration of form in relation to the longevity of urban artefacts proposed in *The Architecture of the City*, it is precisely Rossi's formal decisions that created the alienating environment of his piazza.

Rossi's path instead suggested a degree of inevitability to his forms which simply presumed acceptance. This very muteness, the lack of rhetorical flourish, is one of its most tender and enduring qualities. The most evocative elements of Rossi's work, the shadows and the memory, are precisely the elements which had been banished from architecture by modernism. Their use to redefine urban space as a phenomenon of more than quantitative value was perhaps his lasting achievement given the poor quality of much of his constructed work. Yet, as an architect working in the conditions of the late twentieth century, he created urban objects which stood apart from their context. Indeed the domestic objects, especially the coffee pots, which featured in his drawings as equivalents for the elements of the urban landscape, were easily adaptable for manufacture by the domestic appliance company Alessi during the 1980s Milanese design boom. Rossi's objects, domestic and urban, stand for the collective space even as they occupy it, their exaggerated proportions or ungainly symmetry acknowledging the post-war sense of loss of continuity. Rossi's position had a quiet sobriety which distinguished it from the glamour or playfulness of other concurrent branches of Milanese design, such as the sleekness of Achille Castiglioni, or the eclectic attention seeking of Memphis (Branzi 1984). Its recovery of past forms is not dependent on amnesia with regard to the modern city, but the assimilation of its divergent strands. Rossi's modest stance was that the city was beyond the capacity of design as control, that its political status had a symbiotic relationship with its form, where ends and means became one. In a period of great social turmoil and industrial conflict it would be other hands which would deal directly with the more explicit political content of public space.

# 13

# Labyrinths: The city of 'the years of lead'

History is followed and created by struggling with the present toward the future, not with nostalgic memories.
Carlo Scarpa *Il Lavoro Fascista* 19 May 1931 (Dal Co and Mazzariol 1984: 279)

As this history of the Italian piazza approaches the present situation, the physical creation of spaces gives way to their projection and interpretation. The discussion in the previous two chapters, which dealt with post-war reconstruction and the reaction to it, had added few significant examples to the genre but a growing body of critical material was developing which looked beyond the superfice and architectural style to concentrate attention of morphological analysis, and the economic and social causes for the form of urban space. However, the ideological battles of the first half of the twentieth century had not completely disappeared and would make a forceful return to prominence with violent incidents associated initially with the extremes of left and right, then with the mafia and political corruption, and more lately with anti-capitalist activities. The destructive character of these actions from the 1970s onwards would have architectural and urban design consequences in the measures taken to protect financial and governmental institutions, but would also take place in physical contexts which were benefiting enormously from careful restoration programmes as the value of the urban heritage became a significant component of the economy of tourism. The political promotion of these visible remains of civic life has to be acknowledged as the backdrop against which acts of terrorism were undertaken, the fabric of numerous historic centres being taken as symbols of the general docility and conservatism of Italian society by those who wished to overturn it.

In this general context, the individual status of the architect as an artist encouraged to leave his or her mark on the cityscape comes to the fore from the 1960s onwards. Tending to run counter to the essentially anonymous or possibly collective creation of urban space, the recent cult of the star architect has led to the creation of an illusion that the relationship between architecture and politics is an embarrassment. Its overt use presents a playground for kitsch such as was seen with Mussolini's architectural projects, which the sophisticated palate of the politically aware cognoscenti finds distasteful, but which often finds popular approval. Whatever the romantic vision of solitary genius, the star architect can never be isolated from the power elites, and therefore will produce work which is inherently political. Long before the present 'war on terror' political turmoil and violent events left their marks on the architecture of the city, through both destruction and the creation of new monuments. Examples where history has been manipulated are common and we might ask whether the products of today's political pluralism are any more eloquent, let alone authentic, in their commemoration of events?

It would appear that it was ever thus. The founding texts of the Western tradition in architecture, Vitruvius from two millennia ago and Alberti in the fifteenth century, provide precedents for the relationship between the profession of architecture and the needs of the state. As has been mentioned in Chapter 10, dedicating his work to Augustus, Vitruvius made approving reference to an earlier ruler of the known world, Alexander, and his relationship with his architect Dinocrates. The Roman writer's work is essentially a demonstration of how the building and urban projects Augustus was engaged in could be fitted within a philosophical but practical discourse about wise rulership, and how necessary the architect's skills were. With Alberti there is the famous passage, discussed previously in relation to renaissance urbanism, when he referred in a detached manner to the different expressions required in their urban configurations by democratic states and tyrannies, the one so that external enemies can be repelled, the latter so that internal difficulties with a subject citizenry might also be avoided. This was manifested in the various projects for ideal cities attempted during the renaissance, but as we have seen, political engagement with art and architecture found its strongest expression during fascism with that regime's constant requirement for supportive propaganda and projects of construction that defined the image of an efficient state. The regime's relationship to historical culture was deeply ambivalent, at once impatient with elements of the past it saw as decadent (such as the middle ages when Italy was politically impotent) and reverent towards the Roman past, in particular the creation of the Empire under Augustus (which was deemed to have contemporary relevance). Amongst other examples the historic environment of Brescia experienced this dual natured cultural policy in the construction of Piazza della Vittoria as an arena to show both the benefits of fascist progress and its reliance on Roman precedents. However this association between political representation and architectural and urban form did not finish with fascism, although the context of what followed was often more complex. This chapter will detail the relationship of a politically inspired project within the very charged environment of the 'years of lead', the period of two decades from the late 1960s when Italy was beset by terrorism.

The economic history of Italy since the Second World War would commonly be described as a miracle, where recovery from war and renewed cultural confidence was presided over by a succession of short-lived Christian Democrat dominated governments and produced an era of rapidly expanding prosperity. Extensive internal migration from the poor south to the industrial centres of Milan, Turin and the ever expanding Rome shifted the balance of population from rural to urban dwellers, the life of the new city dwellers exposed in the cinema of Rossellini, Antonioni, Pasolini, and especially Fellini in *La Dolce Vita*, the international success of which had provoked global interest in Italian products and design. However the generation born in the aftermath of the war and coming to maturity in the late sixties were to encounter a changed political scene. The disputes of fascists and partisans from an earlier era, unresolved due to the various interventions of German, American or British occupiers, resurfaced in the extreme actions of groups, neo-fascists and revolutionary marxists whom the post-war consensus had failed to satisfy or pacify. As David Moss writes

Between 1969 and 1988 Italy witnessed some 16,000 acts of broadly defined political violence, at a cost of nearly 400 deaths, 5,000 injuries, and damage to property and individual victims estimated at $600 million. Other types of post-war violence (separatism in the Tyrol, Mafia in the South, had had political consequences, but the violence of the period 1969–88 reached more people and represented a more sustained attempt to infiltrate the country's social and political conflicts. Its forms, authors, targets and objectives of terrorism, spread out over two decades, were very diverse. The overwhelming majority of attacks were directed against the property of individuals and organisations by their antagonists on the extreme left and extreme right. In the early years of violence, between 1969 and 1975, these assaults were largely the work of the extreme right accompanied by indiscriminate bombings which left 45 dead and 349 injured. In contrast the years between 1976 and 1982 were dominated by the extreme left and its increasingly lethal attacks on a widening array of human targets (though this period also saw the worst of all massacres perpetrated by the far right: the Bologna Station bomb of 2 August 1980, which killed eighty-five people). (Moss 2001: 221)

While the cold war and its conflicts provided the context for these actions, the settling of scores between left and right saw the Italian state ostensibly pursue a middle path. However collusion between branches of the state and neo-fascists in the 'strategy of tension', designed to prevent an 'historic compromise' between Christian democracy and the Italian communist party would see some outrages actually perpetrated by the right being blamed on the left. The confusing pattern of responsibilities and intentions, as well as the ambiguous direction of the state during continued material prosperity provided the context for an act of memorialization where a famously reticent architect touched upon this lamentable history.

On 28 May 1974 eight people participating in a trade union demonstration were killed by a bomb in Piazza della Loggia in Brescia, with over 100 people wounded. A neo-fascist group claimed responsibility. The site of the demonstration (and the bomb) was significant, as it provided the resonance of an historical backdrop to contemporary strife. Beyond the complex mosaic of iconography and significant monuments, we can surmise that to the left-wing trade unionists the piazza was an authentic urban location, redolent of civic values, although it was a product of Venetian domination of this area of Lombardy from the fifteenth to eighteenth centuries. The mercantile *logge* in Piazza della Loggia provides a sheltered position from which this elegant renaissance space can be surveyed, and it was here that the 1974 bomb was placed (see Figure 4.4). In contrast the adjacent urban space a few hundred metres away, Piazza della Vittoria, still dominated by the empty frame where Mussolini's equestrian portrait had looked down on this example of fascist urban design held very immediate memories of turmoil from the tainted process of the liberation of 1945. In the aftermath of the terrorist outrage the city council, the Comune di Brescia, commissioned the architect Carlo Scarpa (1906–78) to produce a memorial. Scarpa's previous work had included museums in Venice and Verona where the fact of working in precious historic contexts had not prevented him from creating forceful interventions which exposed the relationships between the contemporary museum and the historic city (Tafuri 1989: 111–14).

Between the various poles of debate among post-war architects, which were associated with the sources of patronage available from the major political parties, the figure of Carlo Scarpa stood out as an individual. It is useful perhaps to consider Scarpa's education, since it seems to have formed the working methods which distinguished him from his contemporaries. He had not attended architectural school, but rather the academy of Fine Arts in Venice. Following this experience, his interest in architecture began to develop so that while a student he worked for various architectural offices and later as a site manager on construction sites. In these origins, before the commencement of his own architectural work, we can perhaps see the elements of Scarpa's unique language, a lack of rigid compositional orthodoxy, a delight in the variation of planar surfaces and textures, and a famously lively relationship with the craftsman. As a designer, there was nothing overly precious about his draughtsmanship, indeed alterations were constantly made up to the moment of construction; but at the same time the drawings that do survive for his buildings show a constantly inventive and exploratory sculptural and spatial sense.

A persistent theme which emerged in Scarpa's work immediately after the war was the setting of temporary exhibitions and the permanent adaptation of museum spaces in historic situations, commencing with the reconfiguration of the Galleria dell'Accademia in Venice between 1945 and 1959. This was followed by the renovation of the Palazzo Abatellis in Palermo (1953–54) following extensive war damage, and then the extension to the Canova plaster cast gallery at Possagno in the Veneto constructed between 1955 and 1957. In all these projects, the display of the paintings and sculptures on specific screens and stands developed a language of elemental detail which was combined with a series of wall openings in new surfaces and reconstructed areas. This experience provided him with the aesthetic material which would be used during the series of major interventions in the great fortress of the Castelvecchio in Verona between 1957 and 1974, Scarpa's major architectural achievement (Blundell Jones and Canniffe 2007: 113–26). It was this skill which

13.1 Piazza
della Loggia,
Brescia. The
location of the
1974 bomb is
marked by Carlo
Scarpa's modest
memorial and the
impact left by the
explosion on the
stonework of the
mercantile *logge*.

was sought by the authorities for the commemoration of a contemporary
political event in a carefully preserved historical urban space, the creation of
a contemplative space in a bustling square (Beltramini, Forster and Marini
2000: 432–39).

13.2    Detail of the courtyard of the Castelvecchio, Verona, showing Scarpa's use of paving, shallow pools, low walls and historical fragments.

Scarpa's initial response was to deal with the horizontal surface of the piazza, where the dead had fallen. This involved the identification of those points within the square, and their connection by a small channel of water. Water, as a Venetian canal which could flood the lower storey of a palace, had played a significant role in the design of the entrance and garden of the Museo Querini-Stampalia in Venice (1961–63), and shallow reflecting pools and narrow channels were introduced into the courtyard of the Museo di Castelvecchio. The different qualities of still and moving water had been used to guide the museum visitor's route, in effect creating a subtle labyrinth, a not uncommon device in the motifs of the Italian garden. From the drawn record we can assume that in Brescia the effect would have been similar, those signature devices were to be used in the public realm, and their introduction into Piazza della Loggia was intended to induce a pause in daily life.

An early sketch by Scarpa shows his most dramatic intention. While a vehicular route is retained on north, west and south sides, the rest of the piazza is to be repaved, with a central channel of water emphasizing the axial disposition of the Palazzo della Loggia and the clock-face in the mercantile *logge*. This channel was to meet an upright memorial, roughly aligned with the existing *Risorgimento* monument in the square, and poised at the outer limit of a newly defined precinct stretching to the site of the bomb itself against one of

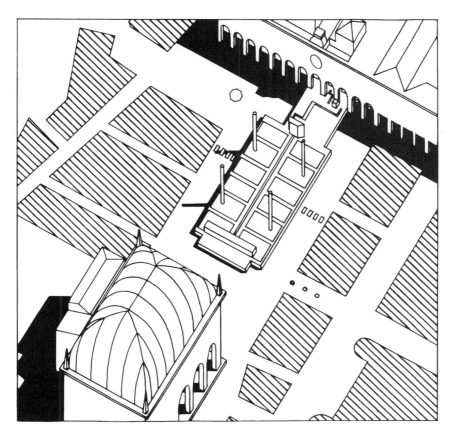

13.3  Diagram of Piazza della Loggia, Brescia, showing Scarpa's initial project to reconfigure the entire piazza as a memorial, with a new rostrum in front of the Palazzo della Loggia.

the piers of the loggia. The square was to be completed by a new podium to be created in front of the Palazzo della Loggia, a gesture to reinforce the use of the piazza for future public gatherings, and conversely to present a democratic platform as an alternative to the *aregno* in Piazza della Vittoria, decorated as it still is with scenes depicting the historical inevitability of fascism (see Figure 10.6). However, this extensive project, resolving the geometrical misalignment of the bomb site by emphasizing the general symmetry of the square through a line of water, was subseqently reduced in scope. Instead Scarpa concentrated on the form of the new precinct on the eastern side of the square sketching an asymmetrical labyrinth which connected the positions where the victims fell. Marble walls, roughly 1.40 metres high, were to bound the visitor's route with the channel of water retained from the earlier project. Scarpa's sensitivity to the location however was uncomfortable with the self-conscious asymmetry of this proposal, and he refined it further into a symmetrical precinct, placed eccentrically in relation to the axis of the space.

This project was developed in Scarpa's characteristic draughting style, where accurate dimensions allowed Scarpa to be more specific in the development of his typical details and combinations of materials. A roughly

13.4   Diagram of Piazza della Loggia, Brescia, showing Scarpa's later project with a labyrinthine precinct around the site of the bomb, enclosed by low walls and featuring a central reflecting pool.

sketched aerial view depicted the overall scale of the proposed intervention, while a plan and most especially a detailed section gave precise information. The rectangular precinct was to be subdivided into five bays, the central one occupied by a basin of water, the others paved. Bronze fixings were to hold double layers of marble panels. A circular opening in the central bay allowed a view into the inner sanctum where a series of columns commemorated the individual victims, columns initially proposed to be obtained from the surplus archaeological remains of Brescia's Roman forum referred to in Chapter 1. The height of the enclosing walls, however, would have created the disturbing effect of the visitors as disembodied heads in the labyrinthine enclosure. The epicentre of the explosion was to be marked by the ruptured stonework of the loggia's pier. Eventually as this elaborate project had little prospect of being completed for the second anniversary of the bombing it was abandoned in favour of a more achievable solution. A newly carved marble column was installed bearing a bronze tablet, and the site of the explosion was defined by an elegant timber balustrade, the project being completed in 1977. The telescoping of Scarpa's projects down to these small elements, however, should not obscure the significance of the image of the urban labyrinth which expediency prevented the architect from employing.

Throughout the evolution of this project Scarpa must have been conscious of the proximity of Marcello Piacentini's work in Piazza della Vittoria, where the architectural compromises of the 1970s were dwarfed by the scale of dubious achievement constructed under fascism. As a young man Scarpa's opinions about Piacentini had been expressed in the joint letter he signed in 1931 as a contribution to the debate about the then direction of Italian architecture. This was exactly the period in which Piazza della Vittoria in Brescia was being completed, and Scarpa's distaste for Piacentini's work was evident, less so for the eclecticism it displayed than for the pomposity with which it dressed itself, and the significance it assumed

The return to the deepest roots of our race, which is being much carried on about nowadays, will always be a return to "the spirit of those forms," and never to the forms of that spirit, as our opponents claim. We rationalists are accused of imitating foreigners, but we ask: how to explain the process by which a design by an Art Nouveau pseudoclassicist from about 1911 or 1914 for a Beaux-Arts palace and a Cinquecento-style imitation for the Banca d'Italia in Rome lead shortly after to the Monument to Victory in Bolzano? Yet these are all works by Marcello Piacentini, the very person who sets himself up as the public accuser of the rationalists.

...While we can give Piacentini credit for having been the first in the academy to attack the architectural decay that existed, why should he now expect younger architects to tag along with the Piacentinism which is now spreading like a plague.

We need fresh air, Excellency, air, air, and what does it matter if it comes from the north? It will, at any rate, be a better antidote to present conditions than anything that His Excellency proposes. Did the Gothic style harm Venice when it gave us the Doge's Palace?

Venice 13 May 1931 = IX
Carletto Scarpa et al.
(Dal Co and Mazzariol 1984: 280)

The architectural ghost at Scarpa's drawing board in the 1970s, Piacentini's Piazza della Vittoria had both glorified the tenth anniversary of the Mussolinian regime and harked back to the grandeur of ancient Roman precedent. The project itself also has two contradictory aspects. The architecture is lumpen and domineering, but the urban scheme with its connections and vistas to other spaces and monuments possesses great subtlety. This is the legacy of Piacentini's admiration as a young architect for Sitte's morphological analysis of Italian urban form. Although its planning is rather stiff, Piacentini's undoubted compositional skill attempted to imply a history to the completely new space by the variety of roof line, massing and materials. Despite the protestations of the young man, in his maturity forty years later, Scarpa's work would also be described as eclectic, both in the renovation projects and new buildings. The significant difference is between Piacentini's use of eclecticism, particularly under fascism, to reinforce an image of *italianità*, and Scarpa's internationalism, native Italian craftsmen using local materials and techniques to build forms derived from the United States and Japan. And whereas Piacentini's synthesis of Italian forms tended towards the regular and a large scale variety which was often bland at an intimate scale, Scarpa's preference for irregularity and the repeatedly exhausting complexity of his detail and articulation of materials provided more enduring aesthetic satisfaction than that afforded by clever composition. Yet both architects, the senior academician and his younger critic, saw urban space as a realm where the expression of architectonic ideas inevitably had cultural and political interpretations. Piacentini's delivery of a political message was admirably clear, despite the unpleasant nature of what the work had to say in support of fascism. For Scarpa, though, ambiguity was all, even in relation to such tragic events as a civilian bombing he had been asked to memorialize.

The ambiguous relationship between fascism and modernity has been covered at length by many authors since the 1970s. If anything the paradoxes of those ambiguities increased after the fall of the regime. Although the elderly Piacentini was investigated for his complicity in fascist culture, his career continued up to his death in 1960, facilitated by the political support of, among others, the young Giulio Andreotti, the future power broker of the first Italian Republic. The completion of Via della Conciliazione at the Vatican for the Holy Year of 1950 and his collaboration with Pier Luigi Nervi on the Palazzo dello Sport for the 1960 Olympics ensured that visitors to Rome continued to enjoy the urban and architectural design of a skilled if elderly hand. In Venice, however, in 1945 Bruno Zevi records Scarpa's ambition running against the chastened spirit of the times described in Chapter 11.

It is 1945, immediately after the Liberation. As an antifascist, Scarpa is invited to take part in a demonstration of left-wing architects. He listens to populist speeches calling for trade-union struggle, team planning and collective work. All at once he asks to be allowed to speak, stands up, and says, "my sole aspiration is to find a Pharaoh who will allow me to build a pyramid." General frigidity. He leaves the room. (Zevi 1984: 271)

This quest on Scarpa's part countered the general mood, since the appropriation of traditional forms of figurative monumental representation by totalitarian regimes and the primacy of abstraction among artistic avant-gardes after 1945 produced new types of memorial expression. Whereas industrialized killing of military personnel had been a feature of the First World War, the memorials produced in its aftermath had co-opted the classical ideal of the valorous warrior to memorialize the countless number of dead, for example at Lutyens' Thiepval Arch on the Somme (1927–32) and Piacentini's Arch at Bolzano (1926–28). Conversely, the civilian dead of World War II, be they victims of air raids or racial and political ideology presented a new species of war dead. The bureaucracy of the Holocaust ensured that the victims' identities were known even if their physical remains were scarce, as the nazis had intended. The aesthetic of departure and loss, often removed from the site of death, therefore came to the fore and could be expressed in such works as Pingusson's Monument to the Deportees in Paris (1962), as well as those of BBPR in Milan and Carpi. This spatial dislocation encouraged a desire to create an empathetic response from the viewer or visitor, sometimes by

13.5  Memorial in Piazza della Loggia, Brescia. A detail of the mercantile *logge* showing Scarpa's dedicatory marble column and timber barrier.

the use of resonant text, but more often by some type of disorienting spatial configuration in which the unfamiliar language of the contemporary artist could be given the opportunity to build bridges of signification between event, artist and viewer.

Scarpa's interest in monumental forms informed much of his work, but what is the significance of Scarpa's choice of the ancient symbol of the labyrinth for the memorial in Brescia? The mythical origin of the labyrinth is that it was created by Daedalus, the first architect, as the lair of the Minotaur, the monstrous product of the unnatural union between Minos's queen Pasiphae and a bull of which she had become enamoured. Every ninth year seven youths and seven maidens were sent by Athens to Crete as sacrificial victims to be devoured by the Minotaur. One year the hero Theseus was sent, he entered the labyrinth, slaughtered the Minotaur and found his way to safety through the thread provided by Minos's daughter Ariadne. The content of this myth, bestiality, terror and treachery cannot be separated from its location, the labyrinth as an architectural and urban type. As Peter Eisenman writes in the introduction to the English translation of Aldo Rossi's *The Architecture of the City*

...the labyrinth, Daedalus's creation can be considered emblematic of a humanist condition in architecture. But this is not the spiral's only meaning. As an unfolding path or route, the spiral has also been interpreted as a psychological figure, the symbol of a process of transformation. Thus we are obliged to interpret (Rossi's) use of the image...in two ways: first in terms of the spiral as a mausoleum, as representing a symbolic place of death, in this case – even if unconsciously on his part – that of humanism; and at the same time, in terms of the spiral as labyrinth, as representing a place of transformation. (Eisenman 1982: 3)

Scarpa's proposed use of the labyrinth as a motif for his memorial cityscape has parallels in the use of its form in the garden maze. Iconographically this can be traced to its appearance, for example, in the renaissance text *Hypnerotomachia Poliphili*, and he had implied it in the garden for the Brion-Vega tomb (1969–78). As a memorial form it had already been used by BBPR in their 1963 monument to the victims of the fascist transportation camp at Fossoli constructed in the courtyard of the castle in the nearby town of Carpi, outside Modena, where the concrete panels are inscribed with the names of the camps where the victims were incarcerated or were exterminated (Jehle-Schulte Strathaus and Reichlin 1995: 70–71). However, in Brescia Scarpa used it as a metaphor for the city and political life. During this period of the mid-1970s, the Italian city was a site of death, with almost ritualized political violence, as left and right took it in turns to sacrifice the vulnerable and unsuspecting to their causes. In subtle reference to the myth of the labyrinth the architect transformed these events into a poetic image of the mirrored confusion of left and right routes, and the men and women caught up in them. Scarpa's labyrinth might be interpreted as expressing the political symbolism of Italy's post-war course between communism and capitalism, fascism and democracy, and the monster at the heart of Italian society – political violence. The negative aspects of this ambiguous symbol, though, have their positive counterpart, as a warning and a petrification of conflict and threat. With reference to its exploitation in antiquity, Joseph Rykwert comments in *The Idea of a Town*

The labyrinth,... had also this double function – apotropaic and regenerative.

It was apotropaic in that it both contained the menace enclosed, and also excluded outside attack; regenerative in that the inwinding and outwinding of the cord which the dancers carried in some forms of the maze-dance, was assimilated to the umbilical cord and to the skin-shedding snake. The dance wound in to a place of death which was also a source of riches and fertility... (Rykwert 1976: 129)

To adapt this interpretation, Scarpa's proposal can therefore be read as a symbol of regeneration as well as a memorialization of tragedy. The labyrinth asks a question, demands an answer to the riddle of its form. In the context of 1970s Brescia the question was how civil society, embodied in the dignified renaissance architecture of Piazza della Loggia, could withstand this period of instability. As a town which had grown up from Roman foundations, the historic centre of the city contained the two characteristic urban forms, the dense pattern of closely packed blocks and the clearly defined public open space of the city squares. In a book such as *Socrates' Ancestor*, Indra Kagis McEwen's discussion of classical architecture and city planning, they are described as labyrinths and dancefloors, the spaces respectively of the struggles of everyday life and the ritual celebrations of the festival (McEwen 1993: 57–64). In the absence of a built labyrinth, albeit as the result of the exigencies of time, the space Scarpa eventually created for the commemoration of the dead, with its new column, its fractured pier, its elegant balustrade, is accompanied by the labyrinthine fabric of Brescia itself and the questions the city of the past poses for the contemporary urban world. Scarpa's intentions are ostensibly elegiac and artistic, but, notwithstanding the absence of a pharaoh, their conception introduced into the contemporary city an ancient device for contemplation on political rituals.

In commemorating an event such as the Brescia bomb and its victims, the artist and architect faced three issues which all impinged on the work produced. Those issues were, firstly, the difficulties of representation which follow on from the historical context of World War II, secondly, the appropriateness of the artist's personal language of expression and lastly the desire to produce a reading of the event in question which fitted within a broader urban narrative. In the case of Scarpa's language of expression, and operating at the more isolated scale of a specific terrorist outrage, a highly selective process created meaning in an urban space. Firstly the materials used were often local and familiar and when not, such as with reinforced concrete, were treated as objects of traditional craft skill. The eclecticism of the choice of forms, redolent of the spoliastic practices of medieval Venice, held in balance influences from modernity, particularly the Viennese Secession, De Stijl and Frank Lloyd Wright, and from the traditions of China and Japan. An intense familiarity with local conditions, however, did not prevent Scarpa from confidently introducing the new and unfamiliar, as at the museum spaces of the Castelvecchio in Verona, to create a new perception of the existing context. Scarpa's technique was to reveal the process of construction of his own objects and spaces so that by extension the story of other constructions was revealed. This narrative intent, the conscious telling of the history of a place as well as the specifics of an individual project, helped Scarpa situate his project within the historical matrix of Piazza della Loggia. A provocative attitude to public space which Scarpa shared with the demonstrators and bombers, saw the piazza as an arena where the personal becomes political and the collective affects the individual. The labyrinth, at once both recognizable to the group and highly personal would therefore seem an appropriate choice for the public function which Scarpa had proposed but did not execute, and as the symbol with which his son Tobia chose to mark his father's tomb.

# 14

# The piazza and the politics of the present

Although the Italian piazza remains a significant object of study, recent decades have not seen the development of significant new examples of the genre (Aymonino and Mosco 2006; Alessi 2007). This situation contrasts with, for example, that in Spain during the same period where the impetus which stimulated a renewed architectural and urban exploration was the opening up of culture following the death of the dictator Francisco Franco in 1975. Italy's own release from fascism, happening three decades earlier, however, had not coincided with a period in civic culture which valued and reinterpreted the spatial lessons of the traditional city. This ambivalence, an appreciation of the historic phenomenon of the piazza, and at the same time the treatment of the defined urban space as a mundane form with irritating and immovable constraints presented a conflict which has not yet been resolved. The sophistication of such personal readings of the political role of urban space as were discussed in the last chapter is only one aspect of the present situation of the Italian piazza, which broadly has two possible versions. Firstly, there is the widely held assumption that the type of enclosed public space that the piazza represents has become an outmoded form which is strictly an historical phenomenon. Changes in the planning of cities, their servicing, their architectural character, their traffic systems, the communicative aspects of the public realm, and shifting social patterns all serve to create a different type of urban space which is less tangible, less constrained by issues of time and place, a civic arena which tends towards the commercial and the virtual. Secondly, and directly opposed to the former, there is the position that the lessons such piazze contain present an exemplary type of public space which demonstrates that variety, flexibility, historical memory and contemporary aspiration, the most everyday events and the most sacred spaces might be layered into each other and create richly inspirational spaces which continue to demonstrate the importance of the physical experience, in terms of the authenticity of the familiar and the directness of sensation. Curiously, these two positions seem equally valid, and are not necessarily as mutually exclusive as they might at first appear. One can, of course, enjoy the facilities of an existing space without regarding that experience to be replicable in new situations. The experience

14.1   Campo del Gesu, Venice, with temporary election hoardings.

can be accounted for by the consolation afforded by nostalgia. It is perfectly possible to hold both views simultaneously, a phenomenon I would ascribe to the strangely fascinating power of the piazza, its ability to subsume all types of phenomena into a sense of a shared experience, be it local, national or even international.

Italy's political scene in the last two decades has been dominated by a general economic stability but a growing disaffection for the ideological labels of the past. In the mid-1980s Italy enjoyed renewed success on the international scene, the Italian national football team winning the World Cup in 1982 and its economy outstripping that of the United Kingdom with unprecedented governmental durability at home under the socialist prime minister Bettino Craxi between 1983 and 1987. But as the uncovering of the corruption scandal known as *tangentopoli* ('bribesville') began to spread from Milan in the early 1990s a political crisis within the Italian Republic loomed. A vacuum opened up in the centre of the political world with the collapse of the Christian democrat and socialist parties, both heavily implicated in the corruption. Evidence came to light that agents of the state had manipulated the terrorism of extreme right and left for political purposes, the so called 'strategy of tension'. The collapse of the Soviet Union in 1991 had propelled the immensely influential Italian communist party into rebranding itself as the party of the democratic left, separatist groups in northern Italy, the *lega nord* sought to free itself from the economically weaker south, while simultaneously the neo-fascists sought to claim democratic credentials as the *alleanza nazionale*. Fighting back against the anti-corruption investigations the media magnate Silvio Berlusconi, who had benefitted from the Craxi years, founded a political party *forza italia* on a vaguely optimistic agenda and briefly held office as Prime Minister in 1994, returning to office with a parliamentary majority between 2001–06. However, his hold on office remained dependent on keeping the mutually exclusive coalition partners of separatists and post-fascists happy, while emphasizing the alliance with the United States and participating in the 'war on terror'. The rebranded left held office ineffectually from 1996–2001 and returned to power with the narrowest of fragile majorities in 2006. By this date the aspirations for political transparency and clean government had evaporated under the impact of Berlusconi's personality, the consolidation of his control over the media and a comfortable economic stagnation and he returned to power in 2008.

The slow transformation in the relationship of public space and Italian political life is perhaps no better illustrated than by two experiences which mark the beginning and end of the research which produced this book. At the beginning of that process – in July 1993 – there was the chance to catch an historic form of political life in its dying days through witnessing a speech by the ex-Communist leader Achille Occhetto in the Sala dei Notai in Perugia. The hour long address was relayed outside to Piazza IV Novembre via a video link, but there was no question that the authentic experience was live, in the hall, where an agitational fervour greeted every statement of intent. The only hint of show was the fine tailoring worn by the senior party officials, and the blood red shirt of an aged female member of the party faithful who enthusiastically cheered each phrase. The zeal of a revolutionary meeting was achieved, although spontaneous action was not really the order of the day. This meeting took place in a period of realignment in Italian politics during the *tangentopoli* scandal before the advent of Berlusconi as a direct political figure.

Fourteen years later in July 2007 I had the chance to witness one of his rallies in Piazza del Plebiscito in Naples (see Figure 0.5). A poster campaign around the city announced his arrival, a stage was erected over two days with San Francesco di Paola as a backdrop, and on the evening of the speech the party faithful gathered in a festive atmosphere with banners, balloons and entertainment provided by crooners belting out easy listening standards. Video screens magnified the real presence when *il Cavaliere* spoke. The usual justifications and attacks on the government and the judiciary were duly framed in sweeping shots of the rapturous crowd for Berlusconi's own television channels before the rally was concluded with the *Forza Italia* party song and people clambered up to the stage to shake, and be recorded shaking, his hand. The messy actuality of the event could be edited out of the broadcast version to present a more sanitized and motivational experience for the remote viewer, but when viewed from the windows of the Palazzo Reale the shade of a Murat or a Bourbon would have recognized the type of political space they had created entering its third century.

The relationship of this shift in use to the physical attributes of the public realm might at first be hard to discern, obscured as it is by the benevolence which has continued to flow from the membership of the European Union. As well as the encroachment of commercial material in traditional urban spaces the understanding of urban values is also under threat from the type of commercial space common to the cities of the leading developed economies. Historic environments have continued to be preserved and continue to serve their original social functions, but the influence of the only remaining global political and economic superpower, the United States, continues to make itself felt in the development of business districts and peripheral areas of the major cities. The cultural value of Italian urban centres, most especially their value to the tourist economy, has preserved them but the ill defined edges of the cities have not been as immune from unsuitable development. In this context the elements of public space are often appropriated as a component of the developer's armoury in creating a successful segment of the city, yet they are exclusive environments without the diversity which authentic urban situations contain as a matter of course. A case in point, intended to be built on former industrial land, is the projected *Citta della Moda* proposed by the American architect Cesar Pelli in 2004 for a site in northern Milan, on behalf of the American developer Gerald Hines. The north American ethos of the design, transplanted to its north Italian context, will be an alien introduction to an undistinguished part of the city dominated by transport infrastructure for rail, metro and car. The intention is to connect the site in front of the commuter terminal Stazione Garibaldi to the entertainment and retail centre of the city in the Via Brera and Via Montenapoleone districts, and also to the bureaucratic and administrative centre in another new development (by the American architects Pei Cobb Freed) which will extend the functions of the Lombard regional government in Gio Ponti's Pirelli Tower. Essentially an office development, the *Citta della Moda* has been envisaged as a spiralling enclosure of office buildings around a circular space. The city of Milan had adopted a master plan produced by Pier Luigi Nicolin in 1991, and following the fallout from the *tangentopoli* scandal and in the very different political circumstances of the 2001–06 Berlusconi government, the revision of that plan resulted in a dramatic increase in scale for the proposed buildings (Nicolin 2007). The developer's requirement to accommodate 3,000 cars to make the office buildings attractive to occupiers, and the simultaneous inability to place them underground because of the rail and metro infrastructure lines resulted in the decision to place the principal public space two levels above ground. Whereas this strategy will allow the space to communicate easily with a new urban park currently under development, dubbed the 'Library of Trees', the creation of the podium will effectively isolate the new public space from the surrounding quarter. Repeating the impermeable design solutions which characterized the megastructures of previous decades, the deliberate creation of a lack of integration between parts of the city though its public spaces is unlikely to be ameliorated substantially by the introduction of exclusive shops as a screen to the parking decks.

In the more ephemeral presence of advertising the global dominance of Italian fashion brands present an ideology which mitigates against the inclusive nature of traditional urban space. In current urban practice the restoration of historic structures (and indeed the construction of new buildings) often takes place behind giant advertising screens (de Giorgi 2004). At the beginning of the 1990s lengthy conservation projects often took place behind well crafted timber hoardings which attempted to minimise the visual disturbance caused by construction projects. At ground level they would attract the usual type of graffiti and fly posting, often political in character, which is common in Italian city centres. The relative discretion of this strategy however has since been abandoned, having a noticeable impact on their attendant public spaces. The first version of this process was the creation of hoardings which replicated the architecture of the original building creating a two dimensional simulation of the actual situation, a falsification which would fail to register in tourist photographs. The sponsoring of such virtual images and the projects they announced then encouraged a more commercial manifestation of the same principle where major brands could be advertised in these prominent urban locations. Those very brands play a significant role in the urban scene, since as with any advanced capitalist society, Italian urban culture is veiled in the images and signs of consumerism.

This, of course, has been the case since the end of the nineteenth century, when campaigns of poster advertising and artificial illumination began to

14.2   The Doge's Palace Venice during restoration. To the left of the image is the restored building, while to the right conservation proceeds concealed by a large photographic image of the palace and its arcades.

14.3  San Carlo
al Corso, Milan.
The neo-classical
church adjacent
to a hoarding
advertising
contemporary
Milanese fashion
brands.

intrude on the previously imperturbable urban scene. Elements of this new
language of popular and familiar imagery would be appropriated by futurists
and other avant-garde groups and would also become subject to political
control during fascism. But since 1945 the imagery of a consumer society
has become an established element of urban space, and stands in historic
situations as a jarring reminder of the contemporary world. The predominance
of Italian brands in different product areas, in cars, in fashion, and in domestic
goods, feature as the contemporary equivalent of the dedicatory text, heraldic
imagery and classical iconography. As in traditional environments the text
and images of contemporary advertising serve to connect the present space
to other times and places, the unhindered freedoms of the open road, the
suffocating luxury of the boudoir and the unattainably perfect penthouse. The
presence of such images and advertising slogans are kept under tight visual
control in most protected situations, except during periods of reconstruction,
when the images are inflated to gigantic size to cover building sites.

Occasionally such elements become permanent features of the urban space,
as in the case of the Armani Wall on Via dell'Orso in Milan, which features
building sized advertisements for the latest season's lines of the global fashion
brand most associated with Milan and the design boom of the 1980s. Also in
Milan, adjacent to the basilica of San Lorenzo, the Diesel Wall uses a similar

strategy to provide a display space for contemporary art, but the two examples provide different lessons in the direction of urban space. While the Armani Wall concerns itself directly with advertising and is transparent about its relationship to consumer products, its relationship to urban space is studiously neutral, presiding as it does over a neglected piece of lawn at a busy junction. For an intervention which is so large it is remarkably undemonstrative. The Diesel Wall's relationship to marketing is more obscure, the material displayed on the wall, supplied from an open invitation to artists, having an association with the company through the sponsoring of public space. While the artwork's presence and message is direct, that of the 'subversive' fashion brand is open to more speculation and interpretation. Again, as with the Armani Wall, the direct impact on the space is negligible, hemmed in as it is by tramlines but with the landscape of historical fragments around it there is the possibility of it enjoying a more dynamic relationship with the urban realm. In effect the site is branded, appropriated by the dominating presence of the company's indirect message. Examples of historical largesse, such as that bestowed by the court or the church provide a precedent but where this recent phenomenon differs is in its intentions and its attitude to the use of space. The artworks on the Diesel Wall employ their various means of surface treatment to provoke, in accordance with the preferred attitude of the youth

14.4   Armani Wall, Milan. The permanent advertising for the fashion brands dominates the space at the junction of: Via dell'Orso and Via Broletto.

14.5   Diesel
Wall, Milan.
A permanent site
for temporary
art installations
adjacent to
San Lorenzo
Maggiore.

market to which the products are aimed, but that provocation restricts itself
to the display surface, above the reach of anyone who might want to interact.
The surface of human occupation, directly in the form of the restaurant at
its base, is unaffected, activity neither hindered nor enhanced, just placed
in a form of hybrid artistic and commercial context. In historical examples,
despite the presence of significant iconography, the utility of the space and
the accommodation of its activities is the primary motive and the reason for
their enduring success.

One noticeable aspect of this presence of such billboards in public places is
the collapse of conventional issues of scale. An image, without any change of
detail, can dominate a magazine page, a cinema screen, a television, a computer
screen, conventional billboards or a multi-storey exposed gable wall. Similarly,
in the present time, the experience of an entire city can be edited down to a
brief travelogue in a newspaper supplement. The hierarchies of scale which
traditionally distinguished the city, the building, the sculpture, the painting and
the page have been eroded. Those distinctions between media are increasingly
seen as irrelevant as the city's contemporary appearance is determined by the
brand and what it promises. Through the promotion of tourism in Italy, the
spaces of the historic city have themselves become a brand, offering the cachet
of culture and elegance, although the actual experience of the major tourist

sites is often of crowds of other tourists, high prices for non-luxury goods, and incomprehension in the face of the monuments which are being visited. This experience induces a form of passive appropriation which remains disengaged from the spaces visited and content to retain its image as a postcard or a souvenir. But there is another aspect to the negative tone of the foregoing paragraph. In the most popular spaces, Piazza del Pantheon in Rome, Piazza San Marco in Venice, the Campo in Siena, the crowds do eventually move on, the souvenir sellers and hawkers of counterfeit goods along with them, and the physical spaces remain more or less undefiled, and it is this quality of endurance which gives them their ultimate character. It is risky to make generalizations, but the discreet integration of a piazza with its containing city, the length of time spent in the design and construction of the place and the ambiguity with which it accommodates different functions are what differentiate such spaces from the functionally specific, provisionally constructed and attention seeking urbanism of the present day.

This contemporary situation has its theorists, for example in the position recently espoused by Andrea Branzi that the distinctions between public and interior space of the traditional city will disappear in favour of a continuum in which the viscera of urban functions provide an alternative urbanity.

The quality of an urban place is no longer... formed by the effectiveness of its architectural setting, but rather by the sophistication of its various interior designs, by the products of its shop windows, and also by the public who invade streets and squares, bearing a constant flow of uncontrollable expressiveness. In other words the old city, made of architectural boxes (redundant and no longer perceptible within the context of a complex urban scenario), has been substituted by another, less visible, less flaunted, more extensive and vital city. It supplies emotions, goods and information – but it does not build cathedrals. (Branzi 2006: 46)

While one might observe that the museum building, often part of a broad commercial campaign, has replaced the cathedral as a cultural focus, Branzi draws on the history of the modern movement and its reliance on mechanical metaphors for urbanism, but proposes that the city's hierarchical distinction between different types of space is also a function of the depoliticization of society. What this position ignores, and thereby betrays the aesthetic origin of this theoretical idea, is that the disappearance of any overt political aspect to public space is itself a political symptom of the passivity of populations in established democratic societies.

While that phenomenon has many possible causes, its relationship to the formerly communicative nature of public space is worth emphasizing. New technology, which is spreading the global use of the English language faster than any other previous means of communication, is creating a virtual space which is replacing the common area of the piazza with more compartmentalized communal spaces. The developments of personal multimedia technology during the last two decades perhaps represent a species of threat to the traditional forms of public space encountered in the previous chapters. The phenomenon is twofold, engaged both in the aspect of consumer culture which demands the visibility of the latest product, and in their ability to replace conventional forms of social engagement and encounter through virtual means. While behaviour in public space is subject to change (for example with an increasing sense of isolation produced by the ability to be physically present in one space and mentally engaged elsewhere, and the requirement to ignore one's fellow citizens' indulgence in one-sided conversation, as a form of externalized interior monologue), these recent phenomena are perhaps no more than an extension of the alienation which characterized the period of industrialization. And for all their claims of promoting autonomy, which could be thought of as inimical to traditional forms of urbanity, the collective experiences which are available through such media are largely promoted by commercial interests. The unique situation in Italy is the explicit connection, evidenced through the personality of Berlusconi, of the political sphere and the media. The qualities of traditional space, in the allowance for spontaneity within the public sphere, represent the most direct means of balancing the negative effects of the mediated world, through personal encounters with all the agreements and disagreements, pleasures and conflicts they bring. However, as a site for attempting to create a form of collective experience out of this essentially personal phenomenon, the piazza presents opportunities to house facilities where the creations of the virtual world can be shared. This scenario would see the representational structure of the traditional urban space complemented, or perhaps appropriated by new media, in an extension of the advertorial phenomenon discussed above so that the adaptive potential of urban space finds new ways to express the concept of *polis*. The ephemerality of these spectacular insertions in urban space, and their success in transforming an environment, should not deceive the observer into believing that it offers any true alternative to the tradition of the permanent provision of formally designed public space. The ephemeral, commercial distractions of the piazza create no enduring satisfaction, only momentarily dominating the view of the attention-deficient citizen, and as equally unmemorable as an experience.

Because history as an actor is always a vital element in the experience of a piazza. For example, the project to rehouse the Ara Pacis Augustae (the Altar of Augustan Peace discussed in Chapter 1) has been one of the most controversial projects in the redesign of the public realm in Italy during the last decade. The precinct in which it sits, the Piazza Augusto Imperatore was created in the 1930s to reveal the massive remains of the Mausoleum of Augustus, and unify them with the repositioned and reconstructed Ara Pacis, which had originally been situated in relation to the Augustan sundial. The Mussolinian project had been a typical exercise in urban rediscovery, clearing the dense quarter around the monumental remains, which at that time had a cast iron concert hall built on top of them, having previously served as a fortress and a bullring after being stripped of its original ornaments and contents. The transformation of the site had begun with the creation of the Tiber embankments and the Ponte Cavour after the *Risorgimento* and the

demolition of the baroque steps of the Ripetta, an elaborate piece of urban planning which served as the uppermost port on the river. This topographical fact had been the reason the Mausoleum was built here since stone, including its original adornments of Egyptian obelisks, could be transported by boat and unloaded at this point. The continued use of the port gave the area strategic importance and vitality through the intervening centuries, but all signs of this history were swept away with the exception of the two renaissance churches, San Girolamo degli Illirici and San Rocco, which were spared demolition and integrated into the new monumental precinct surrounding the excavated mausoleum on three sides. The fourth side towards the river was left open for a substantial pavilion housing the reconstructed Ara Pacis, sitting on a base on which was inscribed Augustus's testimony of his achievements, the *res gestae* (Kostof 1978). The original pavilion designed by Vittorio Ballio-Morpurgo was considered no longer fit for purpose and was demolished to allow construction of a new museum with extended facilities which would also provide a more transparent relationship with the existing excavated mausoleum. The American architect Richard Meier who had been a fellow of the American Academy in Rome in the early 1970s, was commissioned in 1996 and the new structure opened in 2006 (Meier 1997; Davey 2006). The Ara Pacis and the *res gestae* were preserved and protected in their original position throughout the lengthy construction process, delayed by legal disputes and government interference. Meier's project was to create a stronger definition

14.6   Piazza di Spagna, Rome being prepared for a spectacular fashion show. The show's designers have complemented the Spanish Steps, a masterpiece of baroque townscape, with a series of temporary obelisks.

14.7   Diagram of Piazza Augusto Imperatore, Rome showing Richard Meier's housing of the Ara Pacis Augustae in its new museum, and the excavated remains of the Mausoleum of Augustus.

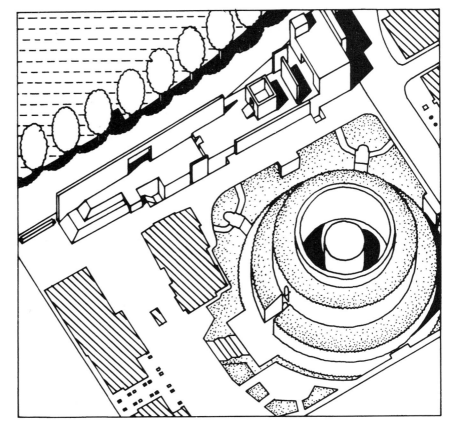

to the square through the creation of a wall stretched from the new pavilion and framing the facade to San Rocco, helping to lessen the intrusive nature of the roadway along the embankment. Future infrastructural plans include the sinking of the roadway into a tunnel so that the relationship between river and square could be improved. The enclosure of the altar within its glazed hall seeks to reinforce the relationship between the sculptural decoration of the enclosing sides which refers to the family myths of the Julio-Claudian dynasty and the view of the Mausoleum of Augustus. That relationship is effectively conditioned by the spatial organization set up in the 1930s, so although the new structure is much larger than the previous arrangement elements are deliberately related to the existing state. The broad flight of steps which approaches the entrance to the new museum are related to the space between the two churches and the boundary line of the Via di Ripetta, with its significant and historic view to the obelisk of Piazza del Popolo. In short the project is somewhat conservative as a work of urbanism, treating an unsatisfactory situation with some care to complete the fascist project for the space. The opportunity has perhaps been compromised which would have given a significant new space to the city, and a significant monument within it given new status. Invention has been exhausted in the creativity with which the conventional language of monumental architecture could form a space, although the respect the new intervention shows to the various histories of the site supports the memorial function of the piazza.

The periods when the piazza as a type has undergone sustained study as an urban phenomenon, in the latter half of the nineteenth century as exemplified by Sitte, and in the post Second World War period with the development of townscape were both periods of immense transformation in cities, when traditional forms of urbanism and society were under severe pressure. In contrast the period of reassessment which took place from the mid-1960s to mid-1990s under the leadership of figures such as Aldo Rossi and the Krier brothers was a period of relative stagnation. In the present time, the urban situation is experiencing a dramatic transformation as new development encroaches on urban centres, but again the piazza features as an identifying characteristic of urban quality, a word which might be applied to the most unlikely open areas of hard landscape and 'space left over after planning', as if the name itself was a guarantee of sophistication and pleasure. In the current confused state of architectural and civic debate, accusations are often made of the same form of discontinuity between intentions and results. Are the variously shaped urban products of today's political pluralism any more likely to survive future criticism? If the formal discipline of previous eras is one element of the piazza's typology which has already loosened, other transformations suggest further changes. The introduction of virtual technology into the life of the square is a phenomenon which has already happened, either through the frequent use of temporary projection screens erected for concerts and international sporting events such as the 2006 World Cup, or as more familiar information points that are an update to the *edicola* or newspaper stand which sits in most popular spaces, and which have provided a comfortable social focus for generations (Severgnini 2007: 217–18). The question arises as to whether treating such features as a more permanent installation will be of great value as urban design elements over time, as technology adapts so rapidly and is increasingly personalized. Can the collective experience of sharing images and information being pursued in the existing public realm, or in the quasi-urban spaces of new commercial developments, have a significant role to play in the piazza's long term future? Is this the appropriate location for continued political discourse or is the future of the phenomenon of the piazza inevitably tied to, and limited by, the rich legacy of its past?

# Bibliography

Ackerman, J.S. (1961) *The Architecture of Michelangelo* (London: Zwemmer)

Adams, N. and Nussdorfer, L. (1994) 'The Italian City, 1400–1600' in Lampugnani, V.M. and Millon, H.A. *Italian Renaissance Architecture from Brunelleschi to Michelangelo* (London: Thames and Hudson): 205–30

Adjmi, M. and Bertolotto, G. (1993) *Aldo Rossi: Drawings and Paintings* (New York: Princeton Architectural Press)

Agrest, D. (1991) 'The City as Place of Representation' *Architecture from Without: Theoretical Framings for A Critical Practice* (Cambridge MA: MIT Press)

Alberti, L.B. (1988) (Rykwert, Leach and Tavernor trans.) *On the Art of Building in Ten Books* (Cambridge MA and London: MIT Press)

Alessi, A. (ed.) (2007) *Italy Now?Country Positions in Architecture* (Ithaca NY: Cornell AAP Publications)

Argan, G.C. (1946) 'The Architecture of Brunelleschi and the Origins of Perspective Theory in the Fifteenth Century' *Journal of the Warburg and Courtauld Institutes* 9: 96–121

Argan, G.C. and Contardo, B (1993) *Michelangelo Architect* (London: Thames and Hudson)

Augustine of Hippo (1972) (Bettenson, H. trans.) *Concerning the City of God against the Pagans* (Harmondsworth: Penguin)

Aymonino, A. and Mosco, V.P. (2006) *Contemporary Public Space: Un-volumetric Architecture* (Milan: Skira Editore)

Barbieri, U. and Ferlenga A. (1987) *Aldo Rossi Architect* (Milan: Electa)

Bass, D. (1997) 'Insiders and Outsiders: Latent Urban Thinking in Movies of Modern Rome' in Penz, F. and Thomas, M. (eds) *Cinema & Architecture: Melies, Mallet-Stevens, Multimedia* (London: British Film Institute ): 84–99

Becker, M.B. (1981) *Medieval Italy: Constraints and Continuity* (Bloomington: Indiana University Press)

Beltramini, G., Forster, K.W. and Marini, P. (eds) (2000) *Carlo Scarpa: Mostre e Musei 1944–1976, Case e Paesaggi 1972–1978* (Milan: Electa)

Benedetti, S. (1973) 'For a Typological Hypothesis in the Restoration of Historic Centers' in Bardeschi, M.D. et al. (eds) *Italian Architecture 1965–1970* (Florence: IsMEO): 164–71

Besana, R., Carli, C.F., Devoti, L., and Prisco, L. (eds) (2002) *Metafisica Construita: La Citta di fondazione degli anni Trenta dall'Italia all'Oltremare* (Milan: Touring Club Italiano)

Bevilacqua, M. (ed.) (2004) *Nolli, Vasi, Piranesi: Immagine di Roma Antica e Moderna* (Rome: Artemide Edizioni)

Blaeu, J. ([1692] 1971) *Theatrum statuum regiae celestitudinis Sabaudiae Ducis...* (Amsterdam, Turin: Edizioni Koller)

Blundell Jones, P. and Canniffe, E. (2007) *Modern Architecture through Case Studies 1945–1990* (Oxford: Elsevier/Architectural Press)

Boatwright, M.T. (1987) *Hadrian and the City of Rome* (Princeton New Jersey: Princeton University Press)

Boyer, M.C. (1994) *The City of Collective Memory: Its Historical Imagery and Architectural Entertainments* (Cambridge MA: MIT Press)

Bowsky, W.A. (1981) *A Medieval Italian Commune: Siena under the Nine 1287–1355* (Berkeley: University of California Press)

Branzi, A. (1984) *The Hot House: Italian New Wave Design* (London: Thames and Hudson)

Branzi, A. (2006) 'The Visceral Revolution' *Domus* 897 November

Bruschi, A. (1977) *Bramante* (London: Thames and Hudson)

Bucci, F. and Mulazzani, M. (2000) *Luigi Moretti, Opere e scritti* (Milan: Electa)

Burroughs, C. (2002) *The Italian Renaissance Palace Facade: Structures of Authority, Surfaces of Sense* (Cambridge: Cambridge University Press)

Canniffe, E. (1995) 'Mannerist Interventions: Three Sixteenth Century Italian Squares' *Urban Design Studies: Annual of the University of Greenwich Urban Design Unit* Vol 1: 57–74

Canniffe, E. (1997) 'The City of False Memory: Piazza della Vittoria, Brescia' *Building as a Political Act* (Washington DC: Association of Collegiate Schools of Architecture): 405–411

Canniffe, E. (1998) 'The Imposition of Order: Autocracy and Architectural Expression in Two North Italian Piazze' *Urban Design Studies* Vol 4: 5–20

Canniffe, E. (1999) 'Recovery Positions: a fourfold model of urbanism' *Transformations of Urban Form* (Florence: Alinea)

Canniffe, E. (2001) 'City and Scene: the theatricality of public space in the Renaissance' *Urban Design Studies: Annual of the University of Greenwich Urban Design Unit* Vol 7: 21–34

Canniffe, E. (2003) 'The Other Rome: Building the Utilitarian City in Trastevere' *The Planned City? ISUF International Conference* 1 Bari: Uniongrafica Corcelli Editrice: 39–44

Canniffe, E. (2006) *Urban Ethic: Design in the Contemporary City* (London and New York: Routledge)

Carandini, A. and Cappelli, R. (2000) *Roma, Romolo, Remo e la fondazione della citta* (Milan: Electa)

Castiglione, B. ([1528] 1967) *The Book of the Courtier* (London: Penguin)

Cheles, L. (2001) 'Picture battles in the piazza' in Cheles, L. and Sponza, L. (eds) *The Art of Persuasion: Political Communication in Italy from 1945 to the 1990s* (Manchester: Manchester University Press): 124–79

Ciucci, G. (1974) *La Piazza del Popolo: Storia, architettura, urbanistica* (Rome: Officina)

Collins, G.R. and Collins, C.C. (1986) *Camillo Sitte: The Birth of Modern City Planning* (Cambridge MA: MIT Press)

Connors, J. (1989) 'Alliance and Emnity in Roman Baroque Urbanism' *Romisches Jahrbuch der Bibliotheca Herziana*: 207–94

Crespi, G. and Dego, N. (2004) *Giorgio Grassi: opere e progetti* (Milan: Electa)

Cullen, G. (1961) *Townscape* (London: Architectural Press)

Cullum, H. (1986) *The Savoy Hunting Lodge at Venaria Reale* (PhD Thesis University of Cambridge)

Cunningham, C. (1995) 'For the honour and beauty of the city: the design of town halls' in Norman, D. *Siena, Florence and Padua: Art, Society and Religion 1280–1400 Volume 2 Case Studies* (New Haven and London: Yale University Press): 29–53

Dal Co, F. and Mazzariol, G. (1984) *Carlo Scarpa: The complete works* (Milan and New York: Electa and Rizzoli)

Damisch, H. (1994) *The Origins of Perspective* (Cambridge MA: MIT Press)

Davey, P. (2006) 'Pax Romana: Richard Meier Triumphs in Rome, Creating a New Shelter and Museum for Ara Pacis' *The Architectural Review* Vol. 220 October

Davies, P.J.E. (2000) *Death and the Emperor: Roman Imperial Funerary Monuments from Augustus to Marcus Aurelius* (Cambridge: Cambridge University Press)

de Carlo, G. (1970) *Urbino: The History of a City and Plans for its Development* (Cambridge MA: MIT Press)

de Giorgi, G. (2004) *Roma: Follie, deliri e contaminazioni* (Rome: edizioni kappa)

de Pieri, F. and Scrivano, P. (2004) 'The Revitalization of Historical Bologna' in Wagenaar, C. (ed.) *Happy: Cities and Public Happiness in Post-War Europe* (Rotterdam: NAi): 452–59

de Wolfe, I. (1963) *The Italian Townscape* (London: The Architectural Press)

Eisenman, P. (1979) 'The House of the Dead as the City of Survival' in Frampton, K. (ed.) *Aldo Rossi in America 1976–79* (New York: Institute for Architecture and Urban Studies)

Eisenman, P. (1982) 'The Houses of Memory: The Texts of Analogy' in Rossi, A. *The Architecture of the City* (Cambridge MA: MIT Press): 3–11

Elsner, J. (1998) *Imperial Rome and Christian Triumph: The Art of the Roman Empire AD100–450* (Oxford and New York: Oxford University Press)

Etlin, R. (1991) *Modernism in Italian Architecture 1890–1940* (Cambridge MA and London: MIT Press)

Evans, R. (1995) *The Projective Cast: Architecture and its Three Geometries* (Cambridge MA and London: MIT Press)

Falasca-Zamponi, S. (1997) *Fascist Spectacle: The Aesthetics of Power in Mussolini's Italy* (Berkeley: University of California Press)

Favro, D. (1996) *The Urban Image of Augustan Rome* (Cambridge: Cambridge University Press)

Feldges-Henning, U. (1977) 'The Pictorial Programme of the Sala della Pace: A new interpretation' *Journal of the Warburg and Courtauld Institutes* Vol 35: 145–62

Ferlenga, A. (1999) *Aldo Rossi: tutte le opere* (Milan: Electa)

Ferrero, M. (2004) *Architetture di Pietra nella Roma del Novocento* (Rome: Palombi Editori)

Filarete (Antonio di Piero Averlino) (1965) (Spencer, J.R. trans.) *Treatise on Architecture* (New Haven and London: Yale University Press)

Flood, R. and Morris, F. (2001) *Zero to Infinity: Arte Povera 1962–1972* (Minneapolis and London: Walker Art Center and Tate Modern)

Foot, J. (2001) *Milan Since the Miracle: City, Culture and Identity* (Oxford: Berg)

Forster, K. (1977) 'Stagecraft and Statecraft: the architectural integration of public life and theatrical spectacle in Scamozzi's Theater at Sabbioneta' *Oppositions* 9: 63–87

Fortini Brown, P. (1988) *Venetian Narrative Painting in the Age of Carpaccio* (New Haven and London: Yale University Press)

Fortini Brown, P. (1996) *Venice & Antiquity: The Venetian Sense of the Past* (New Haven and London: Yale University Press)

Fricelli D.J.M. (1984) *The Architecture of Giorgio Vasari's Uffizi, Florence* PhD Dissertation (Columbus OH: Ohio State University)

Furnari, M. (1995) *Formal Design in Renaissance Architecture from Brunelleschi to Palladio* (New York: Rizzoli)

Fustel de Coulange, N-D. ([1880]1955) *The Ancient City* (New York: Doubleday)

Galli, L. (1975) *Incursioni aeree su Brescia e provincia, 1944–1945* (Brescia: Ateneo di Brescia)

Geist, J.F. (1983) *Arcades: The History of A Building Type* (Cambridge MA and London: MIT Press)

Goy, R. (1997) *Venice: The City and Its Architecture* (London: Phaidon)

Greco, A. (1991) *Foro Italico* (Roma: Multigrafica Editrice)

Grimal, P. ([1954]1983) (Woloch, G.M. trans. and ed. ) *Roman Cities* (Madison: University of Wisconsin Press)

Grant, M. (1970) *The Roman Forum* (London: Weidenfeld & Nicholson)

Guidoni, E. (1990) *L'Urbanistica di Roma tra miti e progetti* (Bari: Editori Laterza)

Gurrieri, O. (1985) *Il Palazzo dei Priori di Perugia* (Perugia: Bevucci)

Hall, J. (2006) *Michelangelo and the Reinvention of the Human Body* (London: Pimlico)

Hart, V. and Hicks, P. (eds and trans) (2006) *Palladio's Rome: a translation of Andrea Palladio's two guidebooks to Rome* (New Haven and London: Yale University Press)

Haynes, S. (2000) *Etruscan Civilization* (London: British Museum Press)

Heater, D. (1990) *Citizenship: The Civic Ideal in World History, Politics and Education* (London and New York: Longman)

Howard, D. (1975) *Jacopo Sansovino: Architecture and Patronage in Renaissance Venice* (New Haven and London: Yale University Press)

Howard, D. (2000) *Venice and the East* (New Haven and London: Yale University Press)

Irace, F. (1994) *Giovanni Muzio 1893–1982 Opere* (Milan: Electa)

Janson, A. and Burklin, T. (2002) *Scenes: Interaction with Architectural Space: the Campi of Venice* (Basel, Boston and Berlin: Birkhauser)

Jatta, B. (1998) *Piranesi e l'Aventino* (Milan: Electa)

Jarzombek, M. (1989) *On Leon Battista Alberti: his literary and aesthetic theories* (Cambridge MA and London: MIT Press)

Jehle-Schulte Strathaus, U. and Reichlin, B. (1995) *Il Segno della Memoria: BBPR Monumento ai caduti nei campi nazisti* (Milan: Electa)

Johnson, E.J. (2000) 'Jacopo Sansovino, Giacomo Torelli, and the Theatricality of the Piazzetta in Venice' *Journal of the Society of Architetcural Historians* Vol 59 No 4: 436–53

Kidder Smith, G.E. (1955) *Italy Builds: Its Modern Architecture and Native Inheritance* (London: The Architectural Press)

Kirk, T. (2005a) *The Architecture of Modern Italy Volume 1: The Challenge of Tradition 1750–1900* (New York: Princeton Architectural Press)

Kirk, T. (2005b) *The Architecture of Modern Italy Volume 2: Visions of Utopia 1900–present* (New York: Princeton Architectural Press)

Kitao, T.K. (1974) *Circle and Oval in the Square of St.Peter's: Bernini's Art of Planning* (New York: New York University Press)

Kostof, S. (1973) *The Third Rome 1870–1950: Traffic and Glory* (Berkeley: University Art Museum)

Kostof, S. (1978) 'The Emperor and the Duce: the Planning of Piazzale Augusto Imperatore in Rome' in Millon H.A. and Nochlin, L. (eds) *Art and Architecture in the Service of Politics* (Cambridge MA: MIT Press): 270–325

Krautheimer, R. (1971) *Studies in Early Christian, Medieval, and Renaissance Art* (London: University of London Press)

Krautheimer, R. (1980) *Rome, Profile of a City, 312–1308* (Guildford and Princeton: Princeton University Press)

Krautheimer, R. (1983) *Three Christian Capitals: Topography and Politics* (Berkeley, Los Angeles and London: University of California Press)

Krautheimer, R. (1985) *The Rome of Alexander VII 1655–1667* (Guildford and Princeton: Princeton University Press)

Krier, R. (1979) *Urban Space* (London: Academy Editions)

Lang, P. and Menking, W. (eds) (2003) *Superstudio: life without objects* (Milan: Skira)

Lombardo, P. (1984) 'Always resound the white walls of the city' in Rossi, A. *Three Cities Perugia, Milano, Mantova* (Milan: Electa)

Lotz, W. (1977a) 'The Rendering of the Interior in Architectural Drawings of the Renaissance' in *Studies in Renaissance Architecture* (Cambridge MA and London: MIT Press): 1–65

Lotz, W. (1977b) 'The Piazza Ducale in Vigevano: a princely forum of the late fifteenth century' in *Studies in Renaissance Architecture* (Cambridge MA and London: MIT Press): 117–39

Lunghi, E. (1994) *La Cattedrale di S. Lorenzo* (Perugia: Quattroemme)

Lupano, M. (1991) *Marcello Piacentini* (Bari and Rome: Laterza)

McAndrew, J. (1980) *Venetian Architecture of the Early Renaissance* (Cambridge MA and London: MIT Press)

McEwen, I. K. (1993) *Socrates' Ancestor: An Essay on Architectural Beginnings* (Cambridge MA and London: MIT Press)

McEwen, I.K. (2003) *Vitruvius: Writing the Body of Architecture* (Cambridge Massachusetts: MIT Press)

McPhee, S. (2002) *Bernini and the Bell Towers* (New Haven and London: Yale University Press)

Machiavelli, N. ([1531–32] 2004) *The Prince* (London: Penguin Books)

Mack, C.R. (1987) *Pienza: The Creation of a Renaissance City* (Ithaca and London: Cornell University Press)

Mallory, N. (1977) *Roman Rococco Architecture from Clement XI to Benedict XIV* (New York and London: Garland Publishing Inc.)

Martienssen, R.D. (1956) *The Idea of Space in Greek Architecture: with special reference to the Doric Temple and its setting* (Johannesburg: Witwatersrand University Press)

Martines, L. (1980) *Power and Imagination: city-states in Renaissance Italy* (London: Allen Lane)

Martini, C. (1970) 'Il Palazzo dei Priori a Perugia' *Palladio* Vol.20: 39–72

Meeks, C.V. (1966) *Italian Architecture 1750–1914* (New Haven and London: Yale University Press)

Meier, R. (1997) 'Sistemazione museale dell' Ara Pacis' *Zodiac* 17

Miller, M.C. (2000) *The Bishop's Palace: Architecture and Authority in Medieval Italy* (Ithaca and London: Cornell University Press)

Morton, H.V. (1966) *The Waters of Rome* (London: The Connoisseur and Michael Joseph)

Moschini, F. (ed.) (1979) *Aldo Rossi Projects and Drawings 1962–79* (London: Academy Editions)

Moss, D. (2001) 'Persuasion by violence: terror and its texts' in Cheles, L. and Sponza, L. (eds) *The Art of Persuasion: Political Communication in Italy from 1945 to the 1990s* (Manchester: Manchester University Press): 221–32

Muir, E. (1981) *Civic Ritual in Renaissance Venice* (Princeton: Princeton University Press)

Mussolini, B. (1936) *The Doctrine of Fascism* (Florence:Vallechi Editore)

Neri, M.L. (1988) 'Potere e cultura comunali: La Fontana Maggiore di Perugia' *Storia della Città* Vol.3 No. 48: 33–44

Nicolin, P. (2007) 'Special Issue: Milano boom' *Lotus 131*: 78–99

Ossanna Cavadini, N. (1995) *Pietro Bianchi 1787–1849 architetto archeologo* (Naples: Electa Napoli)

Panofsky, E. ([1924–5] 1991) *Perspective as Symbolic Form* (New York: Zone Books)

Packer, J (1997) *The Forum of Trajan in Rome: A Study of the Monuments* (Berkeley: University of California Press)

Perez-Gomez, A. (1983) *Architecture and the Crisis of Modern Science* (Cambridge MA and London MIT Press)

Piacentini, M. (1932) "Il Nuovo Centro di Brescia" *Architettura e Arti Decorative* October

Plant, M. (2002) *Venice: Fragile City 1797–1997* New Haven and London: Yale University Press

Pollak, M.D. (1991) *Turin 1564–1680: Urban Design, Military Culture, and the Creation of the Absolutist Capital* (Chicago and London: University of Chicago Press)

Pollini, J. (1995) 'The Augustus from Prima Porta and the Transformation of the Polykleitan Heroic Ideal: The Rhetoric of Art' in Moon, W.G. *Polykleitos, the Doryphoros and Tradition* (Madison: University of Wisconsin Press): 262–81

Portoghesi, P (1999) 'Birth of the Baroque in Rome' in Millon, H.A. ed. *The Triumph of the Baroque: Architecture in Europe 1600–1750* (London: Thames and Hudson): 33–55

Pozzo, A. ([1693] 1989) *Perspective in Architecture and Painting: An Unabridged Reprint of The English and Latin Edition of 'Perspectiva Pictorum et Architectorum'* (New York: Dover Publications Inc.)

Pugliese Carratelli, G. (ed.) (1996) *The Western Greeks: Classical Civilization in the Western Mediterranean* (London: Thames and Hudson)

Puppi, L. (1975) *Andrea Palladio* (London: Phaidon)

Reed, H.H. (1950) 'Rome: The Third Sack' *The Architectural Review* Vol 107 No 638 February: 91–110

Richardson, Jr, L. (1988) *Pompeii: An Architectural History* (Baltimore and London: The Johns Hopkins University Press)

Robbins, D. (1994) 'Via della Lungaretta: The Making of a Medieval Street' in Celik, Z., Favro, D. and Ingersoll, R. (eds) *Streets: Critical Perspectives on Public Space* (Berkeley, Los Angeles and London: University of California Press)

Rossi, A. (1982) *The Architecture of the City* (Cambridge MA and London: MIT Press)

Rossi, A. (1984) *Three Cities Perugia, Milano, Mantova* (Milan: Electa)

Rowe, C. and Koetter, F. (1978) *Collage City* (Cambridge MA and London: MIT Press)

Rowe, C. and Satkowski, L. (2002) *Italian Architecture of the 16th Century* (New York: Princeton Architectural Press)

Rowe, P. G. (1997) *Civic Realism* (Cambridge MA: MIT Press)

Ruskin, J. ([1851–53]1981) *The Stones of Venice* (London: Faber & Faber)

Rykwert, J. (1976) *The Idea of a Town: The Anthropology of Urban Form in Rome, Italy and the Ancient World* (Cambridge MA and London: MIT Press)

Rykwert, J. (1980) *The First Moderns: The Architects of the Eighteenth Century* (Cambridge MA and London: MIT Press)

Saleri, G. (1838) *Museo Bresciano Illustrato* (Brescia: Tipografia della Minerva)

Salmon, F. (2000) *Building on Ruins: The Rediscovery of Rome and English Architecture* (Aldershot: Ashgate)

Satkowski, L (1979) *Studies on Vasari's Architecture* (New York and London: Garland Publishing Inc.)

Satkowski, L. (1990) *Giorgio Vasari: Courtier and Architect* (Princeton: Princeton University Press)

Scott, J. (2003) *The Pleasures of Antiquity: British Collectors of Greece and Rome* (New Haven and London: Yale University Press)

Scullard, H.H. (1967) *The Etruscan Cities & Rome* (Baltimore and London: Johns Hopkins University Press)

Scully, V. (1969) *The Earth, the Temple and the Gods* (New Haven and London: Yale University Press)

Seavitt, C. (1998) 'Cinecitta' *Dimensions: Journal of the College of Architecture and Urban Planning at the University of Michigan* Vol 2 (Ann Arbor: University of Michigan): 129–36

Sennett, R. ([1977] 1986) *The Fall of Public Man* (London: Faber & Faber)

Sennett, R. (1994) *Flesh and Stone: The Body and the City in Western Civilization* (London: Faber & Faber )

Serlio, S. (Hart, V. and Hicks, P. trans.) (1996) *On Architecture* (New Haven and London: Yale University Press)

Severgnini, B. (2007) *La Bella Figura: An Insider's Guide to the Italian Mind* (London: Hodder & Stoughton)

Spike, M.K. (2004) *Tuscan Countess: The Life and Extraordinary Times of Matilda of Canossa* (New York: The Vendome Press)

Springer, C. (1987) *The Marble Wilderness: Ruins and Representation in Italian Romanticism 1775–1850* (Cambridge: Cambridge University Press)

Smith, E.B. (1978) *Architectural Symbolism of Imperial Rome and the Middle Ages* (New York: Hacker Art Books)

Tafuri, M. (1987) *The Sphere and the Labyrinth: Avant-Gardes and Architecture from Piranesi to the 1970s* (Cambridge MA and London: MIT Press)

Tafuri, M. (1989) *History of Italian Architecture 1944–1985* (Cambridge MA and London: MIT Press)

Tafuri, M. ([1992] 2006) *Interpreting the Renaissance: Princes, Cities, Architects* (New Haven and London: Yale University Press)

Torelli, Mario (ed.) (2000) *The Etruscans* (London: Thames and Hudson)

Trachtenberg, M. (1997) *Dominion of the Eye: Urbanism, Art, and Power in Early Modern Florence* (Cambridge: Cambridge University Press)

Tuttle, R.J. (1993) 'Vignola's facciata dei banchi in Bologna' *Journal of the Society of Architectural Historians* Vol 52 No 1

Vesely, D. (2004) *Architecture in the Age of Divided Representation: The Question of Creativity in the Shadow of Production* (Cambridge MA and London: MIT Press)

Vitruvius (Morgan, M.H. trans.) (1914) *The Ten Books on Architecture* (Cambridge MA: Harvard University Press)

Vitruvius (Rowland, I.D. and Howe, T.N. eds) (1999) *Ten Books on Architecture* (Cambridge: Cambridge University Press)

Waley, D.P. (1988) *The Italian City-Republics* (London and New York: Longman)

Westfall, C.W. (1974) *In This Most Perfect Paradise: Alberti, Nicolas V and the Invention of Conscious Urban Planning in Rome, 1447–55* (University Park and London: Pennsylvania University Press)

White, J. (1970) 'The Reconstruction of Nicola Pisano's Perugia Fountain' *Journal of the Warburg and Courtauld Institutes* 33: 70–83

Wightman, G (1997) 'The Imperial Fora at Rome: Some Design Considerations' *Journal of the Society of Architectural Historians* 56: 64–88

Wilton, A. and Bignamini, I. (1996) *Grand Tour: The Lure of Italy in the Eighteenth Century* (London: Tate Gallery)

Wilton-Ely, J. (1993) *Piranesi as Architect and Designer* (New Haven and London: Yale University Press)

Wittkower, R. ([1949] 1971) *Architectural Principles in the Age of Humanism* (London: Alec Tiranti)

Wittkower, R. (1953) 'Brunelleschi and "Proportion in Perspective"' *Journal of the Warburg and Courtauld Institutes* 16: 275–291

Wittkower, R. (1958) *Art and Architecture in Italy 1600–1750* (Harmondsworth: Penguin)

Wittkower, R and Jaffe, I.B. (eds) (1972) *Baroque Art: The Jesuit Contribution* (New York: Fordham University Press)

Zanker, P. (1988) *The Power of Images in the Age of Augustus* (Ann Arbor: University of Michigan Press)

Zevi, B. ([1957] 1974) *Architecture as Space: How to look at architecture* (New York: Horizon Press)

Zevi, B. (1984) 'Beneath or Beyond Architecture' in Dal Co, F. and Mazzariol, G. (1984) *Carlo Scarpa: The complete works* (Milan and New York: Electa and Rizzoli): 271–72

Zucchi, B. (1992) *Giancarlo De Carlo* (Oxford: Butterworth)

# Index

(References to illustrations are in **bold**)